WHY THE THIRD WAY FAILED

Economics, morality and the origins of the 'Big Society'

Bill Jordan

First published in Great Britain in 2010 by

The Policy Press
University of Bristol
Fourth Floor
Beacon House
Queen's Road
Bristol BS8 1QU
UK

t: +44 (0)117 331 4054
f: +44 (0)117 331 4093
tpp-info@bristol.ac.uk
www.policypress.co.uk

North American office:
The Policy Press
c/o International Specialized Books Services
920 NE 58th Avenue, Suite 300
Portland, OR 97213-3786, USA
t: +1 503 287 3093
f: +1 503 280 8832
info@isbs.com

© The Policy Press 2010

British Library Cataloguing in Publication Data
A catalogue record for this book is available from the British Library.

Library of Congress Cataloging-in-Publication Data
A catalog record for this book has been requested.

ISBN 978 1 84742 656 7 paperback
ISBN 978 1 84742 657 4 hardcover

Cover design by The Policy Press
Front cover: image kindly supplied by www.alamy.com
Printed and bound in Great Britain by Hobbs, Southampton
The Policy Press uses environmentally responsible print partners.

Contents

Acknowledgements

I would like to thank a number of people with whom I had very helpful discussions of the ideas explored in this book. These include Nigel Parton, Mark Drakeford, Walter Van Trier, Sarah Jordan, Rachel Nicholson, Marcus Redley and Jonathan Traub. Many thanks also to Alison Shaw of Policy Press for her help in planning and shaping the book, and to Laura Greaves for all her hard work in its editing. Finally, I am very grateful to Rachel Arnold for her careful typing of my handwritten text.

Introduction

The economic crash of 2008-09 put the UK and US, along with several smaller states (such as Iceland, Ireland and Latvia), back where they had been before the boom years of 2001-07. It exposed as illusory the gains achieved by these economies, with their reliance on their financial sectors and cheap credit, and created mountains of public debt. But, more seriously, it exploded the claims of Third Way governments, especially New Labour in the UK, to have reconciled global markets with new, ethically informed public policies.

The Third Way was a set of ideas and policies, first developed by former President Bill Clinton in the US and former Prime Minister Paul Keating in Australia, which was supposed to have made the liberal left electable, and provided a blueprint for the reform of government in an era of globalisation. Although it suffered setbacks, particularly in the election of George W. Bush to the US presidency, and John Howard as Australian Prime Minister, its political dominance in the UK, and the new regime at the World Bank from 1997 onwards (Stiglitz, 2002) meant that it continued to be deployed, modified and tested, and to influence centrist and liberal left politics worldwide during all the years from 1992 to 2010.

This book argues that the ultimate failure of the Third Way has been a moral one, and that this has stemmed from an inadequate and incoherent analysis of how ethical principles can be applied to the workings of a market economy exposed to global forces. This failure has left whole populations disillusioned about politics in general, and liberal left politics in particular. It remains to be seen whether Barack Obama, as President of the US, can transcend this cynicism, and demonstrate an ability to discover more convincing approaches.

Tony Blair came to power in 1997 with grandiose moral slogans, both in domestic and foreign policy, but the Iraq war and the economic crash left almost all of these in ruins. On the domestic front, improvements in poverty, youth unemployment, workless households and educational opportunity had all been reversed, and New Labour's reforming energies exhausted. Drawing on British, US and other examples, this book seeks to explain why a combination of market-friendly and abstract value-led approaches was always doomed to fail, and what the necessary and sufficient conditions are for morally informed alternatives to emerge.

The Third Way embraced globalisation. In particular, it aimed to harness the neo-liberal regime of freely mobile resources, established under former UK Prime Minister Margaret Thatcher, former US President Ronald Reagan and the International Monetary Fund (IMF)/World Bank Washington Consensus. With Wall Street and the City of London as hubs of financial trading, it promoted these as the centrepieces of affluent Anglophone economies, while simultaneously espousing equality of opportunity and social justice for citizens.

In the UK under New Labour government prudence over public finances switched to massive borrowing on world money markets after its second election; banks were allowed to borrow even larger sums, to fund loans for house purchases and consumer credit. The almost magical ability to make money out of money was hailed as the key to stability with growth (Stiglitz et al, 2006), and was also claimed to enable economic development in the most deprived countries in the world. Finally, when climate change, depleted oil stocks and environmental degradation challenged the sustainability of this economic model, Third Way apologists argued that technological innovation and the collective wisdom of national leaderships could reconcile material advance with ecological renewal.

In retrospect, it was always unlikely that a regime that cherished conspicuous affluence, cut-throat trading, media celebrity and instant gratification would also foster distributive equity, social well-being and sustainable lifestyles. Despite its frequent use of words like 'responsibility' and 'community', Third Way policy documents made no serious attempt to spell out how a creed of self-proclaimed individualism (putting choice, autonomy and property ownership at the heart of its approaches to every issue) could give rise to ethically defensible outcomes.

Why should these self-developing individuals, accumulating portfolios of skills and assets, concern themselves with each other's projects? How might bankers, installed as the key decision makers at the heart of the Third Way model of society, bring about morally desirable goals?

The only answer offered by the economic theorists behind Third Way administrations was that individuals, in making decisions about relationships, associations and collective action, as well as employment, consumption and investment, mobilise information, respond to incentives and strike agreements for mutually beneficial exchanges, that is, *contracts* (Macho-Stadler and Pérez-Castrillo, 2001; Bolton and Dewatripont, 2005; Laffont and Martimort, 2002). If governments can design a legal and organisational infrastructure that provides appropriate information and incentives, these contractual arrangements will supply the optimum possible welfare for all, under the aegis of the almost omniscient banks and financial authorities (Stiglitz and Greenwald, 2003).

The influence of these ideas on Third Way policy formation and implementation is obvious, for example from reading the review of New Labour's reforms and initiatives by David Halpern (2010), one of Tony Blair's close advisers on strategy and performance in government. Even though his book is ostensibly about the 'relationships and habits' that constitute the 'hidden wealth of nations', his account is peppered with references to information, incentives and contracts as the key elements in influencing individual behaviour and aggregate outcomes.

This mindset helps explain the enormous proliferation of legislation, regulation and guidance under Third Way regimes, and particularly under New Labour in the UK. It was as if, by classifying, codifying, monitoring, incentivising and target setting in almost every conceivable sphere of human interaction, government could achieve the complete set of beneficial and positive outcomes. If that notoriously obsessive codifier and Panopticon monitor of social activity, Jeremy Bentham, had been the chief adviser to the Third Way project, he could scarcely have improved on its design.

At the heart of this book's analysis is a distinction between this attempt to regulate all forms of social interaction (formal and informal, economic and relational) by codes, rules, policy statements and abstract 'values' (usually taking the form of business-style mission statements and logos), and an approach to similar activities and issues which relies on interpersonal communication, leading to explicit or implicit standards of behaviour, to which all members of society are accountable (Jordan, 2010). The former is here referred to as 'contractual regulation', although it covers a huge range of law, policy and surveillance, from the criminal justice system to the CCTV cameras in city streets and the documents signed by parents when their children enter a school. The latter is here referred to as 'cultural or moral regulation', although it can denote the standards of behaviour expected of each other by bankers, the staff of businesses, professional colleagues, family members or associates in a cultural or recreational group.

The reason why this distinction is so important is that there is evidence that the wholesale adoption of contractual regulation (as in the business approach to government and the arts, or the legal approach to emotional relationships) can inflict long-term damage on existing cultural or moral modes of regulation. In the oft-quoted example (Jordan, 2008, pp 9-10; Sandel, 2009a) that so neatly illustrates the point, the managers of one Israeli nursery introduced 'fines' on parents who turned up late to collect their children in the afternoon (Gneezy and Rustichini, 2000). The result was that there was a significant increase in parental lateness, which persisted even after the financial penalty on parents was hastily abandoned.

What this example shows, as both I and Michael Sandel have independently argued, is that the substitution of a quantitative, monetary 'price' for lateness for a qualitative, 'moral' sanction of mild disapproval by other parents and staff, gave those faced with the possibility of being unpunctual the option of paying when the 'costs' of punctuality outweighed the 'benefits' of being on time (in terms of economic 'utility'). Once the system that created and distributed regard, respect, the sense of belonging and approval among the parental group was subverted in this way, there was no quick way to revive it (Jordan, 2008, pp 10-11).

In a society where the dominant mode of regulation is contractual (as in affluent Anglophone countries today), moral regulation is particularly vulnerable to the introduction of rewards, penalties, quantified targets, codified outcome measures and so on. The Third Way's programme has largely consisted in substituting systems that deal in abstract rules and economic value (utility, welfare) for ones which deal in specific, interpersonally negotiated standards, creating 'social value' (well-being), which is distributed through interactions between members. In public policy, 'one of the most striking tendencies of our time is the expansion of markets and market-orientated reasoning into spheres of life traditionally governed by non-market norms', making issues about 'the right way of valuing social practices' into ones about incentives and choices (Sandel, 2010).

Because cultural and moral regulation relies on intersubjective communications and accountability among members of a community, it depends on institutions that are different in kind from the ones that sustain contractual regulation. Yet, despite its lofty ethical sloganising, the Third Way has erected a regime based almost exclusively on contractual regulation, assuming that the maximisation of overall utility (in terms of orthodox economic analysis) is the only fundamental goal of a successful society. This is the foremost factor in the explanation of its failure.

Not only has the economic crash exposed the weakness of the theory of information, incentives and contracts which was supposed to supply 'growth with stability' (Stiglitz et al, 2006), it has also been accompanied by a rash of scandals and failures in the fields of health, education and social welfare, which illustrate the unsuitability of wholesale contractual regulation for these spheres of activity. This book examines these calamities, and looks for alternative institutional and cultural approaches that may be more morally and practically robust.

Can the Third Way be rescued?

In the aftermath of the economic crash, a fashionable set of ideas about how to patch up the Third Way model emerged from the literature of 'behavioural economics'. According to this analysis, individuals cannot be assumed to be rational maximisers of their utility under all conditions, so they should be 'nudged' towards socially approved and long-term beneficial actions, through the design of a 'choice architecture' that allows sustainable and morally defensible outcomes (Thaler and Sunstein, 2008). With the shaky recovery, with debt-ridden government and mass unemployment, but allowing high pay and higher bonuses to return to the shored-up financial sector, this approach promises to tame the 'animal spirits' (Akerlof and Shiller, 2009) that led to excessive risk taking, by dealers and borrowers alike, and put the world economy back on a smooth developmental path, within ethically acceptable parameters.

But this is obviously no more than a rejigged version of the same model. It still relies on individuals to make choices based on information and incentives, for the sake of competitive advantage, albeit within systems that are supposed to protect them from the worst consequences of their gluttony, addictive propensities and self-destructive euphoria. The revised model still supposes that an equitable order can be achieved through law and policy, reward and punishment, within markets and market-like systems, without explicit moral engagement, debate or even meaningful understanding of the issues at stake among members (citizens).

This attempt to revamp the Third Way still rests on an overall rationale, applicable to all types of interaction, and derived from economic analysis. It conceives the environments in which individuals interact as undifferentiated, but the individuals themselves as highly diverse, distinguished by their variety of tastes (for commodities and social units) and self-developmental projects. Above all, the model's supposed efficiency and equity still comes about through the decisions of these same individuals, conceived as capable at least of 'bounded rationality' (Thaler and Sunstein, 2008), and therefore still aims to maximise their opportunities for choices (albeit 'nudged' ones).

In the UK, Tony Blair's advisers quickly spotted the potential for behavioural economics. David Halpern, a close policy aide, reports that the pioneer of this school of thought, Robert Cialdini (2001), was invited to 10 Downing Street to consult on his approach to government (Halpern, 2010, p 231); he also endorses Thaler and Sunstein's claim that 'libertarian paternalism' derived from these principles could be the new Third Way (p 233). Halpern links the approach to information, incentives and contracts, in an improved way to 'bend public behaviour to more beneficial outcomes' (2010, p 241).

But if recent advances in neuroscience (Gigerenza and Todd, 1999) and evolutionary psychology (Wilson, 2002) are to be believed, people are not so much *irrational* as moved by social forces – 'group think', 'herd instincts', linking us to the behaviour of others (Gladwell, 2006). Far from being autonomous, independent and unique, our thoughts and feelings are all derived from the collective life around us. We take our ideas, images and desires from the everyday cultural resources available and allow these words, symbols and slogans to 'do our thinking for us' (Douglas, 1987).

In an individualistic, commercial culture, this means that we think and act in terms of the tropes of self-realisation, the fantasies of identity and the banal aspirations of advertisements. We are easily led to believe that we need the latest gismo, fashion item or fancy home adornment. If credit is 'available', we quickly conclude that it is a good idea to borrow to the hilt. Far from being distinctive, original selves, we are individualistic conformists, copies of the marketing profiles of companies that target us for suckers (Jordan, 2004). For example, in Ireland the combination of property speculation and a credit bubble led to a construction boom that by 2010 had produced over 250,000 empty new-build homes, 'ghost estates' on the edges of every town, which stood as huddled collective monuments to the mass delusions of individualism.

New Labour in the UK accepted the new economic settlement imposed by Margaret Thatcher in the 1980s; the Third Way consisted in placating finance capital, allowing it to inflate asset prices and tinkering with the consequences for the poor. John Kampfner, a former editor of the *New Statesman* who left the Labour Party over the Iraq war, writes that the New Labour project assumed that it could change society only by stealth, and that its leaders 'restricted their aims to offering limited palliative care for the most disadvantaged.... Having raised the white flag to the super-rich, ministers asserted their power elsewhere, seeking ever more ingenious ways of telling ordinary people how to lead their lives' (Kampfner, 2010). The stealthy method is perpetuated in 'libertarian paternalism', along with the authoritarian goals.

So the attempt to breathe new life into the Third Way is really pitting these digs in the ribs against the massive influence of global commercial organisations. If the existing dense thicket of laws, rules, charges, fines, surveillance cameras and fixed penalties cannot induce us to act in ethically acceptable ways, are we really to suppose that a few more inducements, or some rearranged 'default options', will make us adequately provide for our old age, or eat more healthily, or reduce our carbon emissions?

Far more significant, surely, is the possibility that the social nature of our thought and behaviour steers us, without conscious effort, into adjustment to others' actions, through awareness of their emotions and responses (Bunting, 2009). We are led, even in a society that promotes difference, to emulate and imitate, to fit in, even when we are urged to compete (Grist, 2009b). Is this laziness, lack of spirit, fear of standing out? Or is it a perversion of something potentially more positive – empathy for others, desire to cooperate and the search for fairness?

These questions push the post-crash debate back into the foundational texts of modern moral, social and political philosophy. Writers like David Hume ([1739] 1978) and Adam Smith ([1759] 1948) were trying to base the order of a future affluent, urban society on the psychological and anthropological evidence available to them at that time. Above all, they wanted to show that *institutions*, like the family, property and markets, could be derived from ordinary human emotions (passions) such as sexual desire, the need for security and admiration for the grand (if often useless) designs of the ambitious minority.

It was this search for human instincts (or drives) towards 'sympathy', 'limited benevolence' and 'emulation' that fuelled their optimistic speculations about the possibility of future societies without arbitrary authority, despotic power or superstitious belief. But by the end of the 18th century, the terror which followed the French Revolution, the imperial conquest of Europe by Napoleon and the beginnings of capitalist industrial production (the machine age), all combined to demand more thoroughgoing analyses of collective life under modern conditions.

It may not be too fanciful to suppose that the period since the collapse of the Soviet Bloc in 1989, encompassing the 'War on Terror', the recognition of climate change and the economic crash of 2008-09, represents another such period of challenge to the intellectual foundations of our society's institutions. In retrospect, the Third Way may seem like the last attempt to shore up a crumbling order of the late 20th century, particularly in its reliance on contractual regulation of collective life.

If indeed our present historical moment marks the last hurrah of Benthamite codification, what approach to human society (or indeed, to what it is to be human, as the Labour MP Jon Cruddas has put it) might provide an alternative? In Part I of this book I consider whether there is anything in the legacy of idealism, Romanticism and collectivism

– the discarded traditions of the 19th and early 20th centuries – that might inform this search.

The reason for turning in this direction is that those commentators most opposed to the manifestations of mechanistic approaches – to government and to the management of production and trade – were convinced that the separation of moral, spiritual and aesthetic considerations from these aspects of human experience would be fatal to quality of life. They insisted, therefore, that the analysis of new phenomena of all kinds, through astronomy, chemistry and microbiology, as well as through voyages of discovery and anthropological observation, should be informed by a full awareness of their cosmological, emotional and social significance for themselves and for their fellow citizens (Whale, 2000; Holmes, 2008).

In other words, they demanded that new science, technology and mass production should not allow knowledge and its application to escape from moral scrutiny of its implications, or to occupy a realm outside that of emotional and social life. This was because they were uncannily conscious of the interdependence of our life – botanical and animal as well as human – on the natural environment, in a way that subsequent thinkers and politicians were not. For example, the great chemist, Sir Humphry Davy, speculated on the existence of a carbon cycle (Holmes, 2008, pp 355-6). The whole tendency of idealist and Romantic thought of the time was summed up at the end of his life by the German polymath, Alexander von Humboldt, mathematician, astronomer, geologist, explorer and anthropologist:

> In considering the study of physical phenomena, not merely in its bearings on the material wants of life, but in its general influence on the intellectual advancement of mankind, we find its noblest and most important result to be a knowledge of the chain of connection, by which all natural forces are linked together, and made mutually dependent upon each other; and it is the perception of these relations that exalts our views and ennobles our enjoyments. Such a result can, however, only be reaped as the fruit of observation and intellect, combined with the spirit of the age, in which are reflected all the varied phases of thought. (von Humboldt, 1849, p 1)

Faced with the challenges of climate change, environmental degradation, limited supplies of oil and water, population growth and food scarcity, the archaic idealism of this passage seems surprisingly closer to the mark than the current economic orthodoxies. Although they dealt in metaphysical claims about hope, faith and spirit, what writers like Samuel Taylor Coleridge, William Hazlitt and Thomas Carlyle were trying to capture – in opposition to their 'mechanical' antagonists – was an account of the ways in which through 'intuition' or 'imagination' people could be moved to act in line with a morality reflecting 'the collective common sense' (Coleridge, 1825, p 82) of interdependence.

In Part I of this book I therefore explore how new evidence on neuropsychological responses and evolutionary biology can be linked to earlier thought about unconscious moral and social impulses, to consider the basis for a new institutional approach to public policy.

New alternatives to the Third Way

What makes the present moment particularly interesting and significant for the development of human societies is that it is not only the Third Way that has failed. The neo-conservatism that dominated federal politics in the US from 2000–08 has suffered an even more humiliating collapse in credibility. Yet it is ironic that, in elections since the economic crash, only that of Barack Obama as President of the US and of Kevin Rudd as Prime Minister of Australia demonstrate any popular revulsion against the extremes of market triumphalism. The political mood has favoured moderate conservatism (David Cameron in the UK), with European variations from the pragmatic Anglophile (Nicolas Sarkozy in France) to the vaudeville baroque (Silvio Berlusconi in Italy).

So one of the crushing disappointments of the Third Way is that it has offered no basis for constructing a successor to the combination of market worship and imperialism into which it mutated during the Blair-Bush years. In spite of its claim to have offered a 'new settlement' between the interests within economy and society, it actually extended and consolidated the neo-liberal order. Under its regime, people committed large amounts of their future earnings to repay the increased borrowing that rising house prices had allowed. The economic crash revealed that it was they who were also bearing the risks associated with cheap credit and overblown consumption, while the rich enjoyed a massive increase in their wealth.

So people were angry and demanded justice; they came to recognise the inequalities and destructive consequences of the boom years. At the time of the economic crash in the UK, personal debt stood at £1.4 trillion. But the social and political infrastructure had been weakened by these developments, and there were no movements at the national or local level through which to express this revulsion or build alternatives.

What was required was 'a deep and long transformation that will bring about a good society', in which interdependency and equality were asserted, and security, respect, recognition and the sense of belonging enabled (Cruddas and Rutherford, 2009).

Two important new books about justice appeared in 2009, both challenging aspects of the dominant thinking of the previous quarter of a century. Amartya Sen's *The idea of justice* (2009) rejected the approach of John Rawls (1971) to deriving the principles of justice from an agreement between individuals in a hypothetical state of equality, where their abilities and interests were not known to themselves. In arguing against this attempt (in the tradition of Hobbes, Locke and Rousseau) to derive just social arrangements from a contract between such individuals, he asserted again the claims of another tradition (of the Marquis de Condorcet, Adam Smith, Mary Wollstonecraft, Karl Marx and J.S. Mill among others) of improving justice by addressing specific injustices (see p 131).

Michael Sandel (2009a, 2009b) argues that the justification of market-based arrangements cannot rest on their abilities to maximise the overall income of societies or the freedom of individuals. This is because justice deals in several different kinds of value at stake in various spheres of social relations, and because social arrangements uphold the virtues required to sustain a good society. Using examples from the economic crash, he appeals to moral arguments based on the sense of injustice and outrage felt by people about bankers' greed, and their undeserved rescue through the subsequent government bail-out.

Both these philosophers offer insights into the way a moral order works, and both criticise the excessive reliance on abstract principles and economic forces for the achievement of socially desirable outcomes. In their different ways, they encourage the recognition of the importance of moral and cultural regulation of economy and society for the sake of a politics of the common good. In Part II of this book I argue for a more limited role for economics in public policy, and for a strengthening of the processes through which wealth and power are made accountable to communities.

As we come to understand better the ways in which people create the sense of such accountability to each other through their interactions, and how this in turn gives rise to a set of standards governing their relationships, the question for the future is how these can be shifted from their present focus on individual self-development and consumption towards collective concern for the quality of life and the environment. In the UK there are the beginnings of some recognition of the need for transformation among Third Way supporters, such as the former

New Labour minister, James Purnell (2010), appealing for 'vitality and vision' in New Labour's response to its crisis.

Purnell argues that this implies a rejection of the managerial vocabulary, the administrative values and the technocratic vision of New Labour in office, and a return to the moral traditions of Idealists such as R.H. Tawney (the 'common view of the life proper to a human being'), and the reciprocity and mutuality of earlier communities. He quotes the reforms urged by a body of associations and groups, the London CITIZENS (www.londoncitizens.org.uk), as an example of a campaign against injustice and for local activism in the wake of the economic crash.

In the meanwhile, and especially in the UK, there have also emerged some outlines of new thinking on the right, which address the problems raised in the previous section and which even look in similar directions for their inspiration. In particular, the work of Phillip Blond (2009a, 2009b, 2009c) sketched (in very broad-brush strokes) a speculative 'Red Tory' approach to the post-crash dilemmas facing a Conservative successor to Gordon Brown in the UK. This addressed both the lack of any convincing moral content in Third Way programmes and the corrosive effects of commercial, corporate and financial rationales on public life and civil society.

Blond draws his inspiration from 19th and early 20th-century critics of the ethos of British capitalism and Benthamite public administration, and particularly from the dissident liberal authors, Hilaire Belloc and G.K. Chesterton, both of whom were novelists and poets as well as social commentators (Blond, 2009b, 2010). In this way he introduces the relevance of ethical, aesthetic and spiritual considerations into his critique of affluent Anglophone societies. He, too, seeks a cultural transformation, in which more aspects of everyday life become imbued with elements of respect, reverence and imaginative appreciation. As befits a former lecturer in theology turned think-tank ideas man and shadow cabinet guru, he frequently refers to the religious basis of many of the proposals for cultural and political renewal.

Among his main principles is *subsidiarity*, originally part of Catholic social doctrine (Blond, 2009a) – responsibility for collective issues of concern and provision should be devolved to the lowest feasible level of organisation, so that local and voluntary systems are always preferred to central and compulsory ones. His reassertion of this priority is based on, among other things, a critique of the incursions of big business and high finance, as much as the state, into the lifeworld. It is for his attacks on the power of large firms, especially banks, to subvert community and individual sovereignty that he claims to be a 'Red Tory'.

Hence his institutional design for an alternative to the Third Way rests on radical devolution of decision making to community organisations of all kinds. He argues for a break-up of the assets of banks and corporations, and a redistribution of the powers of government. In the wake of the crash, he sees an opportunity and a justification for these measures, as a necessary step towards a society in which self-organised groups reclaim control over aspects of their lives that have spun out of their control.

But his most radical proposals concern the ways in which these new organisations might be financed, and the redistribution of resources and credit to disadvantaged individuals. Here he argues for a break-up of the nationalised banks and building societies, giving rise to funds for compensating the poorest members of society for their losses during the crash (Blond, 2009c). He suggests that this redistribution should take the form of 'investment vouchers', and that these should in turn fund local social enterprises, from which all residents of deprived districts would doubly benefit (in income/employment and in quality of local infrastructure). He also proposes asset credits, financed out of local council housing bonds, providing income streams for poor people worth around £10,000; rights for communities to buy up local buildings and land for development; and new variants of community investment funds and pensions.

In essence, Blond acknowledges that Margaret Thatcher's 'popular capitalism', through the trickling down of wealth and income to those with least of each, failed. As he recognises, both ownership of marketable assets and access to disposable income have become far more concentrated in the hands of the best off since the 1970s; in the US and Australia, the incomes of manual workers have fallen since then, and their indebtedness risen, while in the UK, the full brunt of the economic downturn has fallen on the worst-off, and not on those whose recklessness caused it. In this sense, his approach represents a welcome acknowledgement that markets do indeed work to the benefit of the rich and powerful, and increase their domination and exploitation of the poor.

These themes were clearly recognisable in David Cameron's election campaign of 2010, with its emphasis on the 'Big Society' and the devolution of power and control to local and voluntary organisations. Cameron also claimed to espouse a long-term culture shift in favour of 'a national life expanded with meaning and mutual responsibility'.

> We will feel it in the strength of our relationships – the
> civility and courtesy we show each other....This is not the
> work of one parliamentary term or even two.... It will take
> more than a generation. (Cameron, 2009)

Although Blond claims close affinity with Cameron's approach to
well-being, quality of life and the ethic of care, it is a large step from
this to the dismemberment of the City of London and its corporate
industrial offspring, or the radical dispersal of central government
controls over provincial political life. How would the assets supposedly
accruing to poor people be managed, and to whom would those in
charge of them be accountable? Airy ideas of community funds and
social enterprises will count for little, if in effect these resources are
taken over by ruthless entrepreneurs, mafiosi, ethnic overlords or plain
incompetents. Big business became big by defeating and driving out
(or at best marginalising) small business; why should these funds and
enterprises be more successful than their local predecessors, from corner
shops to cooperative funeral clubs? Is the principle of subsidiarity (and
the broad-brush communitarianism which accompanies it) any less
abstract and generalised than Third Way values and mission statements?
Which specific moral principles (as opposed to general emotions
and spiritual attitudes) should be applied to spheres such as income
distribution, work roles, healthcare, education and so on? Blond's
prescriptions give no answers to these questions or clear guidelines
for institutional design on cultural shifts.

Above all, there was nothing in the Conservative election campaign of
2010 to suggest the kinds of radical redistribution of resources advocated
by Blond. This has led critics to see the whole 'Big Society' theme as
nothing more than a cloak for severe cuts in public spending; indeed,
Cameron offered his vision of mutuality and associationalism as an
alternative to the 'Big State'. The nostalgia for a past life built around
village shops, banks and churches represents a form of moral regulation
acerbically rejected by Raban (2010) as justifying an assault on the
welfare state more audacious than Margaret Thatcher attempted. The
savage cuts in public services announced by the coalition government
could be a bonanza for large commercial firms, as well as a blow to
the well-being of vulnerable citizens.

The question of how the devolution of power and responsibility to
communities might be combined with other measures to strengthen
wider solidarities and increase political engagement is analysed in Part
III of this book.

Public policy: structure and themes of the book

In the first of his 2009 Reith Lectures, Michael Sandel argued that Aristotle's account of justice, that each person should receive his or her due, relied on an analysis of the different roles and resources (the responsibilities and benefits of membership) in each sphere of society (Sandel, 2009a). This is the approach taken in this book. If each of the areas of public policy is understood as involving certain social roles, and mobilising certain resources, as well as producing and distributing certain goods for citizens, then we need also to understand the power relations constituted by those activities and distributions, and the modes of regulation on which they rely.

At this point it may be useful to give a very specific example of the form of analysis adopted in Parts I and II of this book. My choice comes from the field of employment, wages and benefits, and is used purely as an instance of the approaches taken to issues of justice, power and regulation in each of the areas of public policy analysed there.

In December 2008 yet another New Labour Welfare Reform Act in the UK enabled benefits administration to be contracted out to private firms, and these to be paid extra bonuses according to their success in placing claimants in employment. Among those outsourced in this way were a group of single parents with children over 11 years of age (to be lowered to seven in 2010) in Doncaster.

This pilot project was filmed in the first of a Channel 4 television series, 'The benefits busters' (20 August 2009). The claimants (all women) were selected for a six-week programme, 'Elevate', run by a company, Action for Employment (A4E), which is the largest in this field, and which won an £800 million contract to run the government's Flexible New Deal Scheme in 2009 (Allen, 2010). From the start of the film, the programme leader, Hayley Taylor, told the claimants that she "would not hesitate to take action ... to suspend your benefits" if she did not receive their full cooperation. In the name of 'tough love', she set about identifying the 'emotional barriers' preventing the women from getting off benefits, and continuing (in some cases for many years) to claim support. She insisted on a strict dress code (no jeans and t-shirts) and used individual 'counselling' to unearth guilt and self-loathing (over debts, drinking and above all unemployment) to change attitudes towards job search among group members.

Declaring her 'bible' to be a book based on the television makeover programme 'What not to wear' (by Trinny and Susannah), Hayley Taylor worked with them, as individuals and in a group, to cajole or chivvy them towards employment, with such insistent questions as

"If you really want a job, why aren't you queuing up at McDonald's or Burger King?" She insisted that part-time work on the Minimum Wage, even with unsocial hours, was better than the shame and stigma of being on benefits, a message reinforced by a visit to the job centre, drawing attention to the degradation of the claiming process and the demoralisation of unemployment claimants on view.

What, if anything, was wrong with the scenes conveyed in this film, from a moral perspective? Hayley Taylor was commended by the women participants to her visiting boss, the owner and chief executive of A4E, in tearful tributes, which in turn moved her to tears. They said that she understood them, motivated them, made them reconsider their lives and re-evaluate their plans for their futures. In many ways Hayley Taylor was the very embodiment of Third Way values, opening up new possibilities for disadvantaged and marginalised benefits claimants.

Indeed, four of the women successfully applied for trial positions, on the check-outs at a new branch of Poundland, opening in the town that month. But ironically, one of them, who had been the most forthright in saying that benefit rates made her and her four children better off than they should be, subsequently turned down the offer because it would have reduced her income.

The questions raised by the programme can be divided into three levels: the institutional, the regulatory/authoritative and the cultural aspects of the scenes shown.

Distribution of roles and resources: work and income
- How should work roles be allocated in society? Should the ownership of assets in property or income from other sources (such as the earnings of partners, parents, etc) allow some citizens complete choice about whether to work, and what to do, and the lack of these mean that others are forced to accept whatever employment (at minimum wages) is available?
- Why should certain tasks (shelf filling, burger serving) be classified as suitable to be rewarded by wages and other tasks (parenting, care, self-provisioning, helping neighbours, community work, cultural activities, political work) be deemed unsuitable for waged reward?
- Is it acceptable that the employment of a considerable proportion of the population should depend on the prosperity of another group of citizens? Should the former group be a 'reserve army' of menials, called up to serve the latter only when they have need of such services, and made redundant whenever they cannot afford them?
- How should the state intervene in income distribution and labour markets? According to what principles (and with what conditions)

should benefits be supplied, and on what terms should employment be subsidised (for instance, by tax credits)?

Regulation and enforcement: power relations
- Should benefits authorities be empowered to reduce or suspend the benefits of those who refuse specific employment or training offers? What rights over choice of employment should claimants have?
- Should private firms be commissioned to enforce low-paid work, and enabled to recommend suspension of benefits? Should they be given incentives to get claimants into employment, irrespective of its quality, or the long-term prospects of improved income?
- Should firms be able to make profits, and their owners and executives to enjoy high salaries, from the enforcement of low-paid work conditions on claimants?
- Should the exercise of power over claimants be organised through systems of contract and incentives, whereas the entitlements of claimants are subject to penalties and refusals?
- Should new groups of beneficiaries, not previously obliged to take employment (as in the case of these single mothers), be required to seek work just as unemployment is rising sharply?

Interpersonal relations: the moral regulation of 'advice'
- Should the 'advice', 'counselling' and 'training' of vulnerable claimants be entrusted to someone whose 'bible' is a television makeover programme? Does guidance over dress sense, identity and personal insecurity supply reliable practice wisdom for work with such claimants, on a compulsory course?
- How should practitioners in this field be accountable for their practice, according to what standards, and to whom?

I would argue that none of the questions raised by this television film is adequately addressed (or even recognised or relevant) in Third Way discourses and policies. Indeed, the stream of policy documents on 'welfare reform' in the UK has consistently sought to justify institutional changes which erode the rights of benefits claimants and weaken the protections for low-paid workers; which give officials more power to enforce conditions and low-paid work on claimants; and now ones which give largely unregulated and unrestrained private agencies licence to practice in 'training', 'counselling' and job placement. The rationale for these approaches is derived from economic theory, but legitimated by a cod morality – the duty to take responsibility for oneself, the obligation not to be a burden on the taxpayer, the state's role in making work the most reliable route out of poverty (DSS, 1998, p 80).

Indeed, Hayley Taylor's version of 'tough love' is probably the nearest possible approximation to how Third Way values look in practice – public policy à la Trinny and Susannah. In Part III of this book I argue that the approaches and methods derived from makeover shows (or banking or retail sales) cannot be uncritically and unaccountably transferred to serious issues of justice among citizens. If they could, then social workers could justify their child protection decisions by appealing to an episode of 'Supernanny', or public health inspectors their decisions by reference to 'Ramsey's kitchen nightmares'.

Conclusions

In the post-crash situation there is renewed interest in how societies can recognise value other than that which is susceptible to cost-benefit analysis, and cultivate virtues which promote the common good. The idea that market relations uphold both freedom and the maximisation of welfare has been discredited by the banking collapse, and along with it the Third Way approach, with its emphasis on choices and incentives in all social relations. But how much scope is there for a rehabilitation of moral and cultural forms of regulation in a world in which each person's version of the good life is to be given the same recognition as every other's?

I argue that moral regulation is omnipresent in social life, and flows inevitably from human interactions of all kinds. Simply in communicating meanings and purposes we construct a moral order, however ephemeral, in our everyday exchanges. The crucial questions are whether this can form the basis for a reliable set of social and political relationships, and how these can, in turn, be sustained by adaptable and coherent institutional structures. Third Way governments turned their backs on these questions because they were convinced that their versions of social justice and equality could be achieved by a combination of economic arrangements and individual self-responsibility, and that community was relevant only for a residue of issues, mainly concerning deviance in deprived neighbourhoods (Jordan with Jordan, 2000).

This emphasis on individuals, their choices, aspirations and achievements, obscured the collective processes at work in every human society. I suggest that the social order is also a moral order of interdependent members giving each other mutual recognition (Honneth, 1995a, 1995b). The rights, regard and honour we accord each other all involve social value (Jordan, 2008). Even though the individualisation of social life has weakened and fragmented the collective expression of our sense of justice and injustice, it is still in ordinary people's consciousness of these ideas that these moral principles can be most reliably found. The task is therefore to see how a political programme for public policies could be built on these intuitions.

The first task in any such project is to identify the forms of value that are appropriate to each sphere of interaction. The economic model on which the Third Way was based emphasised the differences between individuals' preferences, tastes and life projects. But it created a collective environment in which they were required to negotiate these within a homogeneous medium for exchanges – markets and market-like organisations. Everything from schools, universities and hospitals to village halls and allotment associations were to be run as if they were businesses, with business objectives, strategies and roles. Questions about how to define the proper limits of such an ethos, or to seek other, more appropriate standards for these activities, were driven to the margins.

In Part I of this book I consider how the idea of a good society, with relationships appropriate to these various spheres, might be addressed. I argue that certain aspects of social interaction require institutions which make the moral standards required for justice, equality, well-being, respect and the sense of membership recognisable to participants, and to all citizens. These institutions could protect the types of value appropriate to their sphere from invasion by subversive market or individualistic norms.

So, for example, the sense that public life – the way politicians arrange their private financial affairs, or bankers conduct trades, or people behave towards neighbours – needs to be regulated by moral as well as legal and contractual standards can only be made effective if we limit the scope for utilitarian choice, personal advantage and exclusive groupings. This means we have to reverse many of the changes through which the Third Way broke down solidarities and increased inequalities, and create new ways of pursuing collective purposes.

Third Way reforms have made individualism and competition seem 'natural', but changes in our institutions could allow fundamental aspects of our neuropsychology and evolutionary biology to reassert themselves in a more robust and engaged political and community life. The challenges of climate change and resource depletion demand culture shifts that can only be achieved through transformations in the ways we see nature and each other. As Sandel puts it in relation to justice, it 'is not only about the right way to distribute things. It is also about the right way to value things' (Sandel, 2010, p 261).

These issues hovered over the UK General Election of May 2010. On the one hand, the Conservatives attempted to mobilise the notions of civic engagement, community participation and mutualism, as a revived version of one nation Toryism. David Cameron claimed this as a collective project, and the party manifesto pledged to 'develop a measure of well-being that encapsulates social value' (Conservative Party, 2010, p 38). Labour, on the defensive because its economic individualism had left this flank exposed, justifiably drew attention to the absence of any reliable public institutional supports or funding for the Conservative proposals. And the Liberal Democrats, with a far longer track record in community politics, took the opportunity to present themselves as more plausible bearers of these traditions.

The challenge for the successor political philosophy to the Third Way is to show how economic and moral regulation can be combined and balanced in ways that are appropriate to the types of value produced and distributed in each sphere of activity. After all, in 'The benefits busters' example, the 'group counselling' supplied under government contract did indeed involve the deployment of moral standards in an attempt to change both individual behaviour and the culture of the members through interactions involving first shame, and then recognition of change. The issues raised concerned the power relations established through the official status of the 'counselling' process, the sanctions available to the group leader and the questionable origins of the techniques used.

Because the Third Way model saw government as enforcing a contract with self-responsible individual citizens, the Conservatives could describe New Labour in the UK as creating an authoritarian 'surveillance society', symbolised by identity cards, CCTV cameras and unnecessary regulations. They could present themselves as campaigning for civil liberties, as well as for empowering groups, associations and communities – a project to mend a 'Broken Britain' in which bonds of solidarity and trust between neighbours and citizens had been subverted by the Big State. But the Big Society needs to be scrutinised in more detail to examine its credentials for inclusion and fairness.

This book does not simply advocate the substitution of moral for economic regulation. It deals in the far more complex question of how collective institutions can allow these to be balanced in ways that uphold equality and justice, and avoid oppression and exclusion. It is to this task that I now turn.

Part I
A moral order?

Value, virtue and justice

The questions raised by 'The benefits busters' example in the Introduction are ones of political and social justice, equity and fairness among members of a society. But they concern the expression of such moral and social principles through the operation of law and policy, within such institutions as property ownership (including the firm, profit and government contract), employment (wages and salaries, working conditions) and the tax–benefits system (government arrangements for raising revenue from and dispensing income to citizens).

By reference to the example of the Israeli nursery (pp 3–4) in the Introduction, I have already endorsed Michael Sandel's approach to justice as concerned with what members of society value, and the virtues that government seeks to promote, as well as with individual freedom of choice and overall welfare (Sandel, 2009b, p 9). Justice deals in issues about the best way for communities to live together, and what is due to members, both collectively and individually.

Sandel's approach is particularly useful in examining issues of justice in the middle ground between interpersonal relations and ones that concern governments and citizens. Through vivid, telling and memorable examples, he shows that questions about whether profiteering in the aftermath of a natural disaster is justified, whether bankers whose greed caused the economic crash deserve bonuses or whether a professional golfer with a circulatory disorder should be allowed to ride around the course in an electrically-powered buggy, cannot be satisfactorily answered by calculating the utilities at stake among protagonists, or by reference to their individual rights and entitlements. What matters in these examples is the deserts of people who share in certain common risks and advantages of their spheres of life, and who have strongly held views over what they value about these activities and relationships.

Where Sandel's approach is less immediately helpful is in analysing the rights and wrongs of larger-scale issues, concerning the overall benefits and burdens of society's membership, or the role of government, or relationships between societies. For example, it is not obvious how to apply his ideas of virtues, or how to live well together, to questions about climate change, rogue states, terrorism, mass migration or even the tax–benefits issues posed by 'The benefits busters' example.

In this chapter I argue that this is because we first need to understand the role of institutions in fixing the type and scale of value at stake in any set of interactions between members, citizens or strangers. Institutions such as property ownership, markets, tax-benefits systems or even religions, the armed services and sports exist in order to provide ways in which the value attached to people, activities and social units can be identified, produced and distributed according to certain standards. These are moral questions, which institutions are supposed to enable us to resolve, thus reducing conflicts, saving time and improving our quality of life.

One of the most damaging failures of the Third Way has been its attempt to impose a number of overall rationales across the spheres of activity governed by diverse institutions, dealing in very different forms of value. These rationales have dealt in utility maximisation, in individuals' rights, entitlements and choices, in the primacy of employment-derived income as a measure of contributions by citizens and in the corresponding shame and stigma attaching to those who do not contribute in this particular way, or who reject the goals of 'independence' and self-realisation as standards for assessing their life projects.

I argue that these rationales, presented as principles based on 'values', and leading to laws, regulations, detailed targets and standards, rewards and punishments, serve to confuse and obfuscate many of the most important questions at stake in our present moment of development, and especially in the post-crash environment. 'The benefits busters' programme was an example of how these questions are obscured rather than clarified by Third World thinking about social justice.

Because institutions are diverse, and have been derived from different periods of our development as societies, they co-exist in tension, sometimes in contradiction. Because they define, produce and distribute different kinds of value, according to a variety of standards, there are questions that arise in the hinterland between them that are difficult to resolve. Part of the point of public policy is to identify and reason about such questions, ideally to resolve them through the application of principles that allow new institutional developments.

Already this seems to be happening in the post-crash environment, because the consequences of the crash have put intolerable strains on the operation of organisational systems, discrediting the institutions they are supposed to uphold. Here again, an example concerns the tax-benefits system. In September 2009, The Centre for Social Justice (CSJ), a think-tank founded and presided over by the former leader of the Conservative Party, Iain Duncan Smith, recommended a radical integration of the schemes for distributing income to working-age UK citizens with those for raising revenue through deductions from pay (CSJ, 2009). Although its proposals were careful to avoid spelling out all the moral implications of the changes proposed, they do, in fact, address a set of contradictions that were apparent in 'The benefits busters' programme (see pp 15-17).

The real test for any such proposal is whether it promotes a convincing set of standards of behaviour, to which all citizens can hold each other to account in morally defensible ways. If there are issues of value at stake in a particular set of activities and relationships, the institutions in question should clarify both what actions and relationships are valued and why, and how people should respond to and engage with each other across a range of situations.

In this chapter I investigate how moral issues have been obscured rather than clarified by Third Way institutions and discourses, but how in spite of this, underlying ethical questions emerge and demand debate. These include examples from the political, financial and social spheres, where the attempt to regulate in line with contract theory and the incentives facing self-interested and self-responsible individuals have failed to establish a viable order.

Missing the point: justice and MPs' expenses

If democracy is meant to be self-rule – government of the people, by the people, for the people – then the legislature is a supra-institution, presiding over all the other institutions which order the collective life of a democratic society. It is concerned with far more than simply making laws and regulations; it also addresses the relationship between the spheres of social life, and which ways of life should be protected and promoted, and how. It is concerned with standards in public life, and the whole cultural basis for relations between citizens, as well as between officials and citizens.

In the UK, these broader issues are symbolised by the standards and norms of behaviour in parliament itself – rules about parliamentary language and behaviour, modes of address and so on. This is supposed to reflect the venerable traditions of the 'mother of parliaments', but also to be an exemplar of the way in which, within the British democratic culture, citizens are expected to contest and dispute with vigour, but also with respect. Parliamentary procedure and standards are part of what the UK claims to represent in a world of fragile democracies, as the longest uninterrupted democratic legislature to govern over the collective life of a large nation.

But in the summer of 2008, and under a Third Way regime, the UK parliament was overtaken by a crisis over MPs' expenses claims, as *The Daily Telegraph* published a leaked list of most of these, in advance of a sanitised version, due for official publication in the wake of disquiet about numbers of inappropriate items claimed by certain individual members. MPs were shocked by the fury, not just in the media but also among their constituents, over the fact that many had profited by 'flipping' second homes, by switching between first and second homes and by making large claims for gardening and cleaning, quite apart from the more outrageous items such as duck houses and moat clearing, or continued claims for mortgages which had been redeemed.

Then, in October of the same year, the first of several independent inquiries into the expenses system reported its findings, requiring a large number of MPs, including ministers and party leaders, to repay sums claimed for gardening and cleaning. There was considerable outrage among members about the fact that much of this money had been claimed 'within the rules', and approved by the House of Commons authorities at the time. This, it was argued, was unjust, because it applied new rules retrospectively, implicitly penalising members for actions that conformed to the relevant current regulations.

For several weeks the row continued, with some MPs very reluctant to repay the sums demanded, despite their party leaders' insistence that this should be done. Why was there such a gap between the views of the public and those of parliamentarians over the fairness of these rulings?

A number of considerations might be advanced in support of the public's moral intuitions about the justice of these demands for repayment:

- There was always an overriding principle governing expenses claims that they should *all* be wholly and necessarily incurred in pursuit of members' duties as MPs.
- Sir Thomas Legg, who wrote the report, was not, as parliamentarians sought to represent him, an anonymous civil servant and an outsider to the Westminster system, but a longstanding member of the parliamentary committee on expenses, who had been warning for several years that the system was corrupt, and heading for trouble.
- In the case of cleaning and gardening expenses, no receipts were required by the authorities for payments to be made. It was quite possible 'within the rules' to make these claims without any cleaning and gardening being done.
- Public outrage was not so much against the specifics of each claim as against the prevailing acceptance among members of standards

over expenses which were seen as corrupt, and as lacking in respect for voters, and for parliament itself.

• By extension, the public was calling for a public recognition by MPs of their failure to live up to the standards expected of them, and to set an example of how behaviour in public life should be conducted.

More generally, therefore, since parliament symbolises the collective life of the nation, its members should be expected to show proper regard for its honour, reputation and even sanctity. If the UK's place in the world rested partly on the esteem due to its system of parliamentary democracy, then their behaviour had brought the country into disrepute. After all, both World Wars were supposed to have been fought in the name of parliamentary democracy and the rights it upheld.

In other words, 'keeping the rules' was not the appropriate standard to apply to parliamentary behaviour, especially when MPs made these rules for themselves. Justice demanded that they set an example, and conduct themselves in a way that upheld decency, honour and respect for institutions in public life. This was especially applicable to New Labour government figures, much given to pontification about lack of self-responsibility and diligence among benefits claimants, residents of deprived districts, parents, young people and so on.

Above all, the scandal indicated that Third Way methods of regulating public life, through detailed codes and categories, was fundamentally flawed; without the spirit of regard for the sanctity of institutions, and without a culture in which members collectively upheld standards perceived as morally binding, this approach was bound to fail. The public recognised that both of these features were absent from Westminster's collective life.

Also in October, a damaging scandal developed around the Attorney General, Baroness Scotland, who had employed a housekeeper from Tonga without fully checking her immigration status. Not only was Baroness Scotland the chief government law officer, she had also been the Home Office minister responsible for steering through parliament the Act requiring employers to carry out these checks, taking photocopies of documents to verify this had been done. In Lady Scotland's case, it was obvious that the detailed regulation of these matters was not seen as morally binding, even on the instigator of the legislation. If democracy is supposed to be self-rule, then clearly the Third Way version of law making was not effective, even among members of the legislature itself.

Justice demands that some institutions commit members of their sphere of activity (in this case, politics) to a set of moral standards, that is, to the moral regulation of those activities. The legislature is one such institution; although it makes the laws that impose contractual regulation on other spheres of collective life, it should order itself by principles of probity and honour, sustained through debate, public reason and the sanctioning of lapses from the cultural code. The public recognised that, under the Third Way regime, the moral regulation of parliamentary standards had broken down.

In their own defence, some MPs argued that the system was really one of 'allowances', not 'expenses', and that it had developed to compensate for the fact that parliamentary pay had not risen in line with the salaries of comparable occupations. On this account, public outrage had been stoked up by the media, and was based on a misunderstanding of the significance of the disputed claims. But these arguments have been considerably weakened by subsequent revelations about the actions of MPs, including prominent New Labour ex-ministers.

The underlying issue is whether elected representatives (and those given legislative powers as peers) have been conducting themselves (as they are required to do under their ethical code) in ways that put the public interest before their own. Practices which had become part of the routine fabric of daily parliamentary life, because they mirrored the Third Way approach to government, looked shabby or worse when they were exposed to public scrutiny. This was most obvious when the public relations methods used by New Labour to manage communications with the electorate spilled over into the legislative process, in the form of lobbying by commercial interests, and especially when parliamentarians were seen as profiting from attempts to influence the details of legislation – an example of 'the expansion of markets and market-orientated reasoning into spheres of life traditionally governed by non-market norms' (Sandel, 2010, p 1).

On 22 March 2010, the Channel 4 television 'Dispatches' episode 'Politicians for hire' showed MPs, including the former New Labour ministers Stephen Byers, Geoff Hoon and Patricia Hewitt, responding to invitations to join the board of a bogus firm of US 'consultants'. They were seen to boast about how they could help companies and interest groups influence legislation and policy, through their knowledge and contacts, including introductions to ministers and to Tony Blair, in exchange for remuneration of £3,000 to £5,000 per day.

Stephen Byers, former Transport Secretary and Business Secretary of State, described himself as "a bit like a sort of cab for hire". He already held consultancies with the transport company National Express, and with the mining group Rio Tinto. He claimed that he still met Tony Blair regularly, and that he had influenced the Transport Minister Lord

Adonis to fix the terms on which National Express got out of one of their mainline train contracts without major penalties while retaining two others. He also said he had, on behalf of Tesco, enlisted the Business Secretary, Lord Mandelson, to amend proposed new regulations on food labelling. Stephen Byers later stated that these claims were untrue, and they were denied by the ministers and firms mentioned, but the evidence that he attempted to use them for his material advantage could not be denied.

Geoff Hoon, who had more recently been Secretary of State for Defence, said that he was looking for opportunities to translate his knowledge and contacts into money. He claimed that his continued involvement in British and European strategic defence planning put him in a position to advise companies seeking procurement contracts. He argued that the parlous state of public and business finances made many European companies vulnerable to takeovers by US firms keen to expand their market shares. He said he would consider a post as chair of the board of directors of the consultants.

Patricia Hewitt, formerly Secretary of State for Health, who held positions at British Telecom, Barclays Bank, Boots the Chemist and the private health insurance organisation BUPA, claimed she still had access to government and could arrange meetings. Baroness Morgan, a 10 Downing Street insider in the Blair years, who was paid by the Lloyds Pharmacy group, boasted of her intervention in the House of Lords debate about the treatment of children's diabetes.

The three former ministers were suspended from the parliamentary Labour Party immediately after the programme was broadcast, amid fury from their own party's MPs; the former Secretary of State for Justice, Jack Straw, said that they had brought the party and parliament into disrepute. But the former Deputy Leader, Roy Hattersley (2010, p 32), wrote that their behaviour was 'consistent with the New Labour view that politics should be taken out of politics', because government was about running 'UK plc'. If all spheres in society are ordered through the same set of incentives for gains in individual advantage, and all value is measured in the same terms, then such actions are to be expected.

In other words, the expenses scandal was not about a single anomalous instance of self-seeking behaviour among parliamentarians. The head of the new body set up (at a cost of £6.5 million) to regulate expenses claims, Sir Christopher Kelly, commented on the 'Dispatches' programme that the problem was not one of rules, but of the need for a change of culture and behaviour. It cannot have escaped his notice that his staff of 80 (that is, roughly one for every eight MPs) represented a very expensive illustration of what happens when a culture of probity breaks down, and is substituted by one of external contractual regulation.

The biters bit: high-frequency trading

If the legislature is a sphere in which the moral regulation of members, practising democratic self-rule, is appropriate, is it possible to define other spheres of activity in which contractual regulation alone is appropriate, even in terms of the principles in justice? In this section I consider the case of trading in stocks, bonds and currencies by bankers, seen as one of the main spheres in which regulation failure caused the economic crash.

To what extent was this a failure of authorities like the Federal Reserve in the US and the Bank of England and Financial Services Authority (FSA) in the UK, which appropriately exercise contractual regulation, following principles accepted by the Third Way orthodoxy (Stiglitz and Greenwald, 2003; Bolton and Dewatripont, 2005; Stiglitz et al, 2006), and what role, if any, should be played by moral regulation? These are complex questions, but in this section I explore them through a specific example of a growing practice in post-crash trading, involving automatic buying and selling by high-powered computers.

Many of the Enlightenment philosophers, such as David Hume and Adam Smith, explored how contractual relations could replace moral and political ones across a wide swath of interactions in large-scale societies. They argued that the history of monarchical, aristocratic and theocratic rule was one of violence and arbitrary abuse, and that it involved systematic violation of the freedoms of subjects. People could rule themselves, and justice between them be achieved, only if institutions could be established allowing them to interact on the basis of their preferences, tastes and desires, not of those dictated by their rulers' thirst for power, honour and riches.

Hume ([1739] 1978, pp 490-5) argued that private property was the foundation for societies in which peaceful and respectful relations could be sustained, and Smith ([1759] 1948, Part IV, Chapter 1) extended this to trading in markets, maintaining that these institutions allowed resources to be distributed as equitably as was feasible, within economies producing the highest possible output of commodities, given their human and natural resources. Later theorists of property and markets, such as Friedrich Hayek (1976), have described the order established through these institutions as 'spontaneous' and – following Hume and Smith – declared that political attempts to impose 'patterned' outcomes, according to ideas of social justice, infringed the liberties of individual citizens and held down the overall welfare of populations.

These arguments were largely accepted by theorists and politicians of the Third Way (Giddens, 1998; Blair, 1998a). Although they saw an important role for government in achieving equality of opportunity, by investing in education and training, activating benefits claimants and renewing impoverished urban environments, for instance, they considered that property ownership, employment and markets would supply the institutions for most interactions between citizens, allowing them choice and autonomy, and hence diversity in collective life.

After the crash, the debate within Third Way circles was not about whether forms of moral and political regulation should re-enforce contractual regulation in the economic sphere, but rather over the extent and scope of government regulation, particularly in the financial sphere. There were open disagreements in the UK between ministers, the governor of the Bank of England, Mervyn King and the newly-appointed head of the FSA, Lord Turner, about these questions.

However, the issue of moral regulation did arise within the financial sector itself, for instance over the phenomenon of 'high-frequency trading'. In a BBC Radio 4 'File on 4' programme (3 November 2009), an account was given of a secret location in New Jersey, US, where an area the size of three football pitches is given over to high-powered computers, owned by a number of banks and trading companies, and kept in the highest of security 'cages'. These banks of computers are co-located in order to minimise the time taken for communications between them, each trade being done in about 30 millionths of a second (that is, 400,000 transactions a second). They are programmed with algorithms allowing them to buy and sell stocks and bonds, within these fractions of a second, and it is estimated that one system of this kind, making up the third largest floor in the New York stock exchange, represents the equivalent of the whole of London's market – an increase from almost nothing two years earlier. In all, perhaps 70 per cent of US trading was by then high frequency.

From my perspective in this chapter, the interesting thing about this radio programme was to hear pension fund managers and other large owners of stock complain that they were severely disadvantaged by high-frequency trading of this kind, by investment banks and other specialist firms. They said that every time they started to sell stock, the algorithms of these computer programmes automatically locked onto the shares in question, and anticipated their sales by fractions of a second, driving prices down, but they could equally quickly buy again to make an instant profit after the fund had made its sale (thus further reducing the price of the stock). Because these transactions were so cheap, it was estimated by a contributor to the programme that one firm alone had made US$21 billion in a year from high-frequency trading of this kind.

The pension fund managers interviewed for the programme said that 70 per cent of the money made in this way by investment banks, etc, was at their expense. They complained that the practice was 'unfair' – "there's such a thing as fairness, someone has to look out for fairness in the market", one said. The UK Minister for the City, Lord Mynors, said that the ordinary investor or fund manager was hopelessly outgunned by firms that could afford to spend millions on computers and software of this kind.

Some of the arguments against high-frequency trading were utilitarian, and concerned the overall welfare of society. High-speed trading favoured large, established companies with huge volumes of stock; it discriminated against the shares of new, cutting-edge enterprises, with innovative products or methods of production. This handicapped the whole process of creative renewal in the economy, and destroyed future potential for growth, employment and tax revenue, by cutting funds to the big companies of the future.

But other critics used moral terms to condemn the effects of high-frequency trading on the institutional landscape of business. Even if it improved the efficiency of capital markets, it transformed the ownership structure of firms. One interviewee pointed out that it meant few shareholders thought of themselves as owners – how could they, if they held shares for mere fractions of a second? This undermined the whole concept of a joint stock company. Trading was no longer a way of providing capital for businesses; it had become a game between traders. Indeed, one institutional innovation had been the creation of 'dark pools', in which trades were concealed from those outside the circle of computer processes.

But this new development was a breach of principles of justice in markets, argued several fund managers. Dark pools were not right and fair because they were not open. They were not transparent to other traders who were influencing prices. Indeed, the apparent price was not a 'true price', and not a reliable piece of information on which to base a decision about sale or purchase, because it could be affected by the secret intervention of automatic computer-generated trading before other market actors were able to act on it.

This led to a discussion, in the final part of the programme, about how government regulation might correct these injustices. Here most of the experts agreed that it was impossible to effectively regulate the casino activities of investment bankers – in a sense, these banks *were* the casinos in which betting took place. The only hope was to try to ensure that this side of banking did not adversely influence the supply of credit to the businesses in the real economy. This raised the question of splitting off the investment branches of the large banks, in order to ensure that they were not 'too big to fail', and that government was not bearing the risk of their casino activities. But other commentators pointed out that banks would resist this, because high-speed trading was more profitable than loaning money to ordinary businesses. Gordon Brown had also rejected this approach to the crisis, insisting that banks should not be split up, against the recommendations of the governor of the Bank of England.

But this discussion on public policy on risk and its regulation did not address the questions about justice raised by the fund managers. If high-frequency trading was unfair because it breached a fundamental principle of markets, that they should be transparent, involving reliable information in the form of prices, then legislation and penalties should aim to restore fairness and strengthen institutions that uphold it. If it is impossible to outlaw automatic computer trading, the obvious solution is to tax it, making it far less profitable and restoring to the stock market a level playing field, in which pension funds can trade on the same conditions as banks. This solution – a 'Tobin tax', on all transactions in stock and currency markets – had been recommended by the head of the FSA, Lord Turner, as part of his critique of casino banking, a 'socially useless' activity. But this too had been rejected by the New Labour government.

Utilitarian arguments about the effects on overall welfare in society cannot encompass such ideas as unfair trading or socially useful activity, which appeal to quite other standards. The criticisms by Lord Turner and others of casino banking, irresponsible ownership and the decline of shareholder participation in company affairs appeal to notions of justice and accountability among economic actors; they call for institutions which promote responsible governance, community involvement and open dealing by businesses, as part of a democratic public culture. They also see the role of government as enabling these features of collective life, and stamping out new practices and institutions that undermine them.

A similar point of view has been put forward by the hedge fund manager, Eric Lonergan (2009, 2010). He argues that the real purpose of money is not individual independence and the accumulation of assets; it is interdependence and the sharing of risks. Credit is the means of achieving social goals, and finance is a way of avoiding one party bearing all the risks associated with innovations. But this can become obscure to bankers and traders themselves, as in the events leading up to the crash.

All this shows that the economy – firms, employment, markets – is not an alternative form of regulation, substituting contractual for moral and political relations. Economic interactions and organisations involve value derived from cultures, and require standards supplied by moral and political principles. Even fund managers became aware of this, when they were the victims of unfairness. Unfortunately, Third Way thinking about social justice and the social order did not encompass this insight.

The aftermath of the crash has precipitated a debate about how to tighten contractual regulation, but also how moral standards might re-enter the world of high finance. The decision on 17 April 2010 by the US Securities and Exchange Commission to bring an action against the top investment bank, Goldman Sachs, for selling a product made up of sub-prime mortgages which a partner hedge fund had backed to fail, marked a decisive point in the reassertion of controls on these institutions. In the UK, Gordon Brown denounced Goldman Sachs as 'morally bankrupt'. It remains to be seen whether legal controls and ethical standards can really change the behaviour of these 'masters of the universe', the inventors of the very derivatives that brought about the crash (Tett, 2009).

Do markets and choice promote diversity? The case of bullying

One of the most common arguments for contractual regulation, and against moral and cultural regulation, is that the former allows a diversity of preferences and tastes that the latter cannot. In this view, a market order enables people, all of whom have different conceptions of the good life, and of how to realise their full personal potentials, to choose their own paths for achieving these. This is because markets enable them to carry out advantageous exchanges of all kinds with others; money supplies a common means of exchange, allowing all to reach an equilibrium over the utility they derive from the resources available to them. In this sense, markets allow *both* diversity *and* a common measure of value among individuals with a variety of beliefs, goals and lifestyles.

By contrast, it is argued, societies with an official religious or political version of the good life are intolerant of creative, original or eccentric individuals, and tend to persecute both them and minority groups. The Soviet system of state socialism, especially during the period of Stalin's Terror, is cited as an example of this. In today's world, Iran and

Zimbabwe serve as examples of how a single religious orthodoxy or political party can suppress dissent in the name of a morality (of faith or of distributive shares) that claims a monopoly of virtue.

But this view does not capture the complexity of how conformity is produced and enforced in *all* societies, not simply in single-faith or one-party states. The social order of commercial societies is sustained through cultural codes that indicate acceptable standards of appearance, ownership of resources, demeanour and speech and so on. All these are derived from the institutions that shape the various spheres of interaction, from families, networks and informal associations to schools and workplaces. The cultures that work through these institutions are made up of elements from many aspects of collective life – markets, advertising, branding, recreational facilities, media resources, sport and the arts, as well as politics and faith.

This means that, in a society ordered around consumption of commercial products, conformity consists in large part of adherence to trends and fashions, ordained by advertising and the mass media generally. The value of particular brands, associated with glamour and celebrity, is absurdly inflated because of their cachet in consumer culture. People are judged and esteemed by what they possess and display, the vehicles they drive and the places where they are seen, rather than what they contribute to the well-being of others.

But this type of conformity becomes dangerous to individual liberty, creativity and originality when it takes the form of persecution of those who do not consume, display and preen in the prescribed manner, or when those who lack the means to do so are excluded from circuits of esteem and social regard, or when those so excluded retaliate by resorting to crime, drugs or violence to compensate themselves for the stigma they bear. In these situations, the insecurity and shame generated by the lack of status-giving resources (either by choice or not) create negative social value, which should be subtracted from any contribution to quality of life achieved by the consumption-orientated mainstream. If the value accorded to comfortably-off, secure property holders, and to the rocket-like bursts of fame and wealth bestowed on celebrities, are the most important sources of intimacy, respect and the sense of belonging to the mainstream of a market society, then these negative aspects must be counted against the total of overall well-being (Jordan, 2008).

An example of the ways in which a culture of conformity to material standards, expressed in terms of clothes, mobile phones or other electronic devices, is the bullying of school children who do not look the same, watch the same television programmes or own the same games consoles as the majority of their peers. Here groups of young people shame, hurt and exclude individuals who do not conform. To do so in relation to ownership of material goods is every bit as unjust and persecutory as to do so on the basis of physical appearance, skin colour, ability or disability or religious faith.

This example shows that justice and injustice in social relations are not only attributes of the political system as a whole – its opportunities for self-rule, for minority rights and for individual liberty – but also aspects of the cultures enabled by many institutions in a society. In the UK, the main gains in justice since the 1970s have been in the ways that women, gay people and black people, along with some people with disabilities, are treated in the public sphere – in shops, offices and other places of employment, as well as in official agencies. But bullying and casual violence still afflict many other situations, including the family home, the school and on the street. The enormous gains in consumption opportunities and in household possessions enabled by the shift towards market relations since the beginning of the Thatcher–Reagan ascendancy has not been matched by improved social inclusion of poor outsiders or disadvantaged groups, nor has it been marked by better manners and consideration in the public sphere.

The Third Way recognised that something needed to be done about these phenomena, but it framed its responses in terms of its economic model of social relations. In the UK, Tony Blair formulated the 'Respect Agenda' in the run-up to the 2005 General Election. His Prime Minister's Strategy Unit gave priority to measures aimed at curbing 'yobbish' behaviour, drunkenness, the targeting of vulnerable individuals and families by groups of youths for bullying and harassment and petty vandalism and theft (Halpern, 2010, p 89). But the chosen methods – CCTV, Anti-social Behaviour Orders (ASBOs), parenting contracts and other 'tough love' measures – were aimed at the actions of individual offenders, to impose penalties, disincentives and surveillance. They did not address the cultural basis of this kind of behaviour, or recognise that it reflected the social devaluation of whole groups and communities. ASBOs proliferated, but cultures of personal disrespect remained; negative sanctions conferred little real stigma in already demoralised districts, and – as Halpern (2010, p 90) later conceded – there was little consideration given to how better standards could be constructed and sustained.

This finally became clear in 2009-10, with the deaths of Fiona Pilkington, a single mother from Barwell, Leicester, who killed herself and her 18-year-old learning-disabled daughter after years of bullying and taunting by youths, during which she made more than 30 requests for police assistance; and of David Askew, a 64-year-old man with learning disabilities who had been baited and bullied by youngsters in his neighbourhood (Hattersley, Greater Manchester) for 20 years. The common feature of these cases was that the authorities had been called over and over again to incidents in patterns of behaviour that had become habitual and almost recreational for local young people.

In David Askew's case, the police had installed CCTV cameras and security lighting in his garden, and had even hidden in his house, but the harassment continued on a daily basis. ASBOs had also been made on a number of his tormentors. Neighbours said that he had been 'baited and bullied' and 'tormented to death – like bear-baiting' (BBC 1 television, 'News', 11 March 2010; Carter, 2010). The 'youths', some children as young as eight, would follow him to the shops, or knock on his windows until he threw out sweets and cigarettes; windows had been repeatedly broken. A police chief superintendent commented that 'It is a sad fact that if people are different in a community sometimes they end up being targeted'.

The same day as David Askew's death was announced, a report by HM Inspector of Constabulary, which was critical of the police in England and Wales for failing to deal with anti-social behaviour, stated that 3.6 million complaints of disorder and harassment had been made the previous year, of which a million had been by people with disabilities. This seemed to indicate that this behaviour had become the norm in relation to vulnerable individuals in such communities, and that the approach to it that consisted in surveillance, police warnings and court orders, had hopelessly failed. The problem lay in the fact that such people were not recognised as full members of the community, worthy of recognition and respect, to be included in circuits of belonging and mutual assistance.

The deeper significance of these attitudes has been evidenced in shocking cases where patients in NHS hospitals have been humiliated, neglected and ignored by staff, to the point of death. The worst such scandal was at the Mid-Staffordshire NHS Hospital Trust, where up to 1,000 avoidable deaths of patients admitted via the Accident and Emergency Department occurred between 2004 and 2008; patients were overlooked by staff while appealing desperately for help, or lying in urine or faeces, food was not served or was left out of reach, and others fell without this being noticed by staff, sometimes on several occasions. Complaints by family members were filed away and unanswered. But in spite of these severe failings, the Trust was awarded the prestigious and lucrative Foundation status at exactly this time by the body charged with its inspection and accreditation. As the Healthcare Commission subsequently stated:

> It was clear from the minutes of the trust's board that it became focused on promoting itself as an organisation, with considerable attention given to marketing and public relations. It lost sight of its responsibilities to deliver acceptable standards of care to all patients admitted to its facilities. (Healthcare Commission, 2009, p 10)

So it was not only members of deprived communities who were failing to recognise their common humanity with people in the most vulnerable situations, or grant them the dignity and respect they deserved. The subsequent independent enquiry into the Mid–Staffordshire scandal found that there was a lack of compassion by staff, and breaches of privacy, with patients 'moved and handled in unsympathetic and unskilled ways, causing pain and suffering; and rudeness or hostility' (Boseley, 2010). The culture of impersonal striving for economic advantage spread its contagion to the hospital's professional staff, whose actions towards some of the most helpless patients veered between neglect and bullying.

After the economic crash of 2009, investigations and reports on scandals around UK quangos (quasi non-governmental organisations) and public agencies (such as the Rural Payments Agency, the Learning and Skills Council and the companies supposed to mark SATS tests and allocate student grants) have repeatedly called for 'changes in culture' in these organisations, in the banks and among parliamentarians after the expenses affair. But all these organisations were regulated by laws, contracts and detailed guidance, according to the Third Way's model – a business order, with behaviour steered through information, incentives and penalties. If these organisations had cultures that permitted such injustices to patients, pupils, taxpayers, electors or deposit holders, this was because the mode of regulation (contractual regulation) had failed to address the moral issues at stake (the human rights of the citizens concerned and fairness between members of society). The cultures of these organisations were largely derived from the prevailing Third Way business model; a shift in culture presupposes the availability of other resources for a different mode of regulation, a moral order.

Conclusions

The grounds for excluding moral considerations from public policy and political life have been explored in this chapter, in relation to principles of justice. Ultimately, the attempt to rely on contractual regulation – law, guidance, targets, penalties, etc – which reached its zenith with the Third Way, was seen as getting around the problems of debating and disputing moral absolutes, such as life *versus* choice in abortion, or the right to die in euthanasia. It is argued that these fundamental disagreements cannot be resolved, and that even more nuanced decisions, not involving 'tragic choices' between rights, are very time-consuming and difficult to settle. So it is more efficient, as well as more diversity-friendly, to leave these matters to private conscience, and to deal with policy issues in terms of individual opportunities for self-realisation and achieving the highest possible levels of overall welfare.

The examples chosen in this chapter illustrate the problems of the Third Way approach. Justice deals in standards that are fundamentally about moral features of collective life, and people recognise moral principles as persuasive. Whether on MPs' expenses, or bankers' trading technologies, or bullying of those who are 'different', contractual methods of regulation do not provide adequate answers. A convincing politics of institutions for social justice demands that challenging moral issues must be tackled through public reasoning.

Furthermore, as Sandel has shown in many of his examples, it is possible to debate and decide about moral issues, even ones over which there are disagreements of principle, once we recognise that each institutional sphere involves particular forms of value, and celebrates specific virtues, all of which are relevant to the collective well-being of a society.

One of these examples is the question of whether same-sex marriages should be recognised in law by the state (Sandel, 2009b, pp 253-60). Sandel points out that there are three possible choices to be made on this question – that only heterosexual unions should be recognised, that both heterosexual and same-sex ones be treated as having the same official status as marriages and that the state treats all partnerships as private arrangements, leaving it to faith groups, kinship and community bodies to decide how to honour (or dishonour) such unions.

One set of arguments for heterosexual partnerships alone to be recognised in law is that marriage essentially concerns procreation and the raising of children. But not all couples who marry have children, and same-sex partnerships may, if the law approves, foster or adopt. Conversely, the state may decide to treat all partnerships alike, irrespective of commitment or duration, but it cannot avoid taking a stance on forced relationships of marriage or (in certain faiths), polygamy, the marriage of minors and other such issues. Therefore it is, if only by default, required to define what is legally permissible in relationships, especially if children are concerned.

Finally, Sandel quotes the decision of the Supreme Court of the State of Massachusetts, which ruled that same-sex marriages were to be recognised as on a par with heterosexual unions because they upheld the virtues of commitment and loyalty for an uncertain future. It ruled that it was these virtues which defined the essential value of married relationships for society, not the bearing and raising of children, for which marriage was desirable but which was not an essential aspiration of every married relationship. Sandel argued that the decision of the court in this case was an example of the application of public moral reasoning to an issue of collective concern to the members of a society, with conflicting principles at stake.

This chapter has emphasised the importance of institutions in questions of justice. But institutions dealing in different forms of value can produce conflicts between priorities and goals for a society seeking a good life for its members living together. Public policy should seek to create official institutions that help to reconcile the purposes and standards upheld by institutions such as the family, the community and the firm. It should aim to allow economic life to be consistent with the value of social relationships.

The example of 'The benefits busters' programme illustrated one case of where a government initiative dealt directly in the family life of single parents, trying to influence them towards employment (of any kind, at any wage, for any hours) as a way of expressing responsible and loving parenthood. It also illustrated a way of doing this, through 'group discussion' and 'individual counselling'. The unstated moral assumption behind this initiative was that the benefits system can be harnessed to the dual task of supporting families through a crisis in their income streams (such as the separation of parents, homelessness or unemployment), and their reactivation (by advice and, in the last resort, sanctions) into the labour market.

The question raised by the CSJ's report *Dynamic benefits: Towards welfare that works* (2009) was whether the institution of means-tested benefits for working-age people, developed piecemeal by Conservative and New Labour governments since the mid-1980s, actually creates a framework for achieving these goals, and respects the value of either family or employment.

After cataloguing a long list of policy failures, in terms of ending child poverty, reducing income inequality, decreasing the number of workless households, reducing the number of young people not in education, employment or training (NEET) and reducing the benefits budget, the CSJ's report outlines an entirely new approach to benefits administration. It declares the goals of this radical reform to be:

- to improve incentives for paid work, and for increased earnings, by reducing rates of benefit withdrawal and the impact of taxes on the incomes of very low earners;
- to reward marriage and savings;
- to redistribute income in favour of the lowest earners doing some paid work;
- to achieve these goals without increasing the benefits budget in the medium term.

In relation to the moral issues raised by 'The benefits busters' programme, the point here is that the report frankly stated that the attempt to drive claimants into work with initiatives of this kind had failed because they gained so little in making the first step into the labour market, as a result of the interaction between very complex benefits and tax rules.

Its proposed reform was not simply a technical fix, simplifying the process of moving into work and making better returns on work effort automatically accessible. It was an acknowledgement that attempts to cajole or chivvy claimants like those in 'The benefits busters' programme are unjust, and do nothing to reconcile conflicts between the value of family life and the value of employment. (Details of the approach proposed in the report will be discussed later in Chapter Seven of this book, pp 163-6.)

The Third Way approach to this issue can be seen as an attempt to apply generalised principles about social justice – that it is best approached through equality of opportunity, not equality of incomes, and that official coercion is justified when people fail to recognise that employment is always an opportunity – to a complex question about the value of different kinds of activity. In the election campaign of 2010, the Conservative Party gave no evidence of having been converted to the approach advocated in the CSJ report. But in his first interviews and speeches as Secretary of State for Work and Pensions, Iain Duncan Smith claimed that the benefits system was 'bust' and that he would use the report as the blueprint for its radical overhaul (*The Guardian*, 2010).

The proposed integration of the tax and benefits systems would aim to make those doing less than 16 hours of paid work per week substantially better off than under the existing rules. This could be a necessary condition for the implementation of Cameron's 'Big Society' agenda. Without it, able-bodied and disabled claimants could be excluded from participation, as part-time workers or as volunteers, in the local, associational, mutual and cooperative activities that are supposed to mend the fractures in 'Broken Britain'.

If the coalition government aims to heal social divisions by finding ways to show that it values those marginalised by the economic crisis, and if the 'Big Society' is to be an instrument for a new form of moral regulation to this end, these institutional reforms might therefore be a first step in a new direction. Although it seems unlikely that the coordination between these two aspects of the new government's strategy was planned far in advance, Cameron and Duncan Smith have a political opportunity that might be a turning point in social policy development. Even if the coalition government does not take this direction, these ideas may stimulate the debate in the Labour Party about its future.

In the next chapter I turn to the Third Way's efforts to operationalise its 'values' in relation to choice, and to how public policy can better deal with the issues raised by apparent conflicts between individual liberty and the common good.

TWO

Snap judgements and rational choices

While I have argued that the failure of the Third Way was ultimately a consequence of its moral shortcomings, it came into being as a moral project, to reconcile individual freedom with collective solidarity and security. It was conceived as a political philosophy to improve social justice and to achieve an acceptable equality (of opportunity, not outcome) in market economies.

No proponent of Third Way ideas was more up-front about his ethical credentials than former Prime Minister Tony Blair. He proclaimed that Labour's values had not changed under his leadership, but that the means of achieving them should change. The Third Way was a project for finding new expression for the values of socialism, feminism, anti-racism and social justice. It 'is a serious reappraisal of social democracy, reaching deep into the values of the left to develop radically new approaches' (Blair, 1998a, p 1).

These ideas were forged together into a programme for 'national renewal' of the UK, aimed at 'rediscovering our true national purpose' (Blair, 1998b, p iii). The principles embodied in this were listed as 'equal value [of each individual citizen], opportunity for all, responsibility and community' (Blair, 1998a, p 3), and were expressed in 'a new contract between the citizen and the state, where we keep a welfare state from which we all benefit, but on terms that are fair and clear' (Blair, 1998b, p v).

In this chapter I show that the attempt to define a new settlement of this sort was a conscious effort to transcend Margaret Thatcher's 'property-owning democracy', by combining individualism with egalitarianism in a new way. As suggested by Perri 6 (2000), this involved the reconciliation of two apparently conflicting 'cultural projects', one concerned with personal self-realisation and rights to autonomy, the other with membership and community. The attempt to do this through abstract general principles, combined with detailed codification, legislation, regulation, prescription, reward and punishment, marked out the Third Way as a utilitarian project, in the tradition of Jeremy Bentham.

Within this tradition of political economy, choice is central for individual liberty and rationality. Each citizen is morally sovereign, and is protected against arbitrary and invasive authority by freedom of choice, across a broad range of private and collective issues. Human beings are conceived as utility maximisers, implementing preferences across a number of goods, including facilities they share with others. The ideal society is one in which there is least constraint of choice, with the proviso of the least possible harm to others. This includes the lowest feasible cost of law and regulation, as well as public provision for goods not efficiently supplied by markets.

But in practice, the combination of capitalist means with utilitarian ends has led to a very extensive infrastructure of rules and organisations, supplying the information, incentives and penalties required by this form of social order. Contractual regulation has high transaction costs, not only from lawyers and accountants, managers and inspectors, but also in the form of insurance against the consequences of greed and folly – as both the US and UK discovered after the banking catastrophe of 2008-09.

Passing judgement on the Third Way 15 years from its original conception, Matthew Taylor, who was a close policy adviser to Tony Blair, comments that the individualism which triumphed in the 1980s remained the dominant cultural feature of the New Labour years, and that the egalitarian values proclaimed by Tony Blair failed to gain any real purchase in the social order, either in the UK or the US. Personalised consumerism was simply reinforced by focus group politics and the internet.

> The culture of the City represents the most extreme version of individualism triumphant. All that mattered in the City was individual ambition. There was no egalitarian belief in a wider social or moral purpose for banking, nor was there any effective hierarchy as the rules didn't work.... Every banker believed they had an unlimited capacity to generate wealth and increase their earnings. To have a major area of activity dominated by a single frame of human relations is rare. To then give those in that area the power to influence the well-being of billions of citizens is – as we have now come to understand – a disastrous error. (Taylor, 2009, p 222)

With remarkable symmetry, a commentary from the Conservative camp has reached similar conclusions about Thatcherism. The self-proclaimed 'Red Tory', Phillip Blond, argues that Margaret Thatcher's attempt to dismantle the authority of the monopoly state, and redistribute its powers and resources to individual citizens, failed because the 'free market' collapsed into monopoly finance, big business and deregulated global capitalism. Instead of empowering individuals and voluntary associations, Thatcher created the perfect conditions for self-interest, and a collective environment in which both state and corporations accrue power at the expense of atomised ordinary people (Blond, 2009c, p 1). Blond's explanation of the financial crisis indicates his view of the Third Way's failure to challenge the Thatcher legacy:

> [T]he great housing crash is primarily the result of the absorption of all local, regional and national systems of credit into one form of global credit.... [T]he strategy of market manipulation deployed enormous amounts of capital in speculative arbitrage (just five US banks had control of $4 trillion of assets in 2007). (Blond, 2009c, p 2)

So Blond sees the New Labour regime in the UK as a triumph of speculation and monopoly in the name of free trade and modernisation. He calls for a break up of the big banks and industrial corporations, and a redistribution of all kinds of assets and powers to local community funds and associations, making money work for the many, not the few.

But if the Third Way's attempt to fuse individualism and egalitarianism has failed, we need to examine in more detail which aspects of the utilitarian approach to public policy (seeking to maximise overall welfare) have let it down, even by its own standards. As both Taylor and Blond conclude from the economic crash, individualism under a finance-dominated version of global capitalism is deeply flawed, harms the well-being of citizens and leads to a degenerate public morality. But what are the fatal weaknesses of the model, which betray its economic functioning as well as disabling its moral compass?

In this chapter I analyse the growing evidence from neuropsychology and other sciences that one of the weaknesses in the economic model of the social order is its naïve and mistaken view of *choice*. As I show, there is now massive evidence that most choices are not rational and calculative, as economic theory assumes. They are intuitive, instant, snap judgements based on unconscious social learning and the observation of barely noticed cues. Often, they cannot be accounted for by the person who makes them, and longer deliberation and accountability (being able to give reasons for a decision) can give *worse* outcomes, in terms of consciously intended purposes or objective facts (Gladwell, 2006).

All this has ambiguous moral implications. Snap judgements are partly pro-social – they reveal a degree of sympathy and benevolence, as well as an intuitive ability to 'read' others, rather as Adam Smith supposed divine wisdom to have written into human nature (Smith, [1759] 1948, p 35). But they are conservative, relying on rules of thumb derived from experience over time and – as David Hume ([1739] 1978, p 490) suggested – they demonstrate the 'limited benevolence' which confines trust and reciprocity to small circles of known others. Hence they tend towards the exclusion of strangers and outsiders. Larger solidarities require charismatic leadership or social engineering to achieve sharing of resources and risks.

Judgement can be refined by selective experience (think food and wine), it can be extended and trained (for the work of police officers, firefighters, social workers and so on), and – given the right institutional framework – can overcome prejudice and conservatism. But all this requires the intelligent design of experience, education and mind-broadening interactions, with the aim of equipping people with increased resources and improved skills in deploying them. Cultural changes of the kind mentioned at the end of Chapter One require such measures.

The assumptions about rationality in choice that underpin economics and utilitarian approaches to public policy have been largely unchallenged for the Anglophone countries for 200 years. The last time they were disputed in their totality, as providing a basis for law and government, was in the era of the Romantics, when authors like Samuel Taylor Coleridge, William Hazlitt and Thomas Carlyle contested with Bentham and his followers. Less radical challenges came at the end of the 19th century (by neo-Hegelian Idealists) and during and after the Second World War (by socialist collectivists).

I argue in this chapter that the present moment is an opportune one for a new challenge, focused on the failure of the Third Way. The Romantics, notably Coleridge, were right to try to identify intuitions, near-instinctive responses, emotions and aesthetic feelings, and something like a collective unconscious, as important indications of the shortcomings of rationalist accounts of choice. They were also right to be critical of abstract values and general principles, because they seldom enter into the snap judgements by which we live – racists and non-racists make the same choices in the heat of an emergency situation where racial stereotypes can affect perceptions.

But they were wrong to assume that those non-rational elements could supply the basis for morality and political justice, for the reasons noted above. A politics of the common good requires *both* the mobilisation of snap judgements derived from social experiences *and* the intelligent design of a collective infrastructure that promotes solidarity.

Launching the young: equality of opportunity?

The Third Way's project for fusing individual choice with equality and social justice redefined the central terms of the debate between liberalism and socialism. In his statement of Third Way principles, Anthony Giddens, a leading influence on Tony Blair, wrote that:

> ... the new politics defines equality as inclusion and inequality as exclusion; inclusion refers in the broadest sense to citizenship, to the civil and political rights and obligations that all members of society should have ... it also refers to opportunities and to involvement in the public space. (Giddens, 1998, pp 102-3)

But his definition of equality in relation to exclusion qualified this in important ways:

> [E]xclusion is not about gradations of inequality, but about mechanisms that detach groups from the social mainstream. (Giddens, 1998, p 104)

He explained that this implied that public policy should focus on making such groups more employable through education and training. 'The cultivation of human potential should as far as possible replace "after the event" redistribution' (Giddens, 1998, p 101). In what he called the 'social investment state', equality consisted in getting citizens better equipped for participation in a competitive economic environment, and specifically in the 'knowledge economy' (that is, a post-industrial labour market).

In view of Tony Blair's emphasis on education as the flagship of New Labour's programme, and in particular on the expansion of higher education places, considerable media attention focused on the revelation, not long after his accession to the office of Prime Minister, that his wife, Cherie Booth QC, had purchased a fairly luxurious flat in Bristol for their eldest son, Euan, who was about to study for a degree at the University of Bristol in 2002. The flat was large enough to let out rooms to several fellow students, and critics suggested that this revealed the extent of the advantages enjoyed by the UK's 'First Family' in comparison with the average household, an opinion reinforced by the publication of other details of Cherie Booth's lifestyle, including the employment of a style coach/image consultant, who also turned out to have close connections with a controversial Australian entrepreneur. Her defenders pointed out that she was a distinguished barrister, an expert in human rights, and commanded a higher salary than her husband; why should she not spend it as she chose, including providing for her children?

In fact, many better-off parents were buying houses or flats for their student offspring at that time. It made sense to do so, given the rising prices of housing, the imperative of getting a foot on the property ladder, the costs of student life (defrayed by renting out rooms) and so on. But an uncomfortable feeling remained that, just as fees were being introduced for university study, and most students were graduating with considerable debts to the student loan organisation, this case highlighted inequalities of opportunity.

Unease of this kind has been increased during the post-crash period because the prospects for students paying off this debt are now bleak. Whereas even recent graduates had good chances of getting salaries sufficient to pay off their indebtedness and to buy a house soon after graduating in the boom years, unemployment rates among those coming onto the labour market in 2009 reached 20 per cent, and many others were taking low-paid posts, such as security officers or door-to-door salespeople. So the advantages bestowed by parents who could afford to buy houses for their student offspring can now be recognised as enormous; indeed, they appear to be breaches of the principle of equal opportunity for all.

In my generation, studying in the 1950s and '60s, although fewer school leavers went to university, most of those who did got grants to cover their living expenses, and their educational costs were paid in full. This, along with the rapid expansion of public sector professional employment (in education, health and social work), explained the higher rates of social mobility in the UK in that period than occurred under New Labour.

The rationale for making students (or their parents) pay the costs of their higher education is that at this stage (unlike primary or secondary schooling) the private benefits they gain from their degrees are around the same level as the social benefits (increased productivity in society as a whole) taken over a working life. Graduates enjoy significantly higher longer-term earning power than those who start work on leaving school.

But this is partly because (unlike in the post-war period) almost all forms of employment are now available only to people with paper qualifications to undertake them. This credentialism leads to an over-qualification game, where competition for better-paid work means that higher and higher levels of education and training are required, as is becoming obvious in the post-crash economic environment. Forty years ago people of good ability were able to get on without degrees or diplomas; now only those with 'good' degrees from 'leading' universities have access to the most sought-after positions, and even quite humble posts demand recognised credentials.

The Third Way's notion of equality of opportunity was part of its attempt at a 'new settlement' between the types of social relations patterned by two different cultural traditions (and their 'thought styles'). Following Émile Durkheim (1912), anthropologists such as Michael Thompson et al (1990) and Mary Douglas (1996) postulated a fourfold division of such elements in the social order, all of which are present in complex modern societies, but which must be constantly balanced, fused and managed in any successful and sustainable institutional regime (6, 2000; Jordan with Jordan, 2000, p 43; Taylor, 2009, p 221) (see Figure 2.1).

According to the Third Way thinkers who shaped New Labour policy in the UK, the Second World War had created the conditions

Figure 2.1: Thought styles/cultural projects

Fatalism	**Hierarchy**
Individuals make themselves. No form of morality is reliable. Luck or fate determine outcomes. Institutions are incidental. Change is random	Individuals should observe standards and norms. Institutions should reinforce rules, punish wrongdoing and reward virtue. Change comes from leaders and rulers through authority, expertise and regulation
Individualism	**Egalitarianism**
Individuals should pursue their own projects. Institutions should prevent them from violating each other's right to do so. Individuals drive change	Individuals are made by communities. Moral character is the product of membership and belonging. Institutions should protect communities. Changes come from the bottom up, through strong values and solidarity

favouring a fusion of hierarchy and egalitarianism in the post-war period, during which the welfare state was constructed. The institutions of the post-war settlement (national economic management and planning, corporatism, public services and reliance on experts and professionals) were compatible with the cheerful fatalism engendered by the war, rationing and the Great Depression, but their early success created more favourable conditions for individualism, and their manifest failure in the 1970s gave Margaret Thatcher's blend of individualism and hierarchy its opportunity. The Third Way represented a reinterpretation of Labour's socialist values, incorporating much more individualism, and little fatalism.

The problem for Third Way administrations both in the UK and US was that they built no effective institutions for achieving equality of opportunity. Indeed, ideas of community, membership and belonging were applied to public policy only in their initiatives for deprived districts, where the attempt was made to mobilise residents with a stake in order and improvement towards controlling crime and deviance, and regenerating their economies and physical infrastructures (see pp 129-30). But all their other reforms of their public sectors actually assisted abler and more ambitious members to exit from such communities, and to move to districts where their aspirations could be met through their individual efforts. Indeed, the Third Way emphasis on self-responsibility and putting the family first strongly reinforced the individualistic elements in its policies (Waddan, 1997; Jordan, 1998). By its second term, New Labour's communitarianism, always conservative in its approach to regeneration (Driver and Martell, 1997; Jordan with Jordan, 2000), had become focused on security and anti-terrorism, rather than social inclusion (Jordan, 2006a, Chapter 11).

As a result, parents competed more desperately for the best schools and the best university courses for their offspring. They were willing to move house, change faith or tell lies (*in extremis*) to achieve these goals. The values of egalitarianism meant little or nothing in an institutional environment giving such important positional advantage to those who succeeded in competition for educational assets. And by the time that New Labour fell from power, a study by the Office for Fair Access revealed that the most advantaged 20 per cent of sixth formers were seven times more likely to get places at leading universities than those from the lower 40 per cent – a wider gap than when New Labour came to power in 1997 (Shepherd, 2010).

Even in the early 1990s, this orientation to family life and labour market access had become the dominant one in middle-class culture in the UK (Jordan et al, 1994). The reforms of the public sector that promoted choice over these and other collective facilities made equality, mobility and inclusion even more difficult to achieve. People who described themselves as socialists agonised about the dilemmas they faced over such choices, but most were unable to resist the opportunity to advance the interests of their family members over those of others. The Third Way reforms consolidated this situation, making the unequal competition for positional advantage less agonising and more accepted.

Instinctive wisdom: snap judgements

The example of choosing a school or a university for your children highlights the importance of an adequate analysis of how such decisions are made by citizens. Third Way theory suggests that people's values – their commitment to such abstract principles as equality and justice – shape the way that they decide on such issues. As I argued in Chapter One, however, most of our choices are based on habits or rules of thumb, derived from the cultural resources provided by institutions, which 'do our thinking for us' (Douglas, 1987, p 65).

Indeed, the cultural theories introduced in the previous section insist that this is necessarily so, because the social order relies on deep-seated patterns ('thought styles') which find their expression in such institutions as family, kinship, community, firm and nation. Fatalism and individualism respond to any choice by reference to individual character and private assets; hierarchy and egalitarianism look to the standards and resources of the group. Conversely, fatalism and hierarchy are concerned with security and the preservation of order, individualism and egalitarianism with change and improvement.

New Labour acknowledged that it was attempting to bring about a culture shift in the UK, notably through its reforms of public services (DSS, 1998, p 26). Political speeches and policy documents argued that its values and visions could penetrate both the methods used by staff of benefits agencies, health facilities, schools, social care services, child protection and asylum support teams, but also people who used these services, making them both more aware of the potential for improving quality of provision and more self-responsible in their actions. But any link between the organisational changes demanded by Third Way thinking – increased managerial control, new quality standards and performance indicators, targets for outcomes, rewards and penalties – and the values on which they were supposed to be based relied on the cognitive and emotional processes by which staff and service users reached their decisions.

If we consider the culture shifts achieved under Margaret Thatcher's leadership in the UK, or under Ronald Reagan's in the US, these built on pre-existing changes in the thinking and behaviour of middle-income citizens, which in turn were influenced by the changes in economy and society. The increase in the incomes of white-collar workers and skilled, technical operatives, rising home ownership levels, educational aspirations (especially for women and upwardly-mobile minority ethnic groups), and the corresponding decline in labour unions, working-class identifications and associations, and class-based mobilisations more generally, all made the shift towards individualism, consumerism and a business orientation to government more acceptable.

In spite of this, in the UK the *Social Attitudes* surveys of the 1980s revealed the persistence of ideas about social justice, the redistribution of income and the protection of vulnerable populations from unemployment and poverty. All this would have indicated an alternation between Conservative and Labour governments. But in fact, the pro-market regimes of Margaret Thatcher and John Major served four terms in office, balanced mainly by a predominance of Labour and Liberal Democrat local authorities, and some cultural influence of the churches, the BBC and the intellectual elite.

When my colleagues and I interviewed better-off (middle-income and above) couples in the early 1990s about their choices over income protection in old age and illness, healthcare, education and social welfare provision, they struggled to explain their choices in terms of their values (Jordan et al, 1994). Many said they were collectivists and egalitarians, even socialists, but they still sought to advantage their families over others, who lacked the resources to compete. They explained that, given the current institutional context of competition and insecurity, they had to put their own family first. Conversely, poor couples interviewed on the same range of topics often deployed an individualistic rhetoric of self-responsibility and family priority to justify such practices as working while claiming benefits, or continuing to claim when low-paid, part-time work was available (Jordan et al, 1992).

In other words, choice is deeply influenced by the cultural resources available to members of a society at a particular moment, and these are largely supplied by the institutional framework – markets, property and employment terms, as well as political systems, ideological constructions and the infrastructure of public facilities. When invited to reflect on their choices, more self-aware respondents in our research studies often noticed conflicts between their ethical commitments and their behaviour, and found them difficult to account for in morally adequate ways.

This has two obvious implications. First, cultural change usually starts with behaviour, leading to habits and unreflective patterns, only later resulting in changes in ideas and values. People who still thought of themselves as socialists were making choices as Thatcherites. Second, the institutions and cultures that allow us to interpret the world, and give our actions meaning, are emphatically *not* of our choosing. They are 'given' to us, and we must make the best of our lives within them. The space for our personal moral commitments within this collective landscape is limited.

These cultural insights are complemented in interesting ways by evidence from social psychology and neuropsychology. Martin Gladwell (2006), a journalist on the *New Yorker* magazine, has assembled findings about how lay people and experts make judgements and decisions – both intuitive ones, which they have difficulty accounting for but which turn out to be right, and considered ones, which turn out to be wrong. These include the purchase of fake artworks by distinguished galleries and collections, which other dealers and artists instantly recognised as frauds; assessments of university teachers by students on the basis of video clips, which turned out to be similar to their evaluations at the end of a whole seminar of classes (Ambady and Rosenthal, 1993); and the discovery that gamblers reacted to a rigged game (both with physical stress and in their choices) many plays before they consciously decided to adjust their strategies. Gladwell calls the ability to make 'fast and frugal' choices of this kind evidence of an 'adaptive unconscious', which does most of the work of making everyday decisions about our orientation to the social and physical world without our conscious involvement (Wilson, 2002).

Gladwell argues that these phenomena indicate that our instincts and intuitions are more influential on who we are and how we respond to our world than our lofty values and principles, and that it would be more productive to focus on snap judgements and their refinement in attempting to influence the quality of our lives. He claims that 'there can be as much value in the blink of an eye as in months of analysis' (Gladwell, 2006, p 17).

This applies to the study of many other kinds of interaction, Gladwell argues. Speed daters end up choosing partners quite unlike their original 'specifications'. Tennis coaches who can predict faults as players serve are unable to account for their own predictive abilities. But Gladwell also shows how snap judgements can lead to the selection of good-looking, apparently distinguished, but actually very incompetent candidates for high office, or reveal unconscious prejudice in the perception of character traits and abilities. The disturbing thing is that it shows that the unconscious influences on our choices may be utterly incompatible with our stated conscious values (Gladwell, 2006, p 85).

These unconscious prejudices also powerfully predict how we act in an emergency and unplanned situations. And they also influence, for example, the way that salespeople target more vulnerable, less advantaged customers for less favourable deals, or successful people choose others in their own image (in terms of non-relevant characteristics) for top jobs.

The optimistic part of Gladwell's message is that intuition and unconscious judgement can be refined and trained, not by rationalisation or reflection so much as the cultivation of close attention to the bases of snap judgements – empathy, close observation, respect and attentiveness, the hallmarks of good practice in the human service professions. In this way, the pro-social elements in adaptive unconscious are constantly reinforced by good habits. Snap judgements are not used as excuses for lazy, routine or self-protective actions. Instead, they raise awareness of the seemingly non-rational and emotionally driven elements in our judgements of situations and people.

Gladwell also suggests that training for other kinds of work, such as the armed forces and emergency services, can overcome anti-social prejudices and the fears from which they derive; they can help people become counter-intuitive when the situation demands. Bravery in the face of enemy action or natural disaster requires this.

The evolutionary basis for these capacities to respond to people and situations seems to lie in the advantages bestowed by quick recognition of opportunities for reciprocating and cooperating with others. Although this requires an environment in which scope for empathy and collaboration allows these responses to be cultivated and refined, the 'social brain' hypothesis now forms the foundation for programmes of research which are influencing thinking about policy and government (Grist, 2009a, 2009b). One line of thought derived from this research focuses on the relationship between the two hemispheres of the brain, and how the potential for empathy and responsiveness of the right hemisphere can complement the organising and rationalising capacities of the left hemisphere (McGilchrist, 2009). This is developed later in Chapter Three.

However, the Third Way adopted an interpretation of these findings from Cialdini (2001) which distinguishes between 'automatic' and 'deliberative' functions of the brain, and saw the former as 'lower' and the latter as 'higher' (Halpern, 2010, pp 229-44). In this approach, the goal of policy is to anticipate and harness certain 'lower brain' choices in some situations (through 'choice architecture' such as default options), and to 'give the higher brain a chance' by encouraging individual citizens to be more self-reflexive and self-responsible. The combination of paternalistic 'nudges' and rational individual choices aim to improve the effectiveness of Third Way methods of influencing citizen behaviour.

These rival interpretations of recent research echo far older antagonisms between philosophers and poets about the significance of our apparently instinctive responses to each other and to the wider social world. As we shall see in the next section, the early 19th century was a period in which ideas about intuition, the emotions and the collective unconscious were strongly asserted as the basis for morality and good government, against an approach from which the Third Way was ultimately derived.

Utilitarians and Romantics

The progressive, reforming agenda of the Third Way was framed in terms of organisational change as well as the reinterpretation of values. In line with the innovations of Joseph Stiglitz and others in the theory of information, incentives and contracts, it emphasised the importance of addressing 'information asymmetries' through the role of banks and governments (Stiglitz and Greenwald, 2003). With banks using their access to financial data on risks and potential profits to allot credit, and the government to regulate and insure the banking system, the structures for 'stability with growth' were to be put in place (Stiglitz et al, 2006).

Of equal importance was the provision of information on which citizens could base their choices. On his time as a policy strategist at 10 Downing Street, David Halpern wrote that, 'Perhaps the single biggest marginal impact that government could have on boosting economic growth, and on the performance of the public sector, is fostering an expansion in citizen–consumer information' (Halpern, 2010, p 48). Along with the subtle manipulation of incentives, this would allow inefficient suppliers to be squeezed out, 'creating a hot-house to catalyse the development of services and products'.

> Similar general arguments apply for public services, with league tables being just the beginning of this journey. In twenty years' time, who can doubt that individual teachers, doctors, policemen as well as schools, hospitals and police Basic Command Units (BCUs) will have online reputations that will grow and change over time, providing detailed

feedback to service deliverers, purchasers and citizens alike.
(Halpern, 2010, p 49)

All the reforms of the public sector undertaken under Third Way programmes were aimed at making these organisations more open to the effects of choices by citizens, and managing their work in ways which delivered outcomes consistent with higher overall welfare for populations. So long as citizens could maximise their utility in relation to these services as well as private goods, and could be informed about the quality of what they were receiving from state agencies, greater efficiency in government would contribute to higher living standards.

The idea that human organisations could be rationalised to achieve maximum efficiency through exchanges between individuals in pursuit of their own interests can be traced to the early work of Bentham ([1776] 1832), with his critique of Blackstone's commentaries on the English law. Bentham regarded the common law as a Gothic monument to confusion and obfuscation; law and regulation should consist of precise codes of rules, rewards and punishments, so that people could understand situations and see reasons to reach agreements. However, Bentham's ideas remained marginal to political debate and public consciousness until late in the first decade of the 19th century, when they were quite suddenly taken up by radical middle-class writers and activists, campaigning for reform of the whole political system.

This movement was opposed by the leading Romantic authors and poets of the time, notably Hazlitt and Coleridge. They counterposed an organic view of social institutions to the 'mechanical' model espoused by Bentham, and deployed the concept of 'imagination' as the link between everyday collective life and government, in an attempt to fill the gaps in political culture and social cohesion left after the French Revolution and the beginnings of industrialisation (Whale, 2000, pp 11-12).

The next 20 years marked a 'culture war' between utilitarianism and Romanticism, with Bentham being drawn into a direct attack on music, literature and poetry, which he called the 'arts and sciences of amusement':

> [T]hey are useless to those who are not pleased with them; they are useful only to those who take pleasure in them..., the value which they possess is exactly in proportion to the pleasure they yield.... Prejudice apart, the game of push-pin [a pub game] is of equal value with the arts and sciences of music and poetry. If the game of push-pin can furnish

> more pleasure, it is more valuable than either.... The game
> of push-pin is always innocent.... Indeed, between poetry
> and truth, there is a natural opposition: false morals, fictitious
> nature. The poet always stands in need of something false.
> (Bentham, [1825] 1832, pp 253-4)

This utilitarian assault on the elitism and mystification of the arts has echoes in today's clashes about the value of television shows like 'The X factor' versus 'high culture' – the opera, ballet and classical concerts, for example. But at a more fundamental level, it was about the nature of human beings and their societies. Hazlitt attacked utilitarianism as cold-blooded calculation, ethically indifferent to the *moral* wrongs done, for instance, to African slaves, counting only the pleasure and pains involved among populations. A far more reliable way of understanding the deep issues at stake was available through 'natural' human emotions – morality is 'instinctive' and works through sentiment in the bloodstream. Imagination gives us ethical capacities, intuitive perceptions of whether a particular event is an instance of a general norm or an exception. It is a habit, a reflex, and comes through an 'intercommunity of feeling', but based on the local and particular, on experience (and therefore limited) (Hazlitt, [1825] 1932, pp 49-51).

The similarities between this view of moral awareness and Gladwell's 'snap judgements' are too obvious to labour; they illustrate how the debate between utilitarians and Romantics has recurred in modern commercial societies, coming to the fore in periods of rapid economic and social change (Whale, 2000, pp 2-20). During that formative period of political crisis and industrial transformation, Coleridge, the leading public intellectual of the day, argued for 'hope and faith' as the instrument of continued amelioration and refinement, and trusted in the 'collective, unconscious common sense' of the people, against the mechanistic and materialistic basis for the new reform movement (Coleridge, [1810] 1969, p 82; [1818] 1969, p 193) – a natural morality, resisting measurement by mathematic calculation, and rejecting generalised abstractions.

This clash of cultural overviews was later recognised by John Stuart Mill as a battle for the soul of Britain, and experienced by him as a crisis in his own soul. Brought up as a strict utilitarian, and with Bentham as his influential godfather, he experienced a nervous breakdown in his twenties, from which he recovered through reading Romantic poetry. He came to see Bentham as incapable of self-reflection or self-knowledge, and acknowledged that he himself had undervalued poetry, and 'the imagination generally as an element of human nature' (Mill, 1864, p 113). Mill saw the two philosophies as concerned with different kinds of value, and sought to balance them, ultimately recognising aesthetic value only as a kind of personal therapy, of psychological rather than political and social relevance (Whale, 2000, pp 183-6).

Finally, it was left to novelists to synthesise the two approaches to the social order, and to provide a kind of imaginative link between them. In the work of Jane Austen and Sir Walter Scott, there was a conscious effort to supply a stabilising influence on British society during the dislocations of the French wars and the political unrest that followed them. As reading novels became a new, unifying feature of British culture, Austen's portrayal of families and friends learning sensibility and morality through reading and criticising together provided such an exemplar, while Scott specifically claimed that his later novels embodied the true 'new legitimacy' – 'an ideological basis for consolidating economic and social power in liberal middle-class hands' (Burgess, 2000, p 190). Conversely, in Ireland a new 'national tale' told of collective resistance to British rule through the novels of Maria Edgeworth, Sydney Owenson and Charles Robert Maturin, prefiguring the politics of protest under Daniel O'Connell (Ferris, 2002).

The Third Way's utilitarian approach has failed. No coherent alternative has appeared, partly because there is less trust in popular sentiment and instinctive morality than there was in the Age of Romanticism. Governments fear nationalism, bigotry and fundamentalism; they look nervously at phenomena like the culture war in Pakistan between Taliban iconoclasts and the liberal cultural establishment of the visual arts, music and theatre in Lahore. The whole issue of how to reconcile utilitarian with aesthetic value with be analysed in Part II of this book.

Conclusions

The Third Way's abstract statements of values were not convincing in their link with public policies. In this and the previous chapter we have seen that equality of opportunity was not implemented in line with people's moral intuitions. Even stock market traders and pension fund managers baulked at the inequalities they faced in competition with investment banks and specialised funds.

All the philosophical traditions briefly reviewed so far have made substantial contributions to social and political institutions in the Anglophone countries. The early Enlightenment exponents of natural or human rights, such as John Locke and the Marquis de Condorcet, provided the intellectual foundations for the US constitution. The theories of utility of Hume and Smith, modified by Bentham, supplied the principles for sanitary and public health measures in cities, basic education, and eventually, mediated by Fabian and collectivist analyses, Social Insurance and the New Deal. The Romantics contributed to the emancipation of slaves, the early Factory Acts and – through the British Idealists at the end of the 19th century – to social work, community development and the public service professions.

Because the Third Way embraced a form of economic analysis that was supposed to supply the basis for new, more effective public institutions, providing growth with stability and better-quality social services, it has been doubly damaged by the economic crash. Not only was its competence for managing the economy discredited where, as in the UK, its proponents were in power; its version of public sector reform and the maintenance of the social order has also come under scrutiny. The latter, too, was derived from the same set of concepts – information, incentives and contracts – so a steady stream of scandals and failures reflects back to systems for computerisation of data, electronic surveillance of staff, target setting, external imposition of quality standards, accreditation and inspection detailed regulation and guidance, league tables of performance and contracting out of tasks.

Both types of criticism of the Third Way model of government therefore focus on its failure to achieve the outcomes that its values were supposed to require through the economic means it adopted. Indeed, some of this critique has deployed ideas from the Romantic tradition, arguing – as did the likes of Hazlitt, Coleridge and Carlyle – that society, and indeed the economy, is not a machine whose workings can be made transparent and reliably predictable by clever calculations and managerial techniques, but more like an organism, or a set of complex interactions between natural forces, like the weather (Waldrop, 1994). On these analogies, economists themselves, and especially governments, should seek to understand processes of development, to

> ... concentrate on explaining and modelling the major dynamics and likely emergent patterns in economic systems, and spotting the probable tipping points and "trip wires" leading to potentially exponential change – so as that, forewarned about them, we can be wisely adaptive to unfolding trends. (Bronk, 2009, p 132)

Part of this shift towards a more organic approach would be to build more realistic assumptions into the microfoundations of economics, and of the management of the economy, ones which better reflect the recent insights about choice and other aspects of social behaviour discussed in this chapter.

> This will enable them [economists] to specify the rules of the economic game well enough to capture the main *social* factors, such as language, institutions and norms, which structure people's behaviour in practice; and it will help them capture the *social* element in the formation of individual expectations and strategy. For, as economic agents, we often make use of rules of thumb and route-maps that are socially formed; and we deliberate on our course of action within social networks that shape our beliefs, our expectations, even our preferences. (Bronk, 2009, p 133)

An obvious application of this whole approach might be to environmental issues, especially climate change. It was not economists – with honourable exceptions such as James Tobin (Nordhaus and Tobin, 1972) – who drew attention to the threat of global warming, but now that it is there, they might usefully focus on modelling the responses of individuals, firms and governments to it, and how the social influences on human behaviour on carbon emissions, waste and over-consumption generally might be better understood and influenced.

Even more obviously, both economists and governments might show more awareness of the connections between such patterns of behaviour and the financial folly that led to the crash. For instance, the environmental charity Friends of the Earth has revealed that most of the trading in carbon emissions – which allow dirty industries in rich countries to buy permits to discharge from developing countries – is in fact carried out by financial intermediaries, who slice and dice these licences, packaging them up into products much like the mortgage-backed derivatives involved in the financial crash of 2008. This involves risks of another such crisis, because those purchasing them cannot know what they are buying. With global carbon markets anticipated to reach US$17 trillion in the near future, the seeds of another economic crash are being sown (BBC Radio 4, 'Today', 5 November 2009). The challenge of environmental issues for the legacy of Third Way public policies will be analysed in the next chapter.

In terms of social policy, the Third Way failed because its generalised value statements did not really impact the trajectory of development established under Margaret Thatcher. Its economic thinking, based on the modifications in neo-liberalism and the Washington Consensus made by contract theory in the mid-1990s, still set all its main agendas.

Only after the crash have these orthodoxies been questioned, and then in pragmatic, sometimes panicky, ways.

Yet the available critiques of these ideas have also been incomplete. From the Conservative side in the UK, they have focused on the failures of collectivism and state control, rather than the inadequacies of market economics and the theory of contracts. David Cameron has, without adequately disowning Thatcherism, made it clear that he considers that the Third Way led to a fracturing of social bonds that now requires a break with the spirit of its reforms. In this he draws some of his inspiration from Benjamin Disraeli, a leader whose political and cultural roots lay in the Romantic Age, and a novelist who in his time out-sold Charles Dickens.

Yet the social changes of the past 20 years seem to owe more to the revolution brought in by neo-liberalism and individualism than to New Labour. David Blunkett, a politician who came into prominence in public life as the leader of Sheffield City Council in the early 1980s, has said that his inspiration came from Marx and Methodism – a mixture of economic radicalism and social conservatism. But he remarked that he had seen a shift in the party within which he rose to become Home Secretary towards an accommodation with global capitalism, but promoting a continual break-up of working-class solidarities, in favour of a more diverse, fragmented social order, leaving people with more choices and options among lifestyles, but also more vulnerable to market forces.

The consequence of this has been that it is more feasible for those attacking the Third Way for its social failures to propose a revival of associationalism and mutuality at the local level than to appeal to a vision of more inclusive, universal national or international solidarities. This has been clear from the failure of New Labour in the UK to mobilise citizens for a scheme for sharing the costs of social care (as was established in the Scandinavian countries, Germany and the Netherlands in the 1990s), as it was from the resistance to Barack Obama's attempts to create a universal healthcare system in the US (see pp 103-4). People feel no embarrassment in refusing to pool their risks with those they perceive as different from (that is, less fortunate or prudent than) themselves.

This explains why, in his election campaign of 2010, David Cameron picked up many of the themes of the 'Big Society' notion of devolution to communities and cooperatives, but made no mention of the CSJ's proposals for tax-benefit system integration. His speeches had echoes of Phillip Blond's writings, both in his implicit appeals to the Romantic discourses of Coleridge and Carlyle, and the later dissident liberalism of Hilaire Belloc and G.K. Chesterton, but also in his faith in local groups, voluntary organisations and social entrepreneurs. He sought to strengthen the bonds between diverse populations, but not to redistribute resources or change systems in ways that might enable this.

On the other hand, Cameron emphasised his commitment to introducing a married couple's tax allowance, and increasing the threshold for inheritance tax (later dropped in the coalition agreement with the Liberal Democrats), both of which sat uneasily with the CSJ proposal. Indeed, when the former policy proposal came under attack from the other two parties, Iain Duncan Smith stepped in to suggest that the allowance be restricted to poor couples with children, a much cheaper option, and more consistent with his redistributive agenda (BBC Radio 4, 'Today', 18 January 2010).

The Big Society programme is clearly more than a cover for Thatcherite public sector cuts, savage though these have been. David Cameron's speeches on the theme (for instance, on 19 July 2010) repeatedly emphasised a 'shift in culture'. Early moves by the coalition government to reform education (acadamies, free schools) and the NHS (funding redistributed to GPs) both reject the New Labour model of public services and bypass its organisational structures by using a different kind of regulation, involving professionals, parents and patients (see p 202).

The moral vision that is supplied by localism and the promotion of voluntary association has a close horizon, especially in a period when global economic forces exert such dominant sway. To be effective in collective action at this level, people need strong institutional supports, derived from broader solidarities, and especially from economic security. In the next chapter I consider how the illusory nature of individual independence and self-reliance that is fostered by the promotion of an order constructed out of personal choices is reflected and expanded in the environmental challenges that we now face.

THREE

Nature, science and cosmology

In this chapter I turn to a more fundamental failure of the Third Way – its inability to recognise and challenge tendencies in global capitalism that threaten future well-being. This is certainly not the Third Way's failure alone, but I argue that its understanding and response to these threats has been mistaken and misleading; a new way of thinking, and a new policy response, is urgently required. The obvious manifestation of this inadequacy is the coming environmental catastrophe, but the issues are broader and deeper even than this.

When the first Third Way regimes came to power in the early 1990s, ecological questions were still seen as marginal to mainstream politics. With the honourable exception of Al Gore (1992), they did not figure prominently in Third Way literature; for instance, Tony Blair's (1998a) essay, *The Third Way: New politics for the new century*, made no mention of them, and referred to 'boosting the science base' as 'a key government priority to keep Britain internationally competitive' through a 'path-breaking public-private partnership' (p 10).

In so far as environmental threats were recognised by Third Way thinkers, these were analysed within the framework of a 'risk society' (Beck, 1992). The combination of global economic integration and the individualisation of everyday life – each relying more on active choices over friends, networks and associations, rather than on tradition, habit and community – exposed people to risks which were difficult or impossible to measure and assess (Giddens, 1991, 1994). Global production gave rise to environmental risks which were qualitatively different from the more localised ones associated with earlier phases of capitalism – their effects were often invisible, pervasive and long term.

The paradigms for such risks in the early 1990s were the BSE scandal in the production of beef and bio-engineering, notably GM crops (Giddens, 2000, pp 136-45). These examples indicated that risks might be present before scientific evidence was available to guide individual decisions, so the self-reliant consumers who made up modern societies were unable to make rational choices about even such banal items.

The Third Way's response to this analysis of risk in all such issues was to argue for 'environmental modernisation', which aimed to reduce the harmful impacts of degradation and the distortion of natural processes.

> But it seeks to escape the value-driven basis of existing environmental discourses.... First, it is intended to "go with the grain" of globalisation.... [It] gives a central place to the perception of risk and scientific uncertainty, and makes risk management a key policy field.... [And] it is firmly a modernist project, accepting the central role of science and technology in tackling as well as contributing towards environmental problems. It sees the future as essentially optimistic and environmental problems as soluble. (Jacobs, 2001, pp 328-9)

This passage, in an essay on 'The environment, modernity and the Third Way', quite specifically argued that 'an extension of the Third Way into the environmental arena is what is required' (Jacobs, 2001, p 329), and that 'the discourse of environmental modernisation offers the Government new ways of approaching the environment as a political subject' (p 329). It applied a paradigm from the Third Way's economic model, using the Giddens notions of individualisation and risk to issues such as climate change (still seen as unsubstantiated by scientific evidence) and resource depletion. It sought to develop environmental policy, 'connecting it to other issues, and making it a central part of the New Labour project' (p 329).

This contribution to *The global Third Way debate* (Giddens, 2001) was therefore aimed at absorbing environmental issues into the established framework of modernisation, globalisation and individualisation. It rejected the normative claims of the ecological lobby (sustainable development, the needs of future generations, the quest for harmonious co-existence with other species) as 'utopian' and 'idealistic' (Jacobs, 2001, p 317).

The attempt to interpret and respond to new phenomena, such as global warming and climate change, in terms of a set of organisational (managerial) concepts from the sphere of business and marketing was a symptom of a deeper weakness of the Third Way. This turned on the manner in which evidence was used for policy development. Although it claimed that its whole approach was 'evidence based', the way in which data were collected and mobilised through the policy process simply transformed them into justifications for its existing framework of ideas. In his reflections on his years as a policy adviser to Tony Blair, David Halpern (2010, p 54) acknowledged 'the necessary, if not sufficient, role played by the environment in our well-being', but devoted only three out of 265 pages to the topic, and then in the context of the use of information and incentives in policy implementation.

In this chapter I show how the Third Way came to illustrate (almost to the point of caricature) a disturbing one-sidedness in human development, both intellectual and social. This manifests itself in the attempt to rationalise, organise, depersonalise and sanitise all aspects of social interaction. It has been one theme of the transformations that constitute 'modernity', which began with the Enlightenment in the late 17th and early 18th centuries. Technological and bureaucratic ways of thinking and organising society have tended to empty human relations of meaning, and to increase the power of experts, corporations and governments to control both thought and action. It was a tendency identified by sociologists in the late 19th century (Durkheim, 1893; Weber, 1905), but deplored far earlier by critics of capitalism and utilitarianism, such as Coleridge, Hazlitt and Carlyle.

The idea that this trend in historical development, which reached its apogee with the Third Way, is literally 'one-sided' – because it reflects the dominance of the left hemisphere of the brain over the right – has recently been persuasively argued by the psychiatrist and cultural historian Iain McGilchrist (2009). He points out that left-sided interpretations of experience, which fragment the world into 'bits' to achieve certainty, substitute information for knowledge, dismiss new data that contradict established wisdoms, prefer formal systems and paper qualifications to practical expertise, replace the concrete and real by the theoretical and abstract, reduce creative practice to sterile algorithms, virtualise experience itself, replace productive work by planning, strategising, management and proceduralism, which justify and regulate, make all activity predictable, anonymous and depersonalised, and turn society into a machine, valuing precision and efficiency over quality (McGilchrist, 2009, pp 428-30), are all characteristic of the present age.

Although ecology, conservation and biodiversity are the most important instances of this tendency in Third Way policies, the one-sidedness is pervasive and deeply damaging. We have already noted the desire to codify and control every sphere of society, and to impose a mechanically economistic approach, simultaneously business-like, managerial and bureaucratic. This is as significant in what it misses – the early warnings of disastrous extinctions, in the economy as well as in the ecological sphere – as it is in how it attempts to regulate all activity.

As McGilchrist shows, the right hemisphere of the brain is an essential complement and balance to the organising and synthesising processes of the left side, because it supplies the actual sense data and direct experiences from which general principles are derived. It therefore allows a critical view of the overall 'big picture' to be sustained; it enables flexibility of thought, the possibility of alternatives (as against predictability of outcomes), the ability to integrate perceptions and perspectives, the whole (as opposed to the part), context (rather than abstraction), individual differences (cf categories) and personal (versus impersonal) characteristics. It also allows openness to emotional and physical experiences, expressivity and reasoning (as opposed to rationality) (McGilchrist, 2009, Chapter 2).

Many of these characteristics of the right side of the brain define the scientific approach to the world – a constant and relentless set of enquiries, conducted in a spirit of humility and open-mindedness (Angier, 2007, Chapter 1). Others supply the emotional and moral intuitions on which many of the 'snap judgements' identified in the previous chapter are based. Openness to emotional and physical experiences allows us to build a repertoire of responses to social relationships and natural phenomena, rather than relying on a fixed set of rules, based on abstractions.

The history of science reflects the attempt to balance left-sided with right-sided interpretations of the world. Figures like Isaac Newton and Carl Linnaeus were predominantly concerned with order and categorisation; but many of the great discoveries were made by scientists strongly linked to the creative arts, poetry and radical politics. I argue that Romanticism and Idealism allowed a far better balance between right-sided and left-sided approaches to the application of science than the Third Way's 'path-breaking public-private partnership' could accomplish.

In the face of global warming, the relationship between science and public policy should be one that is informed by new moral insights and open to entirely new understandings of our world. It is the right side of the brain that is more capable of the 'frame shifts' (Coulson, 2001) required by environmental challenges, and by those of globalisation more generally. The Third Way's attempt to manage them has courted disaster.

Exploring deep space

In May 2009, the Herschel Space Telescope was blasted into orbit on an Arienne European Space Project rocket from Guyana. On its journey of many million miles, it would use a special silver mirror to pick up the lowest frequency electro-magnetic waves ever recorded, and enable some 250,000 new galaxies, some so far away that they were formed soon after the Big Bang, to be charted. The project was described as filling in the gaps in the map of the universe (BBC Radio 4, 'The Herschel Space Telescope', 18 November 2009).

The telescope was named in honour of Sir William Herschel, whose discovery of Uranus in 1781 revolutionised our understanding of the place of our solar system in the universe, and allowed a new cosmology, including such concepts as 'deep space', to be developed. But Herschel was not a scientist – indeed, the concept had not yet been invented in his time. He was a professional musician, a refugee in Britain from Germany, who, after a period as an itinerant in the north of England, had just landed a regular post with an orchestra in fashionable Bath. His original discovery was enabled by his handcraftsmanship in making the mirrors for large reflection telescopes, which allowed him to observe the heavens in far more detail than had been possible using lens-based refractor tubes. When the leading French astronomer, Charles Messier, wrote to congratulate Herschel on his breakthrough, he addressed his letter to 'Monsieur Hertsthel at Bath', while the representative of the Royal Society wrote his to 'Mr William Herschel, Musician, near the Circus, Bath' (Holmes, 2008, pp 99-100).

The significance of the discovery was that it required a paradigm shift in the Newtonian map of the universe that had been the scientific orthodoxy of the previous hundred years. Herschel was very well-read in astronomy and optics, as well as being (with the help of his sister) a meticulous observer of astronomical phenomena. Responding calmly to the scepticism of other astronomers and commentators about his discoveries, he emphasised that observation with his telescopes was an art, which had to be learned through practice, and compared their use to performance on a musical instrument (Holmes, 2008, p 108). In the following two years, having built a new and even larger reflector near Windsor Castle, where he had been appointed Royal telescope maker, he charted the whole night sky with his sister, with maps of huge star clusters or galaxies outside our own (the Milky Way).

In his scientific paper 'On the construction of the heavens' (1786), Herschel postulated a changing, evolving universe, like a huge living organism. He argued that nebulae were active gaseous processes, from which new stars were forming, replacing those that died – he called them 'the laboratories of the universe'. Above all, the existence of nebulae outside the Milky Way implied that the cosmos was immeasurably larger than Newton had supposed, and his (under) estimate of deep space, some 6,000 or 8,000 times the distance of Sirius, revolutionised orthodox cosmology.

Indeed, Herschel's discoveries reverberated around the scientific community, all over Europe, in those days still closely meshed with the philosophical, political and artistic community. Erasmus Darwin (grandfather of Charles) wrote his poem 'The botanic garden' in 1791 in celebration of a new sequence of continuous creation:

> Earths and each sun with quick explosions burst,
> And second Planets issue from the first,
> Bend as they journey with projectile force,
> In bright elipses their reluctant course....

It was after visiting Herschel, and looking through his massive 40-foot telescope, that Joseph Haydn (on his triumphant stay in London) composed his oratorio 'The creation' (1796-98), in which the abundant richness of the universe is celebrated. This appropriately closed the circle which began when Herschel, at the behest of George III, had chosen no longer to 'sacrifice his valuable time to crochets and quavers'.

But Herschel's discovery of Uranus remained the inspiration of artists and poets for a whole generation, and was interpreted through the Romantic view of the relationship between science and nature. Coleridge remembered being taken by his father to look at the night sky in this new way (at the age of eight) on the banks of the River Otter. Byron paid a visit to Herschel in 1811; and Keats' poem, 'On first looking into Chapman's Homer' (1816), referred to the discovery of Uranus directly:

> ...Then I felt like some watcher of the skies,
> When a new planet swims into his ken....

The defining feature of this relationship with nature was that *love* of natural phenomena (a term used by Herschel in his 1786 paper in connection with the creation of his new, enlarged universe) was combined with scientifically informed cosmology. Herschel developed his organic and botanical metaphors for the nebulae and the emergence of new stars in his later, more reflective papers. Since some galaxies were clearly far older than others, some dying and others being born, it implied that astronomy was like the observation of a garden over a huge time span, with specimens from each period of its evolution. Their age could be identified through observation, and thus they could be classified in an almost botanical manner (Herschel, 1811).

This revolutionary view of an evolving, enormous universe, in which the earth and mankind were peripheral, not central, implied the existence of both 'deep space' and 'deep time' (Hoskin, 1963, p 130) – some of the stars he was observing were emitting light from almost two million years ago. But the spirit of science demanded equal reverence and wonder for the most commonplace of objects in nature. Writing in 1830, Herschel's son John argued that the most 'trifling natural objects', like soap bubbles, apples or pebbles, revealed scientific laws:

> ... to the natural philosopher there is no natural object unimportant on trifling.... A mind that has once imbibed a taste for scientific enquiry has within it a source of pure and exciting contemplations. (Herschel, 1830, p 14)

In all these respects, Sir William Herschel demonstrated the combination of right-sided and left-sided thinking postulated by McGilchrist as a requirement for balanced human development. As a musician, craftsman and observer, he always sustained his right-sided connections with physical, practical expertise and the discovery of new phenomena, while his left-sided activities were able to synthesise his findings into a theory of an evolving universe. Above all, he sustained the sense of wonder and appreciation of all the phenomena he studied, and this communicated itself to his younger admirers and collaborators. He shared this combination of very different forms of activity and thought with other leading figures of the age, such as Sir Joseph Banks (explorer, botanist, anthropologist and entrepreneurial President of the Royal Society for 42 years); Benjamin Franklin (revolutionary, pioneer of electrical engineering, inventor of the lightning conductor and President of the US); and Sir Humphry Davy (experimental chemist, inventor of the miners' safety lamp, poet and fly-fisherman).

Apart from the identification of such natural forces as electromagnetism, this period marked the emergence of three concepts crucial for the pursuit of ecological sustainability. *Evolution* was recognised as a process, both in plants by Charles Darwin's grandfather, and in the stars by Herschel. *Interdependence* was a theme of many studies of the organic and inorganic worlds, as expressed by Alexander von Humboldt in the quotation given in the Introduction to this book (p 8). And, more specifically, the *carbon cycle* was identified by Humphry Davy (c. 1799) in his description of the oxygenation of water by aquatic plants when exposed to sunlight, complementing animals' absorption of oxygen and emission of carbonic gas, a natural equilibrium or harmony (Fullmer, 2000, pp 163-6; Holmes, 2008, p 255).

It is, of course, definitive of the Romantic movement that its philosophers, poets and artists embraced the imagination, intuition and emotion as paths to a restorative communication with nature that McGilchrist describes (in a reference to Wordsworth's 'Prelude') as 'the relationship between the two hemispheres [of the brain]' (2009, p 377). But much of their original inspiration came from science.

> These scientific activities … pushed literary writing towards new subjects and styles. Works as diverse as Shelley's 'Prometheus unbound' and Wordsworth's 'The excursion' responded to the latest discoveries as they looked out towards the seas in order to probe into Britons' inner selves. Thus, what scholars have called 'Romanticism' arose partly as a response in writing (travel writing, scientific writing, literary writing) to encounters with foreign people and places. (Fulford et al, 2004, p 6)

In moral and political terms, the implications of new scientific discoveries and new aesthetic responses to nature and the wider world were ambiguous and shifting. Up to the end of the 18th century, the conclusions drawn by explorers and scientists such as Sir Joseph Banks, Erasmus Darwin and Humphry Davy to the liberty and abundance of the social life of Tahitians and the discovery of laughing gas were libertarian or revolutionary. They concluded that all this was evidence of Jean-Jacques Rousseau's account of our origins as noble savages and of the dawn of a new 'electric age', whose patron was Benjamin Franklin (a knowledgeable student of indigenous North American cultures as well as an experimental scientist). Banks sent an expedition to Tahiti to transport breadfruit trees to the Caribbean in a first attempt at a step towards the emancipation of the slaves, arguing that the abundant food they would supply would make slavery redundant. (Unfortunately, he chose Captain Bligh to lead this mission.) Poets like Coleridge and Shelley wrote enthusiastically of universal liberty, and planned utopian colonies in North America.

But – with the degeneration of the French Revolution into the Terror, and then the rise of Napoleon – all this changed. Led by Banks as President of the Royal Society, and marked by Davy's shift from Darwin's dissenting network of provincial scientists to the official, metropolitan circle, a new political conservatism dominated. One by one the Romantic poets became imperialists and upholders of projects of established religion. The only exception was Byron, whose enduring revolutionary passion was expressed in a poem 'The island' (1820), in which one of the *Bounty* mutineers escaped with his Tahitian bride from the British navy's punitive expedition, and established an isolated enclave of liberty and equality (Fulford et al, 2004, Chapter 5).

So there is no logical connection between science – even the 'balanced' science of the Romantic age – and a particular ethical or political standpoint. But, as I argue in the next section, this balance is a necessary condition for an ethically informed science.

Craft, expertise and tradition

The striking thing about the Third Way's approach to nature and the environment was its determination to *modernise* them (along with every other aspect of life on earth). Explicitly in the case of Jacobs' (2001) essay, and implicitly in Blair's (1998a), the Green agenda was dismissed as backward-looking and unsuited to a globalised world, which required ecological policies to be integrated into an advanced technological response to all the challenges of an integrated world economy. Specifically, the concepts of risk management and individualisation were imported from Giddens' (1998, 2000) analysis of late modernity, to absorb 'environmental modernisation' into the Third Way programme.

The clear assumption behind the Third Way's approach was that science was an integral part of the modernist agenda, changing from traditional aspects of collective life, industrial processes, labour organisation and state organisation to ones which were more suitable for this new age. The Third Way was designed to adapt the political left's response to:

> [T]echnological advance and the rise of skills and information as key drivers of employment and new industries, [are] in destroying patterns of employment and placing an unprecedented premium on the need for high educational standards for the many, not the few.... The science base – funded by the public and private sector – is critical to commercial innovation, and the government has significantly strengthened both its funding and the degree of public-private partnership. (Blair, 1998a, pp 6, 11)

This is a characteristically left-sided assumption in McGilchrist's terms. It ignores the fact that science must always (as it did in the Romantic age) rely on those kinds of energetic direct observation of nature and the universe, and the craft skills of expert practitioners, for much of the knowledge that feeds it. James Lovelock, who discovered that CFCs had caused the hole in the ozone layer and formulated the Gaia principle of self-regulating interdependent life forms, made all his own instruments; he said that science must engage the hands as well as the brain (BBC 2 television, 'Beautiful minds', 14 April 2010). Above all, science must be alive to evidence of the harmful effects of human activity (including scientific and technological activity) if it is not to take humanity down the road to planetary destruction. Until quite late in its development, the Third Way was reluctant to recognise this.

But Blair's declaration also reveals an uncritical attitude towards global capitalism that runs deeper than the environmental question. Scientists were achieving their breakthrough discoveries just as early capitalism was taking shape, but the response of these scientists to industrialisation and urbanisation was not one of unequivocal celebration.

This was particularly clear in the disputes over the issue of chimney-sweeps, which focused political contest (along with slavery) during the period between 1790 and the early 1830s. Some scientists embraced the utilitarian principle that new technologies could make such atrocities an anachronism, through the redesign of buildings and work environments. Most prominent among these was Count Rumford, an enthusiastic follower of Jeremy Bentham, who introduced a new Panopticon regime into a workhouse in Bavaria, using a 'totalised and technologised' environment to control the poor (Fulford et al, 2004, pp 228-9). At first, Rumford's approach to the application of science to issues of heating and cleaning was widely praised, but doubts about it grew, and the Royal Society for the Encouragement of Arts, Manfactures and Commerce campaigned for other approaches – chimney-sweeping machines, legislation and regulation. Romantic authors such as Charles Lamb, Samuel Taylor Coleridge, William Blake and Robert Southey joined this movement. This opposition to Rumford's methods was swollen when he published a tract called 'Of food and particularly the feeding of the poor' ([1795] 1970), which set out exact ingredients for making soups sufficient to preserve industrial efficiency.

> Philanthropists in Britain were amazed by Rumford's totalised approach. He made it seem as if a marriage between science and the state could transform all aspects of poverty, creating an ordered, harmonious and happy society. (Fulford et al, 2004, p 257)

By the early 1830s, the movement for the improvement of working conditions in factories was a Tory one, as was that for resisting the creation of workhouses under the 1834 reform of the Poor Laws. In 1833, Coleridge, in an address to the British Association for the Advancement of Science, proposed that philosophy and science should henceforth be separated, with the latter's practitioners being known for the first time as 'scientists' as they were no longer part of the quest for 'the one life within us and abroad', from spirituality and theology (Fulford et al, 2004, p 302).

In terms of the issues of sustainability (of both the natural environment and human societies) which are today so challenging for governments, the crucial step in this story was when political economy laid claim to science as the instrument for material progress through modernisation. This occurred during the 19th century, as financiers, industrialists and politicians sought to justify and promote the march of capitalist expansion worldwide, and the rationalisation of social life this entailed. Although – as Karl Polanyi (1944) documented – this was always resisted by a 'second movement' of ill-assorted religious, aesthetic, communal, class-based and nostalgic resistance groups, it became the dominant force in development.

'Scientific materialism' was a German intellectual movement that advocated the application of science to every field of human activity, in opposition to the Aristotelian notions of what is appropriate to achieve justice – a form of knowledge specific to each different sphere (see pp 24-5). Science was seen as a unity, as possessing the only valid method of enquiry, as systematic (ruling out the influence of chance, happenstance or serendipitous by-products of quite other projects), and as above morality (since it provided the foundations for ethical principles) (McGilchrist, 2009, pp 384-5). The Lenin-Stalin version of state socialism was the Marxist equivalent of this type of scientific materialism.

But less philosophical and grandiose versions of imperialistic science-based programmes flourished in the other 'great powers' of the period, allowing dominance over nature, over colonialised territories and peoples, over the working population and their habitations (cities). Mechanisation of production and standardisation of outputs imposed a technological imprint on all the goods manufactured by these processes, and displaced not only the handcrafts and skills by which they were made before, but also the social organisation (guilds, corporations, apprenticeships, etc) associated with those methods. In McGilchrist's terms,

> Its products would be certain, perfect in their way, *familiar*
> in the "iconic" sense (preferred by the left hemisphere),
> not in the sense of "special things that have value for me"
> (preferred by the right); identical entities, rectilinear in shape,
> endlessly reproducible, mechanistic in nature, certain, fixed,
> man-made. (McGilchrist, 2009, p 387)

The fusion of science with global capitalist development therefore co-opted one part of the original scientific tradition, the one which sought to make all knowledge quantifiable, systematic and internally consistent, and cut it off from the other part, which allowed it to recognise random events, to make intuitive leaps and to value anomaly and diversity. It also shed the aesthetical and spiritual connections that were so clear in the writings of William Herschel, Erasmus Darwin, Humphry Davy, Alexander von Humboldt and many others, and the radical political ones associated with Benjamin Franklin.

In some respects – as we shall see in the next chapter – economics as a social science resisted the totalising implications of this approach. The leading economists of the 19th century, such as Alfred Marshall, who are seen as the founders of modern analysis, did attempt to preserve a space for aesthetic, moral and political judgement, as did their early 20th-century followers, such as Vilfredo Pareto, Joseph Schumpeter and Arthur C. Pigou. In this way, economics retained a critical perspective on human development, which – in combination with Idealism and socialism – allowed collective social movements opposed to capitalist globalisation to find expression in public policy and administration.

But the Third Way, despite its claimed links with these traditions, was not part of Polanyi's 'second movement' in any meaningful sense. Instead, its insistence that science (including environmental science) should 'go with the flow' of capitalist development made it part of the totalising and systemising forces at work at the end of the 20th century. This included its approach to science in particular, and expertise in general.

At the level of individual expertise, the Third Way approach emphasised 'skills' which could be of service to the process of modernisation. It aimed to achieve a 'dynamic, knowledge-based economy', in which 'skills and information' were the 'key drivers of employment, and new industries' (Blair, 1998a, pp 6-7), and 'the science base ... is critical to commercial innovation' (p 11). But this gave little recognition to the form of expertise which Richard Sennett (2008) calls 'craftmanship'.

> Craftsmanship names an enduring, basic human impulse, the desire to do a job well for its own sake. Craftsmanship cuts a far wider swath than skilled manual labour; it serves the computer programmer, the doctor, and the artist; parenting improves when it is practised as a skilled craft, as does citizenship.... Social and economic conditions, however, often stand in the way of the craftsman's commitment; schools may fail to produce the tools to do good work, and

workplaces may not truly value the aspiration for quality. And though craftsmanship can reward an individual with a sense of pride in work, this reward is not simple. (Sennett, 2008, p 9)

Sennett argues that 'open source' computer software design, particularly in the Linux operating system, illustrates these features of craftsmanship. It is open to anyone, but participants focus on achieving quality, in defiance of trends in the commercial software industry, where monopolies dominate (Sennett, 2008, pp 24-7; see also Leadbeater, 2008). Such communities of craftsmen used to be features of large companies and public services in the US and UK, but have been fragmented by companies with a shorter-term focus on profit, growth and innovation, and an outsourcing to subsidiaries abroad (Sennett, 2008, pp 34-5).

Like Malcolm Gladwell, Sennett emphasises the intuitive, 'embedded' and habitual nature of these forms of expertise, the 'interplay between tacit knowledge and self-conscious awareness'. 'When an institution like the NHS, in churning reform, doesn't allow the tacit anchor to develop, then the motor of judgement stalls' (Sennett, 2008, p 50). Staff without this refinement through experience fall back on 'a set of abstract propositions about good-quality work' (Sennett, 2008, p 50), and (under the influence of Third Way principles) replace embedded, tacit knowledge by rational management and planning.

Rehabilitating the right-sided approach

The tendency to overvalue the conceptualising, abstracting and formalising capacities of the human mind is a longstanding and deep-seated one. Because human beings alone among nature's creatures are able to think about patterns of things without considering the characteristics of the things themselves (that is, to apply mathematics, logic and language to the world without reference to any particular content or context), it has seemed reasonable to suppose that we were evolving towards a stage at which the senses and ordinary experiences would become marginal or even dispensable for our needs.

This tendency has been re-enforced by the development of electronic technology, and especially computers, allowing the virtualisation of images, sounds and experiences. Superficially, this seems to have made the physical world, and nature itself, less relevant to survival and well-being. But in fact it points to the opposite conclusion. Descartes predicted that humans would be able to make machines that could embody all the characteristics of animals; but in fact computers can reproduce most features of human abstract reasoning, while the animal-equivalent robots so far invented are scarcely able to move around without bumping into things, let alone to preserve or perpetuate themselves by fleeing, fighting, feeding or mating (Walmsley and de Sousa, 2010).

The rapid expansion of cyberspace and our capacities for creating virtual realities has misled the present generation into neglecting the humbler aspects of human productivity. In the wealthy world, it is easy to forget the physical toil that goes into making the commodities we enjoy, and the craft that underpins our knowledge and skills.

However, in the post-crash environment, some aspects of this imbalance have had to be addressed, especially in relation to issues of sustainability, emissions reduction and resource conservation. Here the link between Third Way thinking and modernisation through the business world model and commercial exploitation of new technology has been modified, in the direction of more local participation, awareness of the physical world and the development of community campaigns and public awareness. In this, expertise in the craft tradition has also been rehabilitated.

Some opportunities for a return to folk methods, craft and subsistence production have arisen from the crash itself. For instance, the motor manufacturing city of Detroit was already experiencing de-industrialisation well before 2008, but since then whole swaths of the city have become wastelands. There is now a local campaign to turn some of these into farms and smallholdings (BBC Radio 4, 'Today', 17 March 2010) so that the 80 per cent African American population can start to reclaim their rural heritage, left behind in the South when they migrated there in the first three decades of the 20th century.

Among many examples of this kind of culture shift, which seeks to mobilise bottom-up responses to the crash, is the attempt to reduce carbon emissions by 10 per cent in 2010 in Stoke-on-Trent. Joan Walley, MP, in the early 1990s a Labour shadow environment minister, hopes to turn the town a 'centre for green technologies and one of Britain's green urban pioneers'; she argues that 'we have to find ways of joining up science, policy, politics and people's lives. A lot of that *has* to be done locally' (quoted by Henley, 2009).

Stoke-on-Trent was one of the earliest cradles of the Industrial Revolution, a coal-mining area where Josiah Wedgwood (the great potter) and James Brindle (the renowned engineer) agreed to develop a 93-mile, 70-lock, five-tunnel waterway in 1765. But its industries have been in decline since the 1960s, and it has become an unemployment blackspot and a graveyard of urban structures. Walley has succeeded in signing up all the main local firms, organisations and government agencies for the project – the Chamber of Commerce, schools, university, college, churches, radio stations, allotment associations, the primary healthcare trust, fire brigade, police, council and Port Vale Football Club (65 organisations in all). Manufacturing companies, including ceramics, also enrolled, seeing their heavy reliance on energy as providing them with an interest in cost savings; one has already saved 25 per cent on energy use and is processing 35 per cent of recycled materials. Environmental charities are contributing to the whole curriculum of Year 7 in one comprehensive school.

Similarly, Newcastle-upon-Tyne has been revealed as the greenest city in Britain by a comprehensive sustainability audit, despite its heavy industrial past, through improving bio-diversity in parks and open spaces, and in the water quality of its river, as well as in waste collection and reducing emissions (Wainwright, 2009).

The revival of fruit and vegetable growing, and of the allotment movement, has been another response to the crash, and to the environmental crisis. Allotments, many of which had become derelict or sold off by councils since the 1960s, are now in short supply relative to this new demand. The National Trust has begun a scheme to provide land for allotments on its properties, and some landowners, large and small, have joined a Landshare movement to enable more self-provisioning.

Such participative initiatives, mobilising local groups and populations as well as public organisations in post-industrial urban areas, balance the dominant emphasis on modernisation and technology in the Third Way's original programme. With each new piece of evidence on climate change and resource depletion, the imperative of shifting attitudes and cultural practices over consumption and emission becomes clearer. For example, a report from Uppsala University in Sweden argued that the estimates of future oil supplies provided by the International Energy Agency (IEA) are far too optimistic, and that by 2030 the 105 million barrels predicted for global production is more likely to be 75 million (*The Guardian*, 2009). In face of the need for such cutbacks, the homespun approaches of Stoke and Newcastle are important complements to high-tech, huge-scale projects for renewable energy production, such as the US$400 billion plan by a consortium of German financial and engineering companies, the DESERTEC Industrial Initiative, to provide 15 per cent of Europe's electricity through a series of linked solar power plants in the Sahara. These will use mirrors to concentrate the sun's rays on a fluid container, super-heating the liquid to drive turbines; the power generated will then be transported via high-voltage cables to Southern Europe (Seager, 2009).

An interesting aspect of the post-crash situation is whether this combination of high-tech green projects and crafts-based local initiatives can restore the balance in future development, and in how science and industry supply the means for improved quality of life. Evidence of the renewed interest in traditional expertise (in cooking, vegetable growing and handcrafts) suggest that this is partly related to environmental concerns, and partly to reduced incomes, but one hope must be that it will allow these arts to be rediscovered, just as they were in danger of being lost. In addition, demand for craft products, such as cheeses, yoghurts and cured meats, and for allotments and opportunities for city farms, indicate the beginnings of such a revival.

Finally, expertise itself is being reassessed, in the light of disappointing results from the professionalisation of service roles and the rationalisation of service organisations. As Sennett (2008) argues, expertise in human communication and therapeutic relationships cannot be acquired by studying general principles; it demands reflection on experience, the cultivation of a repertoire of responses and an environment in which colleagues uphold practice excellence.

More radically, expertise may often be applied in more imaginative ways than are currently enabled by service organisations, which favour the 'delivery' of rather impersonal 'packages' of care, education or treatment. For instance, horse-riding or sailing may be more therapeutic for people with physical and intellectual disabilities than clinical physiotherapy or training. Children and young people with serious spinal or limb deformities have mastered riding and sailing, and shown benefits from energetic participation in these sports which outweigh those of therapy (BBC Radio 4, 'You and yours', 25 November 2009).

These are all small-scale examples of a cultural shift that recognises the value of activities that connect people to nature, and to folk and craft skills that were in danger of being lost, particularly in the Anglophone countries. In Europe, and especially Southern Europe, cultures of food production and appreciation have survived at a local and regional level. These are now linking with movements in the UK and US to revive and strengthen the interest in such methods and tastes.

The Third Way did not recognise the potential relevance of these activities for well-being, or for the sustainability of the economy. While local environmental projects and initiatives have thrived in the UK under New Labour, there has been no effort to incorporate a practical, hands-on, empirical approach to policy or government into its management of public life. As Halpern's account of 10 Downing

Street since 1997 bears witness, the Third Way was about 'strategy', 'performance', 'innovation' and 'delivery' (Halpern, 2010, pp 266-77). Government continued to be seen in terms of the management of contracts, information and incentives, with some additional sophistication brought to these tasks from behavioural economics and 'choice architecture' (Halpern, 2010, pp 231-51). Faced with evidence of unhealthy lifestyles, poor learning outcomes or disorderly behaviour, the New Labour response was to look for ways of getting people to commit themselves to contracts to improve themselves (p 245). It was seldom to look for ways of enriching and diversifying their experiences of social life, or of the natural world.

Conclusions

The environmental crisis highlights the importance for future politics of an approach to government that incorporates a genuine spirit of scientific curiosity and humility, and a world view that is open and adaptable to new evidence. The Third Way was in fact remarkably rigid and closed in its interpretations of human and natural phenomena, because it was based on a purely theoretical model of the relationships between the elements of society and nature it wanted to transform. Although its most spectacular failure was the economic crash, this was symptomatic of the weaknesses of its analyses of all complex interactions, which resulted from reliance on a few narrow assumptions, elevated to grandiose principles for redesigning the world in its image.

One of the great challenges for the future will be to combine large-scale interventions, involving highly sophisticated technology, with very small-scale, personal adaptations in behaviour that require cultural change to become established. The first, 'geo-engineering' projects, which will aim to alter the whole environment in order to slow climate change, involve a high risk of unintended consequences, and hence require very wide-ranging and comprehensive assessments of their impacts on the planet, which go far beyond the cost-benefit analyses favoured by the Third Way. The second need to achieve forms of moral regulation whose very existence the Third Way has discounted.

These challenges represent the policy counterparts to a set of discoveries that have shaken the scientific world in recent years, destabilising the established model of the universe and the laws of physics. Cosmologists had, since Einstein, relied on a 'standard model' – a mathematical account of how the whole universe came to be as it is now. This postulated the formation of a kind of fog in the fractions of a second after the Big Bang, which eventually coalesced into nebulae over billions of years. But a series of observations since 1980 have produced findings inconsistent with the standard model, indicating that it is wrong or incomplete, and a number of adaptations in it, using new hypotheses, have had to be made (BBC 2 television, 'Is everything we know about the universe wrong?', 9 March 2010).

If the universe started with an explosion, its contents could be expected to be lumpy and messy; but in fact they are almost uniform in temperature and consistency. To explain this, cosmologists have hypothesised a sudden dramatic 'inflation' after the initial slow expansion that followed the Big Bang. Next, galaxies on the edge of the universe seemed to be spinning round more quickly than the standard model would have predicted, so 'dark matter' was incorporated to bulk up the universe, in order to restore the workings of the laws of physics – compared with visible matter, five times the quantity of this exotic, unknown substance, not made of atoms as understood, was required. Next, the discovery that the universe seemed to be speeding up rather than running down necessitated the hypothesis of a 'dark energy', acting like the opposite of gravity to repel bodies from each other – a force filling each vacuum in the universe at an accelerating pace. Finally, unexplained movements in the cosmic microwave background seemed to require a notional 'dark flow', another mysterious force which some have argued indicates other universes outside our own.

All this has demanded constant adaptations of the standard model, and openness to the possibility that the study of these new phenomena might turn out to yield a whole new cosmology to replace it. The findings from the Large Hadron Collider experiment might yet have this result. This seems to be the situation in which the social and political sciences should be at present. But the Third Way approach, with its rigid theoretical commitments, is a fetter on such a transformation.

Evidence of this is available in Halpern's (2010) account of the New Labour years, and of the UK government's encounter with the 'Easterlin paradox' of flat-lining levels of subjective well-being (Layard, 2005) during 40 years when they would be expected to have risen in line with higher average incomes. Halpern even refers to the neglected 'economy of regard' (social relationships, culture, moral regulation) as the 'dark matter' of the economy and society (Halpern, 2010, p 54). But instead of addressing the fundamental weaknesses of the Third Way model, he tries to absorb the findings of well-being research into the established framework of ideas on policy and government.

On environmental issues, the Third Way has proved more adaptable. Under the pressure of scientific evidence about the impact on climate, bio-diversity and human flourishing of global warming, and of resource depletion, the Third Way approach to environmental policy has been considerably modified from its original, gung-ho position. A clearer commitment to the reduction of carbon emissions and the protection of the planet's ecology was taken by New Labour in the UK under Gordon Brown's administration. But the most significant question for the future is whether Barack Obama can steer the US beyond the tentative moves in this direction taken in the Clinton years, away from the climate change denial and oil guzzling that characterised the Bush ones.

During his campaign for the presidency, Obama gave a pledge to cut US energy use by 80 per cent by 2050, by raising the effective price of fuel. To achieve this, he would make renewable energy production profitable, and introduce a cap and trade system that would put a price on carbon emissions from fuel use. Coal-fired power stations would not be banned, but would simply be far more costly to run. Obama acknowledged that his scheme would make electricity much more expensive, but insisted that these costs could be defrayed by other measures, including greater efficiency in use. In California, for instance, where 23 per cent of energy is generated from renewables, and only 17 per cent from coal, 'home weatherisation' has saved up to 60 per cent on electricity bills, and US$10 billion overall has been saved. California is consequently 40 per cent more energy-efficient than other US states, has among the highest electricity prices, but almost the lowest bills (BBC 2 television, 'Can Obama save the planet?', 25 November 2009).

In attempting to legislate for his cap and trade scheme in 2009, Obama relied on promises of incentives and opportunities for energy companies and households, and on a campaign by 2,000 young activists, Power Shift, which was given open support from his administration. Members of his staff argued that the cap and trade transformation would bring about an 'economic revolution', as important as the Industrial Revolution, and that this was already under way. For instance, in Texas (the oil state) in the past eight years, the construction of 2,500 wind farms, supplying one million homes, has allowed the US to overtake Germany as the leader in this field, partly because, as governor, George W. Bush legislated that power companies must provide a quota of renewable energy (BBC 2 television, 'Can Obama save the planet?', 25 November 2009).

The automobile industry in Detroit has also, belatedly, shifted towards an eco-friendly strategy. General Motors has committed vast investment. With the rise in fuel prices, it now supports Obama's initiative; its new high-powered electric car will make a substantial contribution to reducing the 20 tonnes of carbon per person per year discharged by each North American citizen (compared with 6 tonnes by each Chinese one).

But Obama had to go to the Copenhagen Climate Change Summit meeting without congressional approval of his cap and trade bill. Although the House of Representatives narrowly passed it in June 2009, the Senate Democrats were divided, with those from West Virginia, a poor state with low wages but 28.5 billion tonnes of coal and over 30,000 mining jobs, bitterly opposed. Even more difficult for Obama was the fact that the coal lobby, which took out television advertising against the bill, commanded more popular support than the young eco-activist movement. North Americans were still unwilling to give up their fuel-heavy cars and cheap electricity, partly because of the lack of adequate public transport and the poor insulation of many of their homes.

So the need for a cultural change in the US in relation to energy use and emissions indicates that top-down engineering, through regulation and taxation, is a necessary but not a sufficient condition for the shifts required for ecological survival. In this chapter I have argued that the other requirement is that people come to recognise that science is concerned with how nature flourishes, and how human life can enhance this flourishing, rather than with how the world works as a kind of mechanism or mathematical model.

This means that science must be part of an approach that loves and cherishes the phenomena it studies, and which encourages a wider public to do the same. This was certainly the spirit of scientific enquiry in the Romantic age, when the aesthetic appreciation of nature was an integral part of how natural phenomena – including the chemistry and physics of impersonal cosmic forms – were observed and experienced by investigators. Capitalism, with its relentless drive to dominate and transform nature, has led science away from these priorities, towards a more abstract and systematic view of the world, while recasting those who once lived and worked in nature to produce their livelihoods as technicians and consumers in an artificial, man-made environment.

Every culture, from those of hunter-gatherer societies to the present day, has its own cosmology, its creation stories and narratives of continuity and change. At the dawn of modernity, when scientific accounts of the universe began to be adopted, the pioneers used images from terrestrial natural phenomena – such as waves, magnets and black holes – to explain cosmic forces, and these are still part of our cosmology today. But they also offered us the means of appreciating the interdependence of all the elements in the universe, and experiencing them with wonder and reverence, rather than absorbing them into an abstract or mechanical model.

The Third Way's initial approach to science and nature involved an uncritical acceptance of the impact of global capitalism on the environment. This book argues for a reorientation of public policy, based on something closer to the understanding of scientific knowledge expressed by von Humboldt in 1847. His introduction to *Cosmos: A sketch of a physical description of the universe* was entitled 'Reflections on the different degrees of enjoyment presented to us by the aspect of nature, and the study of her laws', and started by announcing his intention to avoid both 'the superficiality of the encyclopaedist ... [and] aphorisms consisting of mere generalities clothed in dry and dogmatic forms' (p 1).

In emphasising the 'chain of connection by which all natural things are linked together, and made mutually dependent on each other', and the importance of recent discoveries in electro-magnetism, luminous waves and radiating heat, and the 'fruitful doctrine of evolution ... in organic development' (p 56), he went on to explore the 'mutual relation of the ideas and sentiments simultaneously ... excited in the mind of the observer ... from the connection and unity of the impressions and emotions produced ... by analysing the individuality of objects, and the diversity of forces' (p 6).

> It would be a denial of the dignity of human nature and the relative importance of the faculties with which we are endowed, were we to condemn at one time austere reason engaged in investigating causes and their mutual connections, and at another that exercise of the imagination which prompts and excites discoveries by its creative powers. (von Humboldt, [1847] 1849, p 61)

It was this balance between systemising and openness to new phenomena that was missing from the Third Way's initial approach to science, but which is advocated in this book.

Part II
Regulation and relationship

FOUR

What is economics good for?

The Third Way defined itself in terms of 'the conviction that a growing market economy can be reconciled with a good society'; it proclaimed that it was 'at ease with the primacy of the market', but insisted that 'the ethical foundations of socialism – fraternity and equality – can coexist with the freedoms of liberalised markets and liberal democracy' (Latham, 2001, pp 25-6). The most influential economist in the post-Washington Consensus, the former chief economic adviser to the World Bank, Joseph Stiglitz, described the new agenda for global economic development as one in which government and markets were complementary:

> ... [in] some circumstances the new agenda sees government as helping to create markets.... In other areas (such as education), it sees the government and the private sector working together as partners, each with its own responsibilities. And in still others (such as banking), it sees government as providing the essential regulation without which markets cannot function. (Stiglitz, 2001, p 347)

In many ways, the new economic orthodoxy of the later 1990s, which was adopted as its model for public policy by the Third Way, seemed to accept the moral and political principles outlined in Chapter One of this book. For instance, it recognised that *institutions* were all-important in understanding how markets actually distributed resources and incomes, and hence produced the outcomes on which judgements about equity between citizens could be made. Taken in combination with the Third Way's claimed commitment to 'a new social contract between the winners and losers from globalisation' (Latham, 2001, p 28), this new institutional approach could provide the basis for social justice.

However, the range of institutions seen as significant by the new economics – property, markets, contracts, law and government – was far narrower than those reviewed in the analysis of justice in Chapter One. The new economics would have little to say about any of the examples given in that chapter, concerning social relations in legislatures, school playgrounds or even fairness between traders in stock markets.

But even worse, the new approach actually attempted to extend the scope of orthodox micro-economic analysis to spheres from which it previously excluded itself. It sought to explain social behaviour in units such as families, associations, communities and polities in terms of 'information imperfections' (Woolcloth, 1998; Dasgupta, 2000), 'externalities' (Collier, 1998; Foley and Edwards, 1999) or 'extended utility functions' (Becker, 1996).

In fact, the history of economic thought discouraged this kind of imperialism. Although vulgar political economy advocated policies of *laissez faire* in the 19th century, and the standard justification of government intervention in public health, education and social care was crudely utilitarian, the liberal tradition of John Stuart Mill ([1848] 1944, [1859] 1912) recognised that the wider field of social relations was better understood and regulated in terms of moral and political standards. The leading theorists of the late 19th and early 20th centuries, such as Alfred Marshall ([1890] 1927), Vilfredo Pareto ([1916] 1966) and Arthur C. Pigou (1920), insisted that economics alone could not prescribe political programmes, and – following Adam Smith ([1776] 1976) – that considerations such as security, cohesion and the maintenance of culture and character should be at least as influential (Jordan, 2008). Economic theory itself attempted to incorporate some social concepts, such as Marshall's ([1890] 1927, pp vii-xv) preference for biological over mathematical or mechanical models, Schumpeter's ([1943] 1994, pp 79-83) notions of 'organic change' and 'evolutionary processes' and Keynes' (1973, Chapter 16) acknowledgement of the 'complex unity' of the economy (Bronk, 2009).

But the turn towards methodological individualism that underpinned neo-liberal political economy rejected all these concepts as mythical and unscientific. Writers such as James Buchanan and Gordon Tullock (1962, p 4) argued that, because individuals all had different tastes in private and collective goods, all decisions to accomplish purposes collectively must be seen in terms of individual choices, and that government and other social units are properly seen simply as 'the set of processes, the machine' which allows collective action to occur (p 13). This meant that individuals could in principle consent to political institutions, tax rates and organisational systems, so long as these reflected the lowest cost ways of increasing their utility (pp 42-5).

Conversely, attempts to impose patterns (for instance, of income distribution) for the sake of moral, social or political goals, such as equality or justice, were violations of individual liberty (Hayek, 1976, p 68), and many government projects and services were examples of collective action by organised groups, such as politicians, professionals or bureaucrats, to gain 'rents' (higher returns than would be available under conditions of perfect competition) from unorganised individuals (Buchanan and Tullock, 1980).

The new economics embraced by Third Way politicians claimed to have challenged this dogmatic individualism, with its insistence on self-correcting market mechanisms, in important ways. But in this chapter I show that the changes in economic analysis that it initiated were rather superficial. The crash of 2008-09 exposed their ineffectiveness as guiding principles for public policy, while the scandals in the UK public services of 2008-09, whose genesis lay in the years before the crash, showed that they provided a misleading basis of the design of state institutions.

In this chapter I examine three key areas of the new economics' emphasis on institutions – *contracts* (as the basis for achieving efficiency and value for money in the public sector); *information and incentives* (as the basis for choice by citizens over the services provided through government); and *predicting the future* (as the basis for economic management). I argue that the claims made by the new economists, such as Stiglitz, have proved overweening, and that economics should accept a more modest role in understanding the issues which public policy must address, rather than trying to prescribe in detail for government actions.

Contracts: the holy writ

Writing about the significance of institutions in a collection of essays, *The global Third Way debate*, Joseph Stiglitz (2001) defined the new perspective in terms of the special responsibility of governments to 'create the institutional infrastructure that markets require in order to work effectively'. These rely on the security of property rights and the certainty that contracts could be enforced, but they also included the deployment of 'markets and market-like mechanisms' in the public sector, using competition to 'create competing public agencies' and private agents to compete with public services. All these processes brought contractual relationships into the achievement of policy goals, for the sake of 'improving government performance' (Stiglitz, 2001, pp 346-9).

The rationale behind these claims lay in the theory that contracts can be designed to deal with the main factors leading to inefficiencies in large organisations, and especially state ones – above all, the possession by one party of relevant information about the tasks in question of which the other is ignorant ('asymmetric information'). Once this is recognised, contracts can be designed which give the former incentives not to exploit this inside knowledge to the other party's disadvantage (Macho–Stadler and Pérez–Castrillo, 2001, pp 3-5).

This is of obvious relevance for public policy, because governments must induce their employees (civil servants, professionals) to act in ways consistent with their democratically mandated programmes, as has been recognised by theorists for many years (Vickrey, 1945; Marschak, 1955; Hurwicz, 1960). However, the innovation introduced by contract theory in the later 1990s was the idea that contracting with private firms as well as within the public sector could increase efficiency simply by the design of more complete and intelligent contracts to deal with problems such as moral hazard and imperfect information (Laffont and Martimort, 2002; Bolton and Dewatripont, 2005). Indeed, the functioning of the whole economy could be improved by measures of this kind, applied to the relationships between the government, central bank and commercial banks, derived from an analysis of information imperfections and asymmetries (Stiglitz and Greenwald, 2003, pp 3-4; Stiglitz et al, 2006, p 47).

This elevated contracts to a key role in public policy, as the main instruments for achieving 'stability with growth' in the economy, as well as better functioning of state agencies. But – as Mary Douglas pointed out – it gave contracts an almost holy status in the culture of political as well as economic analysis. Contract substituted for moral and social as well as political regulation, for loyalty and solidarity, to the point where only 'one abstract principle is sacred still, the holiness of contract itself' (Douglas, ([1978] 1982, p 192).

This reverence for contracts was indicated when the UK government threatened to introduce legislation to restrict the pay and bonuses of bank employees where these put the stability of the banking system and the security of savers' deposits at risk. The former chairman of the Royal Bank of Scotland (RBS) said in a radio interview that it represented 'a dangerous route' for government to 'tear up contracts voluntarily agreed' (BBC Radio 4, 'Today', 16 November 2009).

Yet voluntary agreement to a contract has never been a moral or legal defence, if the actions agreed between the signatories constitute a danger or harm to third parties. It is wrong and illegal to contract to injure or kill others, or to buy and sell children. It is even illegal to agree voluntarily to sell oneself into slavery. So the idea of breaking contracts which risked others' savings and the stability of the whole economy was perfectly consistent with existing law on contracts, even though it violated bankers' notions of the holy status of theirs. The revelation that Tony Blair's administration drew up a 'contract for Iraq' in 2002, to specify how the Anglo-American alliance would reconstruct that country after the overthrow of Saddam Hussein, does not make their invasion in 2003 either legal or right.

More generally, the problem about contracts is that they can have 'external' costs – effects on others who are not parties to them that are damaging, and may indeed be damaging to the overall efficiency of the economy. For instance, if a large supermarket contracts to buy a piece of land on the edge of a town it may immediately start to affect the profitability of local high street shops, and the value of their premises. This may in the long run allow shoppers to get their weekly basket filled more cheaply, with a greater variety of products, but it may also adversely affect local suppliers (farmers, craftspeople), and involve extra costs, for instance in terms of vandalism and petty crime, as premises in some town centre streets become derelict.

The mechanism by which contracts achieve greater efficiency in the private sector involve 'creative destruction' – the fact that new business developments, such as the one given in the above example, drive less 'efficient' ones out of the market. But this can only work if the whole environment – producers, wholesalers, retailers and consumers – is in a constant state of flux, with signals coming from each part of the market to every other. There must be the possibility that some new supermarket ventures fail, as well as high street shops, and that some local farmers who supply supermarkets, as well as large food companies, may fail too. Only in this way will the whole process benefit consumers, which is its main claim to superiority.

The problem of trying to apply this to the public sector, and to any form of government activity in the economy, is that the government cannot be allowed to fail in the same sense – it cannot be allowed to go bankrupt, even in such extreme cases as Iceland in 2008-09, when mismanagement of the country's financial sector meant drastic devaluation and loss of national income. So the feedback process that is supposed to drive the whole virtuous circle actually stalls when it comes to government. Particular administrations can be voted out of office in democracies, but the institutions of government always remain in place.

This means that a contract with government is not the same as a contract with another commercial firm. In the latter case, a supplier and contractor know that, if their behaviour influences the other party adversely, they run the risk of not being paid, and not getting future contracts. This interest in the other's benefit applies, even where there are loopholes in the contract that might allow wiggle-room to perform one side of the bargain less adequately, or not at all.

The same is not true in government contracts, because suppliers knows that nothing they do will affect the future existence of the government itself, or its overall functioning; equally, government officials know that their agency will still be there, no matter how badly the work is done. No amount of clever drafting of contracts can alter this basic lack of incentives for efficiency, which differentiates the government contract situation from a commercial market.

The most obvious examples of these problems concern defence procurement spending, where government purchase of weapons systems and vehicles (planes, tanks, personnel carriers) often spills beyond both price and time limits. Here the scope for exploitation by the suppliers is made worse by the fact that they are usually very large firms, with something near a monopoly of their national markets. They have little to fear from delays or overspends, especially if they are important sources for employment and expertise in their regions and fields.

But similar considerations apply to larger-scale construction projects. This has been very clear in the reconstruction of Iraq after the war there. Huge US corporations made billions of dollars from major projects, amid suspicion of profiteering and corruption, since prominent members of the Bush administration had stakes in the most successful bidders for the work.

Even when smaller organisations contract to build public facilities, there have been instances of similar phenomena. In Afghanistan, a contract for constructing a village school through foreign aid was placed with a non-governmental organisation (NGO), which subcontracted to another. By the end of the process, in which each party took its 10-20 per cent, there was enough money only to buy the wood for the roof. When this arrived from Iran, it was found to be too heavy to be supported by the mud walls of the school – so it was used as firewood (BBC Radio 4, 'World at one', 19 November 2009).

Much the same applies to government contracts for large-scale computer programs, such as that for the UK national fire service commissioned in 2007 where the requirements were not properly specified and the contractor did not appreciate the complexity involved; the costs have continued to rise because the termination of the contract would involve huge additional costs. Or the English Rural Payments Agency's system under which annual payments to farmers, some for a few hundred pounds, cost £1,200 each to calculate and issue (six times as much as in Scotland). Or the NHS computerised record system, on which details of all test results and treatments are planned to be recorded, now reckoned to be the most expensive IT system in the world, and which may, after several cancelled contracts, never deliver on its promised benefits (BBC Radio 4, 'File on 4', 2 March 2010).

Contract theorists argue that these problems can be overcome by developing the skills of government managers in designing contracts, and by eliminating corruption among suppliers. But the actual effects of the contract culture have been to increase transaction costs exponentially in the public sector. Local authorities and health authorities in the UK have used consultants, lawyers and accountants to try to deal with these problems, driving up their expenditure by more than the savings achieved.

The issue is a structural one. In the theory of the firm, it pays a company to take over a supplier who can gain advantage by delaying a project's completion. In this way, the enlarged firm internalises the costs of ensuring that work is done on budget and on time, through its management hierarchy (Hart, 1995, pp 5-30). But this option is not open to government agencies, which are required to contract with private suppliers under Third Way regulations and 'partnership' policies.

This gives rise to another set of problems, quite apart from the ones identified above. Because government officials must stay at 'arm's length' from those commercial organisations with which they contract for services, they cannot be directly responsible for the standards of practice in those firms, either in relation to service users or to staff. Although this has the advantage of giving politicians an option of deniability when scandals occur, it is a very inefficient way to provide services, and gives suppliers many opportunities to cut their costs in unacceptable ways.

For example, a public sector trade union in the UK revealed that the firm holding the contracts for 16 per cent of all hospital cleaning in the NHS in England and Wales, ISS Mediclean, was employing and exploiting immigrants without proper status. At Kingston NHS Hospital Trust, half of the firm's staff records were found to be fraudulent, and workers were being threatened and blackmailed because of their irregular status by managers, who were creaming off part of their wages. Criminal charges were pending against certain managers (Channel 4 television, 'News', 19 November 2009).

Here again, a private firm would not simply place the contract in question with another company; it would seriously consider taking over the defaulting supplier, and managing its services better. But – as scandals in the public sector over patient safety, social care homes, bail hostels and many other facilities constantly reveal – commercial providers have little interest in improving the quality of their services, while there is no way that government agencies can ensure that these standards are consistently maintained. For example, the death of a young man in a bail hostel in Stockton-on-Tees led to the revelation that the company (Clearsprings) owned over 2,000 houses all over the country in which young people on bail were living, in groups of four or five, without supervision, under a £6 million a year contract (BBC Radio 4, 'News', 28 November 2009).

All these negative consequences stem from an excessive reverence for contracts, seeing them as the main institutional basis for the achievement of efficiency in the public sector. I have argued that contracts are *one* means for reaching efficient outcomes in markets, but that they have to be seen as part of a range of institutions, which include structural factors such as the size and scope of organisations. Applying contractual approaches to government ignores a huge literature on firms and their management in the world of business, analysing when mergers are more efficient, and how transaction costs can be minimised (Williamson, 1975).

Excessive reverence for contracts also leads to an assumption that *external* regulation, through the design of conditions in drawing up agreements and the monitoring of contract compliance, is the best way to achieve good outcomes. This in turn ignores a massive literature on leadership and management in organisations (Bass, 1990), which emphasises *internal* regulation through shared goals and standards. This will be more fully explored in the next chapter.

Misleading information, perverse incentives

An integral part of the theory of contracts which underpinned the new economics as the basis for Third Way programmes for modernisation and reform concerns information and incentives in government policy, and in the choices of citizens over collective amenities. Imperfect information (leading to the asymmetries in information which block advantageous exchanges between contracting parties) was seen as the most important externality causing market imperfections, which in turn are the barriers to perfect competition, and hence to a 'first best' world of Pareto efficiency, where no one could be made better-off without making another worse-off (Durlauf and Fafchamps, 2004, p 16).

In the theory that rose to dominance in the late 1990s, issues for public policy could be largely restated in terms of the principal-agent problem, in which the principal (the government) tried to regulate the behaviour of all other individuals and organisations (the agents) in line with its social objectives, through incentives. To achieve this, it needed to make sure that the central bank regulated the financial sector in such a way that the information these intermediaries held on the credit worthiness of individuals, households and firms was used to maximise their lending consistent with stability and growth (Stiglitz and Greenwald, 2003, pp 3-4, 203-10; Stiglitz et al, 2006, pp 47-8). The government also had to find ways of getting citizens to reveal their preferences for the public goods it was responsible for supplying (Laffont and Martimort, 2002; Bolton and Dewatripont, 2005).

The banking crisis of 2008-09 demonstrated the limitations of this approach. It had assumed that the information required to manage risks in a stable and sustainable way was 'out there', waiting to be discovered, and that regulators who provided exactly the right set of incentives and penalties could induce bankers to achieve this, to the benefit of all. In practice, of course, the financial sectors of the US and UK had borrowed vast sums on global money markets, and used them to create bubbles in their housing and office prices, through the invention of new and opaque instruments ('derivatives', 'credit default swaps') for recycling debt (Fleckenstein, 2008; Tett, 2009).

What the financial crisis and subsequent economic crash revealed was that people's imaginations and creative powers were far more important determinants of the outcomes on which welfare depended than the dominant model allowed (Bronk, 2009). First, the investment bankers, hedge fund managers and market traders who created the new instruments did not simply respond to the institutional environment in which they worked; they changed it, by inventing these financial products, which they believed could revolutionise the science of risk management (Tett, 2009).

Second, people – as consumers and savers as well as investors – are not as 'rational' in their expectations of the future as the model supposes. The assumption that they will not make systematic errors (that they will use available information to correct for past mistakes) gives rise to the notion that only random shocks will drive the well-regulated economy off course. But, as a series of economists since Keynes have recognised, expectations of the future are informed by sentiment and rumour as much as by information (Keynes, 1936, pp 152, 163; Shackle, 1992, p xvii). Imagination often plays a bigger part in the construction of future expectation than information (Shackle, 1992, pp 8, 366). This feature was exacerbated during the bubble by the opaque nature of derivatives such as credit default swaps – even the managements of the banks and insurance companies creating them did not understand them, let alone the people taking out the mortgages which were being sliced, diced and sold on in this way (Thaler and Sunstein, 2008, pp 256-7), the so-called 'bounded rationality' problem.

Third, there is an inherent tension between the idea that markets tend towards equilibrium (which is fundamental to micro-economic theory), and the notion that economic growth relies on innovation and creative destruction. In the former, efficiency is derived from the hypothesis of perfectly clearing markets, with no future uncertainty (Walras, 1877), and through all agents being assumed to optimise their trading possibilities and satisfy their preferences as best they can, even in imperfect markets with sub-optimal equilibria. But innovation which relies on creative destruction (Schumpeter, [1943] 1994) may demand an institutional infrastructure quite different from that which aims at efficiency through steady expansion. The Third Way seemed to oscillate between these views of economic stability and dynamism, and the crash indicated that its claims to have achieved the former were undermined by its often unwitting promotion of the latter, especially in the financial sector.

Indeed, just as the new economics claimed to have reconciled growth and stability through its intricate model of government (as the insurer of last resort), central banks (as regulators and planners) and banks (as holders of key information for loans to innovators), all this was subverted by a contribution from the more radical wing of the economics profession.

Buchanan and Vanberg (1991) argued that the information on which markets were supposed to rely could not be discovered in the ways that might lead to incremental efficiency gains; it had to be created through projecting into a future still to be realised. The idea that market imperfections arose from 'information problems', and that these could be reduced by better knowledge leading to gains from trade, and hence an equilibrium, was rejected. Instead of a set of goods to be allocated, market actors dealt in a future to be created, and to the challenge of responding to others' innovations.

So the idea that information is a key to improved performance in the market sector of the economy, which is fundamental to the new economics, has come under increasing scrutiny from both those who follow Schumpeter and from the methodologically individualist school (Bronk, 2009). But its application in Third Way public policy is even more problematic.

The notion that efficiency in the public sector can be improved if citizens are allowed to reveal and follow their preferences for the goods supplied by government has been at the root of reforms since the late 1980s in the US and UK. Influenced by Wicksell ([1896] 1958), public choice theorists followed two lines of thought. In the first of these, it was claimed that – under a set of conditions including zero costs of moving and a lack of externalities between jurisdictions – people who could move between local authorities on the basis of the quality of their collective facilities (their physical infrastructures and their public services) as well as their rates of local taxation, could in principle select the jurisdiction which maximised their utility over public goods, and fully consent to its regime (Tiebout, 1956). This approach was developed by a number of economists, and applied to private developments and gated communities (Foldvary, 1994). In order to take advantage of these potential gains in utility to all citizens from free movement between jurisdictions, they should be fully informed about the range of options open to them.

Second, other economists drew attention to the fact that certain collective facilities which had been treated as public goods could in fact be reserved for fee-paying members, because those who could or would not pay could be excluded. Although the initial example chosen was a swimming club (Buchanan, 1965), other theorists soon applied the idea of 'clubs' to schools, hospitals and care homes. In this branch of economics, efficiency gains were claimed where a 'club' could specialise in supplying the facilities and services which were required by particular groups, because of their abilities (such as a specialist sports or science school) or needs (an amenity or enterprise for highly intelligent people with physical disabilities). Here again, an informed public was a precondition for these improvements in efficiency.

The Third Way approach to public sector reform carried forward the pursuit of these principles, introduced under neo-liberal governments, in more systematic ways. In the UK, the whole emphasis on modernisation was justified in terms of choice for citizens, and matching provision to the preferences and aptitudes as well as the needs of service users (see, for instance, DH, 1998, 2005).

In order to supply the information on which choices were to be made, the systems for inspecting, managing, measuring and changing outcomes established under New Labour in the UK were pervasive; they required staff to pursue and record specific outcomes and standards, and their agencies to provide information about these to central databases. These requirements changed the ways in which practitioners did their jobs in many ways. It was not simply that they focused on achieving specific targets (such as reducing waiting times in the NHS or achieving grades in SATS tests); they also spent far longer in recording these activities in standardised ways. This became a focus of the critique of social work practice in the scandal over the death of Baby Peter in Haringey (Jordan, 2010, Chapter 1).

But it also had direct effects on the behaviour of citizens, many of which were unintended. Especially in the field of education, parents moved to districts where they could gain access to schools with better examination results. This drove up prices of houses in those districts, and meant that better-off people were advantaged in competition for the most desirable schools. Conversely, it accelerated processes of social polarisation which were already happening in the 1980s and early 1990s (Jordan et al, 1994), leaving concentrations of disadvantaged people in the districts with the less successful schools and other public amenities.

In other words, the provision of fuller information about public facilities often gave perverse incentives and had socially undesirable consequences. Teachers were encouraged to teach to specific tests and assessments, rather than to educate children more broadly. In some cases they cheated to help students get better grades (Levitt and Dubner, 2006). School rolls became polarised between those with aspirational and those with unmotivated pupil populations. Health professionals were incentivised by managers to achieve specific targets, and came by this prioritisation to neglect others, such as patient safety, as in the Mid-Staffordshire scandal (Healthcare Commission, 2009). Inspections of child protection services and hospitals focused on paper assessments of standardised checklists, and were often poor reflections of actual practice.

Many of these consequences were the results of differences between the goods distributed by governments, and those available in consumer markets. The resemblances between hospital or school places and concert tickets or restaurant tables are very superficial; the idea that better information can produce 'market clearance' does not apply. In the case of treatment for illnesses, people's 'preferences' cannot be ranked. For the most serious conditions, they need immediate, good quality care, not a range of options. As was seen during the scandals over patient safety in the UK in November–December 2009, information is useful more to learn which hospitals to try to avoid than which to choose.

In the case of schools, the main difference lies in the 'positional' nature of those with the best exam results (Hirsch, 1977; Jordan, 1996). A good school is not valued simply for the quality of its education, but also for the advantages it gives over other future applicants for jobs and university places – hence for access to better careers and incomes. The socially undesirable consequences of publishing league tables for the sake of easier choice stem from the fact that better-off parents, who are better aware of these positional features of good school places, also have the best opportunities to take action to secure them. Information plus mobility equals inequality, with all its unwelcome social consequences (Wilkinson and Pickett, 2009).

Predicting the future

The new economics claimed to have rectified weaknesses in the theory of self-correcting markets. These adjustments allowed governments that followed certain broad principles, about balancing private with public actions, strengthening institutions and improving regulation, to achieve 'growth with stability' (Stiglitz et al, 2006). The future would become manageable and relatively predictable, so that, for instance, Stiglitz felt able to write that, 'I am confident that the coming decade will certainly see enormous growth in the developing world and a reduction of poverty' (Stiglitz, 2001, p 356). There would, in Gordon Brown's hubristic phrase, be 'no more boom and bust'.

But earlier theorists had warned that these claims rested on models of the economy as a machine rather than a complex organism, or on mathematical formulae underpinned by heroic (that is, unrealistic) assumptions (Bronk, 2009). These warnings came from Romantics such as Johann Gottfried von Herder ([1772] 1969), Samuel Taylor Coleridge (1810) and William Hazlitt ([1825] 1932), but also from Alfred Marshall ([1890] 1927) and John Maynard Keynes (1936); they are now augmented by analyses from a very different source – 'complexity theory'. Here a new approach to economics argues that random events can shift the path of the whole economy in ways that relate to the specifics of a particular time and place (such as Silicon Valley in California in the 1980s), and that this is not susceptible to the abstract analysis preferred by economists since the 1970s.

> To the extent that small events determining the overall path always remain beneath the resolution of the economist's lens, accurate forecasting of an economy's future may be theoretically, not just practically, impossible. (Arthur, 1990, p 85)

Using non-linear mathematical and computer techniques, theorists from this school used analogies from biology, meteorology and physics, to model economic change as a dynamic, 'organic' process which is constantly evolving, through bursts of creativity and extinction, as in biological ecosystems (Waldrop, 1994, p 119). This implies an approach to the future that combines mechanical and organic metaphors in its use of computer modelling, but only by accepting indeterminate outcomes between chaos and stasis (Waldrop, 1994, p 294).

> The important conclusion is that ... economists *can* hope to simulate the full dynamic nature of social and economic organisms with mechanical models, but only if they stop trying to make them deterministic and predictive of a unique equilibrium outcome or steady-state; they need to experiment with modelling behaviour according to rules of behaviour and interaction that allow clear (and observed) patterns to form but do not imply a single optimal outcome. (Bronk, 2009, p 130)

This implies that the kinds of quantified predictions of the trajectory of the economy over a period of years, which have made up the approach to public policy of governments since the Second World War, are likely to mislead. Not only are the shocks which disrupt growth difficult to foresee, as the crash demonstrated; even the clusters of success through 'increasing returns', where innovators interact to produce sudden spurts in development, are equally unpredictable.

But this does not imply that economic modelling is useless for public policy. The fact that economists should not even try to make *ex ante* predictions of the future, or to make 'scientific' tests of their predictions, does not represent a humiliating fall from grace, or a reduction in its status as a discipline. Other sciences do not attempt to predict with any great degree of accuracy, but instead aim to explain outcomes after the event. This can give rise to useful understanding of patterns that may occur in future, such as the sequence of asset bubbles being followed by crashes. If economists could explain and model the tipping points in such processes, this would be of more assistance to policy makers than their very unsuccessful efforts at precise prediction (Bronk, 2009, pp 131-2).

After the crash of 2008-09 there was a revival of the old joke, which in one of its variants went 'Why were economists put onto this earth? To make astrologers look good' ('The West Wing', series 1, episode 1). A more recent version gave the answer as 'To make weathermen look good' (BBC1 television, 'Paradox', 24 November 2009). But this analogy would not be so discreditable. If economists were to recognise that the phenomena they model are more like weather than like the atomic structure of matter, then their work would be more valuable for policy makers.

If complexity theory provides a more appropriate model for micro-economic as well as macro-economic analysis, this is because individuals, as well as firms and governments, interact in ways that attempt to anticipate each other's strategies, or even fantasies, for the future. In business this may amount to something like playing chess (Waldrop, 1994, pp 150, 253); in many other spheres it relies on how we understand and respond to others' snap judgements and rules of thumb – socially influenced decisions and behaviour patterns (Bronk, 2009, pp 132-3).

The implication of these ideas is that the elaborate abstract models and pseudo-exact predictions which have been fashionable in economics should be set aside in favour of a closer study of empirical data, and a willingness to learn from other, more applied activities (such as the management of avalanches or forest fires) about how to avert catastrophes. Economists should be more aware of the limits of their science.

Keeping economics in its place

Under Third Way regimes, economics not only aspired to guide government according to prescient knowledge and prescriptive principles; it also invaded the spheres of society previously shielded from its rule. Because the Third Way regarded itself as a modernising and reforming force, and saw markets as the means to sweep away arcane and protectionist practices, and business management methods as driving efficiency, it was blind to the destructive and corrupting potentials of economic logics.

In retrospect, it seems extraordinary that in the UK in particular, with a whole century of socialist thinking and organisation to draw on, New Labour can have so studiously ignored the known harms and hazards of capitalism. But it was almost a fetish of the reformers to turn their backs on their party's traditions, and embrace the very dragons that it came into being to slay. If this was most obvious in its dealings with banks and the City, it extended into the harnessing of private firms and business principles for transforming every part of the social system.

This pride in its radicalism was, in truth, little more than hitching a ride on the 'creative destruction' of capital's drive to create 'One Big Market' – the original First Movement of Karl Polanyi's *The great transformation* (1944). There should be no shame in acknowledging that much of the motivation for an ethical socialism is backward-looking, derived from the desire to protect human value from the incursions of impersonal economic forces. As Polanyi pointed out, a large part of the impulse to resist the advance of globalising forces stemmed from the recognition that they swept away archaic social institutions and practices through which such value was honoured, created and distributed among members of social units.

As the historian Tony Judt (2010a) has pointed out, the left has an interest in conserving its legacy of achievements in the fields of equality and social justice, and this involves the constant reassertion of the need to subject economic life to moral rules.

> We take for granted the institutions, legislation, services and rights that we have inherited from the great age of 20th-century reform. It is time to remind ourselves that all of these were utterly inconceivable before 1929.... [I]n truth the democratic left has often been motivated by a sense of loss; sometimes of idealised pasts, sometimes of moral interests ruthlessly overridden by private advantage. It is doctrinaire market liberals who for the past two centuries have embraced the relentlessly optimistic view that all economic change is for the better.... From the war in Iraq through the unrequited urge to dismantle public education and social services, in the decades-long project of financial deregulation, the political right – from Thatcher and Reagan to Bush, Blair and Brown – have abandoned the association of political conservatism with social moderation which served it so well from Disraeli to Heath, from Theodore Roosevelt to Nelson Rockefeller. (Judt, 2010a, p 4)

The irony of the Third Way's radical reformism in the UK was that, while the market-minded programme of Margaret Thatcher provoked resistance from the public sector, rallying around its distinctive culture and ethos, the New Labour government was successful in subverting this in the name of modernisation. The price for the enormous expansion of budgets that took place in its second term was the creation of management and contractual systems that institutionalised its economic approach. These undermined the traditional moral and cultural codes that had regulated schools, hospitals and universities, and even the voluntary organisations that came to rely on government contracts for their funding. As Michael Sandel argues, this has led to an urgent need to define the moral limits of economic reasoning, and those spheres that should be protected from market logics and management business practices. In these, the issues:

> ... are not only about utility and consent. They are also about
> the right ways of valuing social practices.... As marketised
> social practices may corrupt or degrade the norms that
> define them, we need to ask what non-market norms we
> want to protect from market intrusion. We need public
> debate about the moral limits of markets. (Sandel, 2010, p 4)

To an extraordinary extent under Third Way regimes, the approach
based on information, incentives and contracts penetrated the public
sector and public life more generally. Its criteria for efficiency became
the only standards to which staff were accountable. Electronic systems
for collecting data were deployed as the means for surveillance and
control, and targets ensured that outcomes were measured and costed.

These processes often displaced the actual goals of organisations,
sometimes in ludicrous ways. In a move unprecedented since the Second
World War, a few weeks before the Iraq invasion, the UK government
recalled all its ambassadors for a seminar at the Foreign Office. But
the justification for the war and its geopolitical implications were not
mentioned. Instead, according to the experienced diplomat Sir Ivor
Roberts, Tony Blair and Jack Straw (the then Foreign Secretary) held
forth about 'value for money', 'synergies', 'silos' and other management
concepts, in a session of what he described as 'Bullshit bingo' (BBC
2 television, 'The great offices of state: the Foreign Office, palace of
dreams', 27 March 2010).

But perhaps the most serious shortcoming of the economic approach
underpinning Third Way policies has been revealed by the resistance
to Barack Obama's healthcare reforms in the US (which forced him
to adopt a compromise system), and by the failure of the New Labour
administration to make any progress with a national plan for funding
social care (marked by a Green Paper, which simply postponed the key
decisions about the necessary structures, in the last weeks of the Brown
government). What these showed was that electorates which had been
groomed to believe that they would gain important advantages by
being able to choose the others with whom they would share risks of
this kind were unwilling to accept schemes for pooling their risks with
those of their most disadvantaged fellow citizens. The economics of self-
selected clubs 'undermines the solidarity that democratic citizenship
requires' (Sandel, 2010, p 1).

In the US, insurance interests used the same slogans and rhetoric to
resist Obama's proposals as had proved successful in defeating Clinton's
in the 1990s – why should you have to share the risks of accidents and
illnesses with construction workers and 'welfare mothers'? For citizens

who had paid into schemes that selected others like themselves, and even for some who had not been able to afford healthcare insurance, this appealed to the ethic of self-responsibility, implying that these others had no incentive or motivation to minimise the hazards they faced. These campaigns, together with conjuring up the bogey of 'socialised medicine' and the 'Big State', succeeded in forcing substantial modifications in Obama's original proposals, and protecting insurance companies' interests.

In the UK, New Labour were unable to reach a consensus with the other main parties over how to fund their proposed national care service, and lacked the political will to attempt to push through their own plan. The main disagreement arose because the Conservatives favoured a voluntary insurance principle, despite the fact that the only other major EU country to follow this approach, France, had been unable to draw more than 20 per cent of its population into such a scheme. The most obviously equitable solution, to fund it through general taxation or National Insurance contributions, was not even canvassed. Presumably this was because the dominant economic approach so strongly favoured co-payments and differentiation of risks and benefits. After all, the presiding genius of the Third Way/World Bank economic model, Joseph Stiglitz, had started his career as an insurance economist.

Conclusions

The contribution of economics to the well-being of societies is likely to be enhanced, rather than diminished, if it can accept the lessons of the economic crash. An appropriate modesty, and a look at the history of capitalism, would indicate that surges in the prices of assets and in credit markets have occurred quite often, and that models claimed to eliminate risk are snake oil. As argued in the previous chapter, a truly scientific approach requires practitioners to derive their (falsifiable, and always provisional) theories from observed data, not to devise abstract models based on unrealistic assumptions. The trouble with economics was that it had lost its connection with the true spirit of scientific investigation.

> The prestigious economics journals have been cleansed of all but the purveyors of highly technical algebra. Economic history has been removed from the syllabus because those who yearn for economics to be a hard science believe the past can teach them nothing. (Elliott, 2010, p 24)

The Third Way's reverence for the new economics, and particularly for the institutions of contractual regulation and business management, placed serious constraints on the scope for implementing its proclaimed moral and political principles. Because economists of the new orthodoxy insisted that these instruments supplied the means to maximise the welfare of citizens, particularly by improving the effectiveness of government activities, Third Way regimes gave priority to the application of the theory of information, incentives and contracts to public policy.

In the UK, this allowed the government to suppose that economic growth could be achieved by a combination of making money out of money in the financial sector, and constructing a pyramid of contracts in the public sector. The former turned out to be no more than a speculative bubble, and the latter saw an expansion of management without a corresponding improvement in productivity. As a result, the government has found it difficult to reassert any control over the operations of financial intermediaries since the crash, because they represent a kind of club (or cartel) of traders who continue to bet against each other inside their protective enclave, using taxpayers' money. And the government also faces barriers to reducing costs in the public services, because management structures now represent rigid features of the organisational landscape. Not only are the salaries of senior managers in health authorities, local government and the universities now set at levels close to those of the private sector, they also carried on recruiting more managers even after the crash.

At first the crash brought disorientation to the UK government in particular, because of its enthusiastic adherence to the new economics. For instance, the governor of the Bank of England was initially reluctant to bail out the banks because of the 'moral hazard' of rewarding their reckless risk taking. But – after Lehman Brothers in the US was allowed to fail, which caused the global credit freeze – the New Labour government and the Bank were given little alternative to injecting capital and guaranteeing loans.

Then these policies, along with the 'quantitative easing' through which the Bank of England pumped money into the economy, created entirely new conditions, for which the principles of the World Bank orthodoxy supplied no guide. As we have seen in Chapters One and Two, dilemmas such as whether to allow bankers, who were only still in business because of government rescues and credit creation, to draw massive bonuses from profits swollen by quantitative easing, cannot be answered by economic analysis. Balancing the prospects of getting taxpayers' money back against the sense of injustice felt by entrepreneurs driven into liquidation by the crash, or employees made redundant through the collapse of demand, required another kind of judgement.

Accordingly, when the New Labour government was deliberating the pre-budget report of 9 December 2009, its options were framed in terms of fairness, and the Conservative opposition accepted these terms. While the Treasury was considering how to impose a super-tax on the financial sector (either bonuses or salaries or both) to reduce government debt out of the windfall profits by bankers in the asset boom, the opposition preferred the withdrawal of tax allowances under which the losses incurred by this sector could be offset against profits in good years. Indeed, most of the debate concerned the feasibility of these alternatives and their actual returns to the Exchequer, not their justice. Bankers themselves disputed these measures in terms of the fairness of taxing a single sector (BBC Radio 4, 'Today', 7 December 2009).

These concerns spilled over into the public sector; Gordon Brown, speaking at the Institute of Government, described 'a culture of excess' among executives and senior managers over their salaries. He announced that all civil services and other public sector posts paying over £150,000 a year would require Treasury permission, and that those authorities which wasted taxpayers' money would be named and shamed. This was a departure from the Third Way's reliance on incentives and contracts for efficiency, in the direction of achieving a 'culture shift' towards equality and accountability to moral goals.

Economics can supply important indications of the factors that influence growth and decline in industries, in employment, in incomes, in trade and in government revenues. In this way, the economics of welfare can and should be one of the guides to public policy. But the founders of this branch of the discipline were under no illusions that economics could have the last word on government decisions.

In the very work in which he expounded his famous principle for optimal resource allocation, Pareto (1909, p 2) started by distinguishing between 'customary' and economic behaviour. He gave the example of a 'well brought-up man' taking off his hat and making polite gestures on entering a drawing room, but then retiring to his study to buy a large consignment of grain at a profit. The first kind of action he saw as responding to 'sentiment', to a legacy of beliefs and institutions about social life and relationships which was not susceptible to a regime of efficiency or material gain (Pareto, [1896] 1966, p 103). Furthermore, he argued that government should be at least as concerned with influencing 'interests and sentiments' of this kind through its policies and laws as with achieving maximum overall economic welfare (Pareto, [1916] 1966, p 244).

In the next chapter I support this approach with an analysis of the role of moral regulation, arguing that governments should aim to find a balance between 'external', contractual and legal means of influencing the economy and society, and 'internal', social and cultural ones.

Moral regulation: rituals, symbols and the collective conscience

The moral failures of the Third Way stemmed from its mistaken conception of the process of moral regulation. As its leading exponents claimed, the end of the 20th century marked a period in which society was moving from traditional, collective standards of behaviour, uncritically adopted from family, neighbourhood and class, to individual, 'reflexive', self-responsibility, in which 'we are what we make of ourselves' and 'the moral thread of self-actualisation is one of *authenticity* ... based on "being true to oneself"' (Giddens, 1991, pp 75-97).

In this view, the Third Way was addressing a new kind of society, and had to adapt to 'the changing nature of the family, work and cultural identity' (Giddens, 1998, p 46). As we saw in Chapter Two, its approach lay partly in the assertion of values such as equality of opportunity, which informed its policies on education and welfare-to-work activation. But it also demanded that individuals took responsibility for themselves, in terms of work, saving and updating their skills (DSS, 1998, p 80), and that they participated in civil society organisations (Blair, 1996). Individuals were seen as choosing the associations and activities which reflected their values and identities, in a complex and diverse community. Indeed 'community' was itself a Third Way value (Blair, 1998a), but this took a 'post-traditional' form, moving beyond class issues (Driver and Martell, 2001).

In this chapter I argue that the Third Way's adoption of self-actualisation and self-responsibility as its model of moral regulation meant that it greatly underestimated the importance of emotional, aesthetic, symbolic and ritual elements in the creation of the social order, and above all it discounted collective influences on social relations. By buying into the notion that 'reflexive individualisation' was a wholly new, post-traditional feature of late modern (or post-modern) culture, it mistook a culturally produced dominant myth for a new liberation, in which individuals met as 'real', 'reflexive' and 'authentic'.

Mary Douglas anticipated this development. She argued that market-orientated social relations produced the illusion of rational choice and 'the conviction that we have escaped from the old non-market institutional controls into a dangerous, new liberty'. Believing ourselves to be 'uncontrolled by the idea of the sacred', and that we have achieved 'full self-consciousness', we are in fact simply parroting a 'collective representation' of our society – indeed a form of 'primitive solidarity' (Douglas, 1987, p 99).

All that Third Way theorists were describing therefore was a society in which individuals were competitive and unconstrained by social boundaries, groups were provisional and temporary and status was negotiable. Such societies are quite common in the aboriginal cultures of New Guinea and Indonesia, and there, as in our society, individuals seek status, position and power over each other, as in the cult of celebrity. Furthermore, the idea that a market economy makes notions of sacred value anachronistic is obviously delusional. On the one hand, as we saw in the previous chapter, contracts have come to be seen as sacred (Douglas, [1978] 1982, p 192); on the other, individuals themselves, as sovereign, self-realising and choosing, are regarded and regard themselves as having sacred value (Rose, 1996).

Conversely, the version of morality which was promoted by the Third Way – as a set of attitudes and values through which an individual expresses his or her authentic identity (Rose, 1996, p 1) – implied that it had shaken off its origins in an externally imposed, collective, ritual and non-rational code. This meant that moral regulation consisted of self-regulation, and was accomplished through the processes by which people transform and improve themselves, educating, training and developing themselves, using enterprise and initiative to fulfil their potentials (Rose, 1996, p 154).

On this understanding of morality, the role of government was to provide institutions through which people could exercise autonomy and choice, and achieve self-improvement. Such external regulation as was necessary was ideally exercised through contracts, seen as mutually beneficial, voluntary agreements. But this optimistic view of society was belied by the Third Way's almost obsessive concern with law, guidance, codification and micro-management, which imposed such detailed incentives and requirements on its target populations that it left little room for independent judgement.

This could be explained by the Third Way perception that it had to overcome and defeat a backward-looking cultural legacy of the previous age – the public sector culture of mediocrity and standardisation, and the 'dependency culture' of passive welfare state beneficiaries (DSS, 1998, p 26). Its application of a programme for modernisation was supposed to replace these by features of the mainstream ethic, but this had to be done through the imposition of external standards, into which both public sector staff and service users could grow.

In practice, the tide of regulation and micro-management did not recede over time; it spread across a broader field of social interactions, as more and more spheres of activity were seen as being in need of intervention. On the other hand, government agencies did not become more like businesses, nor service users more like customers, despite the attempt to introduce new terminology, and to rebrand society itself, as in 'UK plc'. What emerged was not a new morality of self-reflexivity and striving for improvement, but a mechanistic reliance on rules and procedures on the one hand, and on cod-commercial logos, symbols and mission statements on the other.

In this chapter I trace this failure of the Third Way programme to the absence of any adequate understanding of how moral regulation works, and how cultural ideas and images can be mobilised to provide alternatives to law, contract and material incentives. The belated recognition in the UK of the need for 'culture shifts' in almost every sphere is a signal that this realisation has finally dawned.

How morality shapes action

The Third Way version of morality was in contrast with the account given by Émile Durkheim ([1893] 1933, 1898). Durkheim recognised individualism as the emerging moral code of the upper middle classes in European countries of his time. But he analysed it as 'a religion in which man is at once the worshipper and the god' because the human person 'is considered sacred in the ritual sense of the word'; it was a code which 'penetrates our institutions and our mores' (Durkheim, 1898, p 46). It provided the constraining moral reality through which individuals understood their world, and within which they felt obliged to act. Above all, in their decisions and actions they felt compelled to account for themselves as authors of their destinies – to say what they had made of themselves (Jordan et al, 1994, pp 24-30).

In other words, Durkheim explained individualism within the same framework in which he understood the religious moralities of earlier periods, and indeed the codes which governed the behaviour of members of hunter-gatherer tribes. Hence he sought to explain the force of morality through rituals and symbols, as much in the society of his day as in past history and among aboriginal peoples. Beliefs and moral codes were sustained by ritual practices, by symbols of the sacred objects of the society (Durkheim, 1912). Ideas could become consecrated in the same way as totems or icons (Durkheim, 1912, pp 243-4).

So Durkheim argued that morality was a *product* of ritual. In simple societies with a strong group identity, rituals such as feasts and celebrations gave a heightened sense of intersubjectivity and energy, conferred on symbols of the group and of goodness (1912, p 242); this was respected and valued for its own sake. But the same mechanisms can apply in individual interactions, which have particular emotional significance (Collins, 2004, pp 42-3). To understand the morality of individualism, we need first to understand how individuals (rather than groups and their symbols) are made sacred.

Here the analysis of morality in the tradition of Durkheim and Douglas focuses on *situations* rather than people – on moments rather than those who are supposed to make them. But these situations are not necessarily ceremonial, nor do they necessarily involve large groups. Erving Goffman (1967a, 1967b) showed how even informal, everyday encounters involved rituals which affirmed the moral order of society, defining (even creating) social reality itself. These rituals can be as stereotyped as greetings and minor conversational routines, but they indicate degrees of intimacy or respect. He adopted Durkheim's view of ritual: '[R]ites are the rules of conduct which prescribe how a man should comport himself in the presence of these sacred objects' (Durkheim, 1912, p 56). Goffman wrote, 'I use the term "ritual" because this activity, however informal and secular, represents a way in which the individual must guard and design the symbolic implications of his act while in the immediate presence of an object that has a special value for him' (Goffman, 1967b, p 57).

Among these sacred objects, honouring what is socially valued by means of ritual, the foremost in modern societies is the individual self; we are required to treat each other as little gods in the everyday encounters and avoidance rituals of our lives (Goffman, 1967b, p 232). When ritual rules are transgressed, people feel moral uneasiness, although apologies can restore the moral order through ritual deference.

One of the most spectacular public transgressions of this moral order occurred during the UK General Election campaign of April 2010 when Gordon Brown, on a televised visit to Rochdale, Lancashire, met a 66-year-old widow, lifetime Labour supporter and former worker with children with disabilities, Gillian Duffy. On camera he dealt politely with her questions about the government deficit and student grants, and only slightly less comfortably with one about the influx of East European immigrants to the district, before complimenting her on her coat and on the aspirations of her grandsons, and getting into his car.

At this point he forgot that he was still wearing a live radio microphone, and asked with audible fury who had allowed this encounter to occur, expressing angry frustration with the aide whom he suspected to have been responsible. In response to a puzzled question from another aide about the problem, he declared the incident to have been 'a disaster', that he was sure it would be broadcast later and that Mrs Duffy was just 'a bigoted woman'.

In a few seconds Brown had thus evinced rage at being filmed with someone not conforming to the accepted cultural stereotypes for televised campaigning interviewees, blame of one of his team for permitting this to happen and scorn for one of his core supporters. Worse still, all these emotional reactions were in stark contrast with the impression of warmth and regard he gave in the interview itself, and the value he appeared to bestow on Mrs Duffy and her family in their interactions. When she in turn was filmed being informed of his characterisation of her, which had been broadcast on the radio soon afterwards, her face and voice registered shock, mortification and outrage. It is hard to imagine that the apologies he made as a 'penitent sinner' in a long visit to her house a few hours later could erase this sense of having been demeaned and devalued by his words.

What this sequence of events revealed was how the moral order which underpins all social relations, including the political basis for democracy, is ultimately derived from the communication of social value in the humblest conversations. Our identities and our roles in society are sustained or subverted in such encounters. In this case, an interview which seemed to maintain Gordon Brown's claims to be a sincere and friendly Prime Minister, who understood and supported pensioners who had worked in social services, and Mrs Duffy's claims to the honour which was due to her as such a voter, were violated by his inadvertently broadcast comments. Although in the event this incident seemed to make little difference to the outcome of the election, it received enormous media coverage and comment because it appeared to reveal a tear in the fabric of the moral order which Brown himself claimed to uphold.

In Goffman's work, the self is constructed in *situations*, through claiming 'face' (whatever value the individual seeks to put on him- or herself). But the scope for these claims is limited by how consistently each can maintain a 'line' – a self-presentation in that particular situation. As the parties to any interaction perform themselves, they jointly construct a social reality which exercises moral constraint on them, and is experienced as external to them. They feel required to perform a 'morally adequate' version of themselves, which is appropriate for the situation, and for the 'face' they have claimed in it (Goffman, 1967a). Gordon Brown destroyed the face he had claimed on the campaign trail by his unguarded comments; Mrs Duffy had hers instantly dismantled by his description of her.

On this analysis, the social order is created by millions of such ritual interactions, although certain large-scale events are of particular significance, and can radically transform it:

> These moments of high degree of ritual intensity are high points of experience..., the key moments of history, the times when significant things happen. These are moments that tear up old social structures or leave them behind, and shape new social structures ... like the French Revolution in the summer of 1789..., like the collapse of communist regimes in 1989 and 1991.... (Collins, 2004, p 42)

On such occasions, the collective nature of the rituals which create the moral order is obvious, as is the emotional intersubjectivity of the experience and the capacity of the occasion to give rise to symbols. But Goffman's work shows that these features are also present in micro-level interactions; even casual encounters require reciprocity in communication, a degree of commitment in the return of smiles or gestures, and often also the evocation of something which symbolises a previous meeting ('wasn't it at X's party we last met...?').

What these analyses provide is an explanation of how we feel compelled to act in certain ways towards other people, often without conscious awareness of any specific 'value' or 'rule' which indicates the appropriateness of this behaviour. We are not polite or deferential because of a belief in the virtue of these qualities, but because of 'habits of the heart' (Bellah et al, 1985), arising from previous interactions. Conversely, we do not often avoid or snub others because they offend our principles; far more frequently we do so because they have been uncivil, or failed to observe the proprieties (such as not detaining us with long and irrelevant accounts of their misfortunes) in earlier encounters.

In all these ways, morality works more like the snap judgements described in Chapter Two earlier; it seems unconscious, and something that comes to us unbidden. But this does not make it any less powerful. Indeed, we feel strongly constrained to give a morally adequate performance of ourselves in almost every situation, including meetings with strangers. We almost immediately determine how to present ourselves, and how much value to claim from the other person (as a competent citizen, an expert, a local, or whatever). This in turn requires a response which either reciprocates, treating us accordingly, or makes a counter-claim, which may implicitly or explicitly reject ours. If reciprocity is established, a 'local interactional order' is created (Warfield Rawls, 1989), one which exercises its own moral constraints on us, even though we have unconsciously, and often unintentionally, constructed it.

For instance, in research interviews my colleagues and I did for a project investigating how better-off couples made decisions about work, pensions, children's schooling and welfare (Jordan et al, 1994), we found that the respondents had clear expectations of how to present themselves as competent interviewees and how to give a morally adequate account of their choices. A few became obviously uncomfortable, almost to the point of distress, when they could not meet their own, self-imposed standards, for instance in showing how a decision to move a difficult son to a private school improved his educational performance (it did not). However, some, whom we called 'heretics', defied what they seemed to know were the expectations of a morally adequate account, giving deliberately flippant or unconventional reasons for their decisions ('I moved in with her because I liked her dog'). Others still (all men) gave terse, unelaborated answers ('purely economic reasons'), which fulfilled the basic requirements of adequacy, but were not competent performances of themselves – we called them 'fundamentalists'. In comparing their accounts with those given separately by their partners, they had been criticised for failing to provide an adequate family income.

So the situation of a research interview gave rise spontaneously to a 'local interactional order' with standards of moral adequacy that were largely self-imposed but which could be breached in some circumstances (where the interviewee rejected its requirements). But in any situation, the moral order may break down because one of the parties does not observe the emerging ritual demands of that particular type of encounter.

I remember with embarrassment being approached by an eminent political philosopher at a conference, when I was talking to a friend. The latter introduced me by saying, "This is Bill Jordan, the well-known...". At this point he paused momentarily, not knowing quite how to describe my diverse academic output, and finally finished, "... athlete". The philosopher responded in kind to the value claimed for me by my friend, saying that when he was young he could run the 200 metres in something like 25 seconds. Rather to my surprise, I heard myself reply, "So could Woody Allen". This was taken as an offensive riposte (although in fact true, I think), perhaps because of the philosopher's (slightly Allenesque) physique, but I am glad to say that we met on a subsequent occasion, when no reference was made to athletics, but he said he had read a useful paper by me in the 1970s (thus restoring the moral order which I had breached with my smart-arse quip).

The fact that I remember this incident so vividly (I can recall exactly where I was standing, and how he approached us) indicates the morally compelling nature of even the most casually created moral order. Equally, it is easy to remember occasions on which someone breached the ritual niceties of a meeting or a conference by saying or doing something quite inappropriate. No doubt the delegates at an Italian trade union seminar recall me walking through the assembly in my running clothes, after having been forbidden to leave by a back exit near where I had changed. They probably also remember me (jokingly) shouting to Guy Standing, who had switched his slot with mine so I had to speak first, "Hey, Guido, bastardo!", which apparently is far ruder in Italian than in English.

However, these breaches were anomalies, in situations where I was a foreigner, and probably forgiven as such. Of more concern are examples of disorder, incivility and lack of commitment (littering, for example) which indicate disrespect for others using a public space. When these actions become habitual and taken-for-granted, they signify a decline in the collective morality which is constructed when people expect certain standards of themselves and each other.

The analysis of moral regulation in terms of ritual interaction also makes sense of the phenomenon of *Generation me* (Twenge, 2006) – the cultivation of a self-promoting, insecure egoism masquerading as self-esteem, which is evident in recent surveys of young people in the US. This was manifested among people with few valid claims to respect and few accomplishments; it represented a fragile, narcissistic attempt to shore up the self, which Twenge discovered in two thirds of college students in 2006, far higher than revealed by her research in 1982. This development has been described as a 'social evaluation threat' (Wilkinson and Pickett, 2009, pp 37-8) – people 'are driven to preserve the social self and are vigilant to threats that may jeopardise their social esteem' (Dickerson and Kemeny, 2004, p 357). They react defensively, and this includes changes in their cortisol levels (Dickerson and Kemeny, 2004, p 377); it reflects the attempt to preserve self-esteem which 'is largely based on others' perceptions of one's worth' (p 357).

In other words, the aggressive and uncivil claims of 'face' habitually made by many young people within recent popular culture can be understood in terms of how they seek value in interactions with others, especially peers. They reflect the anxiety which is generated by an individualistic culture, in which group solidarities and grid roles (positions in gender or occupational hierarchies) do not supply validated claims to respect from others.

Symbols in collective action

So the interaction ritual perspective shows that moral regulation is omnipresent in individualistic societies such as the present-day US and UK, but that it is problematic. At the everyday, local and informal levels, it relies on claims to intimacy, respect and belonging which are made on the basis of the individual – his or her qualities and accomplishments, rather than his or her role in family, on kinship or occupational structure, or on membership of a tightly-knit 'community of fate', into which we are born and remain. So moral regulation has to be performed in myriads of separate encounters, in which individuals claim uniqueness, distinctive identity and a trajectory of self-realisation, yet also claim social value from others for this performance of themselves. The 'little gods' of individualism are therefore insecure and fragile, and the moral order they create is correspondingly brittle, requiring perpetual repair, as members reconstruct their narratives of self, to make them more morally adequate (Hilbert, 1992; Jordan et al, 1994, pp 70-1).

Indeed, a defining feature of this latest version of individualism is the impermanence of the identities and self-narratives of those who undergo constant transformation and reinvention in their quest for social value. These require such processes as cosmetic surgery and style makeovers for their accomplishment, therapy for their maintenance and speed-dating for their communication (Elliott and Lemert, 2005). Because such individual selves are so provisional and transient, insecurity is built into this culture.

But this does not imply that these societies have dispensed with collective experiences, group solidarities and the heightened emotions of the crowd. Instead, it means that these are very diverse, and that people move among them in shifting patterns of affiliation, allegiance and membership. This makes the associational life of individualistic societies more fluid than traditional ones, and implies that organisations are constantly striving to create loyalty among their affiliates (Ahrne, 1990). Part of this process involves the attempt to create enduring symbols, which capture the experiences and emotions of collective participation, and bind people to the group.

In the recent literature of symbols, their central functions have tended to be defined in terms of links they historically provided to the spiritual, divine or transcendent. These were the types of symbols associated with the everyday life of hunter–gatherer societies, including sacred images, gestures or actions (such as dancing), usually derived from nature, linking members of a tribe to the spirits of their ancestors, to the forest and to each other. Mary Douglas (1970) argued that medieval Christianity, both Roman Catholic and Greek/Russian Orthodox, sustained some such aspects of the symbolic in their world views, and used images and objects (as in the relics of saints) as a means of communication with and about the divine. She even went so far as to side with what she called the 'bog Irish' in their respect for rituals like abstaining from meat on Fridays, against the liberalising and modernising reforms of the liturgy and practices urged by supposedly enlightened clergy under Pope John Paul I (Douglas, 1970, Chapters 1 and 2).

A similar view has been urged by the philosopher Roger Scruton (2009) in relation to classical and Renaissance painting and sculpture, in addition to medieval art and architecture. Beauty in the Platonic tradition, as well as the Christian one, was supposed to console us in our sorrows, as well as uplift and inspire us, and hence give us access to transcendent elements in experience. McGilchrist (2009) puts forward a similar point of view; both see the Reformation and the Enlightenment as having subverted or destroyed the power of symbols to transport people beyond the banal and material world of the everyday.

It is true that much in Protestantism was iconoclastic and condemnatory of all kinds of symbolism which represented itself as supplying direct links with the divine through ritual images and actions. But – despite its attempts to substitute a mainly verbal and conceptual expression of worship – it did create new symbols, such as plain architecture and costumes, which represented modesty and purity. Indeed, Protestant art and literature quickly developed images and allegories which symbolised virtues and vices, temptations and victories. The obvious example was John Bunyan's *Pilgrim's progress*, written during one of his 15 years of imprisonment, in which allegorical figures such as giants and dragons, representing pitfalls and evils, were overcome on the Christian's journey through life to the Heavenly City. In the late Enlightenment, natural symbols became significant, and Romanticism heightened awareness of the links between nature and spirituality, in science as well as in art and poetry (see pp 67-71).

In the modern period, political movements have been quick to adopt styles of art and architecture (as in fascism, Nazism and the Socialist Realism of the former USSR) which symbolised their ideologies, and banners which (in rallies and marches) were used to heighten emotion and enhance collective experiences. More modestly, the welfare state in the UK, which was claimed as a democratic revolution, was launched by William Beveridge (1942) as a campaign to slay the five giants of Ignorance, Want, Disease, Idleness and Squalor – a clear reference to Bunyan. Much early literature of the public social services referred to them as tearing down the walls of the workhouse, and releasing people from the Poor Laws (Curtis, 1946), also symbolically Bunyanesque. Indeed, the adoption of the term 'Commonwealth' to replace 'Empire' was explicitly Cromwellian in its Protestantism.

But the period during and after the Second World War was particularly fertile ground for symbols which united whole societies, partly because of the prolonged threat to civilian populations from bombing, and partly because the enemy (with its dreaded symbols) could so readily be portrayed in monstrous images. Even during the Cold War, it was easy to find symbols (bears, hammers and sickles, bombs) for the Soviet threat. With the transformations of 1989, it is harder to mobilise people for collective action on this scale, partly because no such gigantic threat exists. Even during the over-hyped Bush–Blair 'war on terror', only right-wing splinter groups used Muslim symbols to represent threats.

Individualism does not destroy the excitement of being part of a crowd, or a participant in a large collective event. Concerts and sports events are obvious examples, and these now command larger attendances than political rallies, other than specific protests (for example, over the Iraq war or the G20 meeting in London). Musical and sports events allow shared emotions and experiences, which focus on symbols – the performers, players or emblems of their identities and teams. These become 'sacred objects' in Durkheim's sense, and prolong the attachment to them between events and appearances (Collins, 2004, p 83). The Third Way in the UK has made rather feeble attempts to create a sense of 'Britishness' which might imitate these forms of solidarity, but has not been able to discover a compelling set of symbols (images or ideas) around which to mobilise it.

The atrocity of 9/11 in New York created symbols of heroism (the firefighters) and – retrospectively – of national identity. The site where the twin towers had stood became symbolic of remembrance of and solidarity with the victims. Ceremonies have widened the scope of this symbolism, as well as periodically renewing it (Collins, 2004, pp 92-5). Even though the firefighters were doing their job, and it was their training (rather than heroism) which led them into the stricken buildings rather than away from them, their subsequent efforts to find their dead comrades after the collapse of the towers also became symbolic of solidarity (Collins, 2004, pp 93-4).

More typical of the current emergence of symbols, however, has been the division of US society between the gun and anti-gun lobbies. Gun culture claims that its roots lie in the American War of Independence and the Constitution, but the symbols which sustain gun culture are created in the rituals of gun clubs and hunting groups, and revolve around maintaining and displaying guns as well as demonstrating skills in using them (Collins, 2004, pp 99-101). But – as the anti-gun lobby tries to show through its symbols, derived from massacres in schools and streets – these symbols can easily be adopted by deranged outsiders, with exaggerated grievances or ideas of their own destinies. They can also emerge as part of gang sub-cultures in deprived districts, where they become the symbols of criminal solidarities and the causes of hundreds of thousands of deaths.

Third Way symbols (such as the logos and mission statements adopted by the hundreds of quangos and trusts established under public sector modernisation) are not built through interactions of these kinds. They are unimaginative versions of brand images and advertising slogans – attempts to create identities which are distinctive, and which convey an idea of quality. Because they are never used by service users themselves in their everyday interactions (except perhaps satirically), they do not command loyalty or create solidarity.

Indeed, there is a contradiction at the heart of the attempt to create brands and product loyalties, or symbols of facilities such as schools and care companies, when the rationale which is supposed to be expressed by the choice of these products and amenities is individuality and distinctiveness. The branding and logos try to influence a mass target audience to adopt these as elements in an identity and lifestyle which are constantly evolving and transforming as individuals reinvent themselves (Elliott and Lemert, 2005). Indeed, the new culture of individualism demands that people perpetually remake themselves by adapting their appearance, possessions and affiliations, combining items available from mass markets and shared facilities in novel and original ways.

By putting the individual at the centre of the social order, this culture takes each person out of his or her context of relationships and habits, and substitutes processes of flexibility and plasticity, where makeovers of image and narrative, new 'passions' and projects, are parts of the search for self-improvement and self-transformation. Advertising and Third Way ideology have fed this attempt to define all experiences, both positive and negative, in personal terms, removing them from their interpersonal and communal connections. This privatisation of emotions and identities destabilises everyday life rhythms, making people subject to extremes of elation and disappointment, joy and anguish.

How can government influence moral regulation?

I have argued that moral regulation is built up from the smallest-scale and most everyday of encounters between individuals, but that it can transform the whole social order of society, especially when dramatic, large-scale collective experiences create symbols of solidarity, and point towards new kinds of collective action. The examples given so far of the latter phenomena – the events of 1789 in France and 1989 in Central and Eastern Europe, the Second World War and the attack on the twin towers on 11 September 2001 – all arose from major popular uprisings (which went beyond their original purposes), or from external threats. Can governments, through their policies and through collective mobilisations, change or strengthen moral regulation in specific directions, and hence influence the social order in intentional and predictable ways?

In its reliance on contractual regulation, the Third Way implicitly rejected this possibility. Its model of how political life might enter the social world was through the publicly asserted values of the government coming to be adopted by citizens (see Chapter Two, this book). Individuals who were reflexive and self-realising could choose to live according to the principles recommended by the various government agencies, but in practice, many of these concerned the strengthening of their 'independence' and 'self-responsibility' rather than any attempt to mobilise them collectively. Even the value of community-involved citizens being active in essentially socially conservative ways – things like Neighbourhood Watch or local charities (Driver and Martell, 1997) – was portrayed as strengthening the capacities of deprived districts to be more self-reliant.

At first sight, it might seem that the analysis presented so far would not encourage any optimism about the scope for large-scale moral regulation in complex, diverse modern societies. Durkheim's account of rituals and symbols has been characterised as 'functionalist'; it was primarily intended to show how the social order perpetuated itself in traditional societies, in which there was little change over centuries. Furthermore, writers who seek to revive the notion of transcendent symbols, such as Scruton and McGilchrist, appeal to a past European age in which moral regulation was exercised through religious ritual and belief. However inspirational this may have been, in terms of art and literature, it was also deeply intolerant of dissent and diversity among populations.

But as Mary Douglas (1983, 1987) pointed out, Durkheim's framework was intended to apply to the European societies of his time, as well as to those studied by anthropologists in Africa and the Pacific. His 'collective conscience' was embodied in the institutional structures and the popular cultures of industrialised countries; people unconsciously adopted the 'thought styles' characteristic of their social worlds. Although he did not complete his analysis of how this occurred, in economic life in particular, Durkheim was certainly aiming to explain the similarities between forms of solidarity and moral regulation in modern and traditional social relations, as well as the differences.

The manifestations of a 'collective conscience' in today's affluent societies are more likely to be found among football supporters or at rock concerts and festivals than in conventional political meetings. In the UK, 19th-century orators like Robert Hunt, John Bright and William Ewart Gladstone could move thousands to collective action through open-air rallies (and speaking without electrical amplification); and in the first half of the 20th century, George Lansbury and Sir Oswald Mosley achieved much the same. They were all in their different ways able to generate emotion and the sense of belonging to an organic unity of purpose, which nowadays is reserved for those witnessing the deeds of sports teams, or experiencing the excitement of music, in large crowds.

But – as Collins (2004) points out – the processes at work are much the same in both instances. In large assemblies it is not so much the images, words or sounds which evoke responses as the synchronous emotions and actions of the crowds themselves. Chanting and waving add to the ritual elements of the experience, and to the emotional effect of symbols such as banners, badges and slogans. These not only reinforce existing loyalties and solidarities, but also perpetuate the images which bind people to the cause, the club, the team or the group in future.

Sport and music seldom communicate a moral message in the conventional sense, but crowds and audiences have certainly been important in several of the cultural transformations of our times. Paul Robeson's outdoor concerts can be recognised as the progenitors of the Civil Rights Movement in the US; he represented black dignity, pride and the claim for recognition in the generation before Martin Luther King's great rallies. Protests against the Vietnam War in the late 1960s and early 1970s often centred on concerts and festivals. And in the UK, the 1980s saw a cultural transformation among football crowds in which racist chants and insults became unacceptable. Supporters themselves supplied the moral regulation which gave the same respect to black as white players. It is a mark of this that they are now open to the same range of insults from opposition supporters – for disloyalty to former clubs, or for other alleged individual characteristics – as their white team mates, but not to scorn or ridicule because of their skin colour.

Conversely, the ways in which religious worship and ceremony achieve moral regulation bear more similarities to sporting and musical assemblies than many sociologists allow. Here again, it was Protestantism which led the way, after the symbolism of medieval Catholicism went into decline. John Wesley and George Whitefield were the first to undertake open-air services (in working-class communities outside Bristol) in the early 19th century, and the Methodist movement took this practice to the US. After sweeping through New England in a series of revivalist waves, Methodism and Baptism were adopted by slaves in the Southern States to express their spiritual and political aspirations. The form taken by worship in these movements was far more expressive, in terms of singing and crying out, than in the more liturgical Catholic and Episcopalian traditions. The moral message of Christianity, both its requirements for the salvation of individuals and its vision of the good society, was expressed in emotional and physical ways, more like the behaviour of sports supporters and pop concert audiences than the ritual observations of the earlier church services (BBC 4 television, 'The history of Christianity', 6 December 2009).

The idea that religion should be a collective experience through song, dance and speaking in tongues is particularly characteristic of the Pentecostal tradition, the fastest-growing branch of Christianity in South America and Africa. In countries like Nigeria and Ghana, religious life is often expressed through gatherings to which congregations bring their sorrows, frustrations and disappointments, which are then shared in songs and cries, and finally danced on (BBC 4 television, 'The history of Christianity', 6 December 2009). A different variant of this tradition is found in the huge congregations of South Korea, where expressive ceremonial praise and thanksgiving is offered for the achievement of material prosperity (BBC 4 television, 'The history of Christianity', 6 December 2009).

However, the scandals in the Roman Catholic church, first in the US and Ireland and then in Europe, over the abuse of children by priests, and the cover-up of these offences by the church authorities, have reminded the whole world of the dangers of combining moral regulation with unaccountable power. Precisely because codes of behaviour and the value of those who are accepted as upholding them rely on mystique, on rituals and symbols, and on the special status of religious leaders, they can be exploited for purposes of oppression, domination and cruelty. The critique of unaccountable power developed during the Enlightenment was aimed at exposing these features of the authority claimed by monarchs and bishops – the divine right to abuse and torture and the sacred entitlement to rule through exclusion and secrecy. Where moral regulation is exercised by these means, it is indeed pernicious, and was a legitimate target for those philosophers who sought to substitute the milder bourgeois vices of acquisitiveness and vanity for the traditional lust for power and glory of the medieval church and state, and the bloodthirsty religiosity of the 16th and 17th-century civil wars in Europe (Hirschman, 1977).

The Third Way showed that the quest for economic efficiency and individual freedom was not immune from issues of this kind. Contractual regulation, when this was exercised through giant banks or invisible quangos, could be as arbitrary, unaccountable and exploitative as religious authority, if these organisations developed secretive cultures, allowing their leaders to justify gambling away others' money or neglecting vulnerable hospital patients. Moral regulation need not involve the substitution of a zealous set of guardians of orthodoxy for this corrupt rule. But it does require a culture which makes members responsible to each other for standards which are ultimately ethical in their origins.

Although the cultural foundations of his mobilisation of the US electorate were a long way from the political life of the UK, Barack Obama's explicit appeal to the moral and religious legacy of leaders like Martin Luther King in his presidential campaign were clearly of this nature. In the UK, the protests against the war in Iraq, and the climate change protests of the following years, have shown that political mobilisations around moral issues are still feasible.

But before any such attempt is made by politicians, it is necessary to abandon the Third Way understanding of moral regulation as coming about through abstract principles, adopted by self-responsible individuals. Once it is recognised that morality is created in interactions between people, and sustained by the use of cultural codes and repertoires, then its collective nature makes it more democratically susceptible to open and accountable influence from political leaders, and from public bodies of all kinds.

Conclusions

I have argued that moral regulation relies on interactions, which are unavoidably ritual and symbolic in their nature. Individuals claim value whenever they communicate – in gestures and expressions as much as words – with each other, and they produce social value through their communications. In presenting themselves, they attempt to perform a morally adequate version of what they consider their situation requires, and in this way they create a local moral order, which has to be repaired when someone acts inappropriately for that situation.

So even at this micro-level, the social value which is produced is collective in nature, and the moral force of the order created is collective. Cultures are made up of these elements, they are constantly being modified, but supply the collective resources by which we understand the social world and experience it as meaningful. In this sense, governments must always rely on the legacy of interactions in civil society for the words and images through which they seek to sustain order and mobilise populations. But they can also be active in the processes of moral regulation, not so much through homilies and policy statements as by giving opportunities for the experience of shared emotions and symbols which can guide collective life.

In this there are lessons to be learnt from music and sport. Even when these are primarily shaped by naked commercialism, they are capable of inspiring their participants in ethically relevant ways. Just as football in the UK was for most of its history tribal in a mono-ethnic way, but transformed its own cultures into one which now embraces cosmopolitan diversity, so music has come to be truly international, and to celebrate a huge range of talents and cultural traditions.

The Third Way inherited from neo-liberalism a deep distrust of social movements and political mobilisations generally. It sought to confine the labour movement to concerns about wages and conditions of workers, to limit local government to the pursuit of efficiency in achieving target outcomes, the professions to technical skills and competences, and the voluntary sector to the delivery of services under contract. In all these ways it impoverished the moral life of the societies it governed.

In the UK, this opened an opportunity at the centre of the political spectrum, seized by David Cameron. The charges that New Labour had weakened national and local cultures, damaged civil society, and subverted social bonds were central to the 'Big Society' thesis of Phillip Blond (2010, pp7-9). After the destruction of working-class culture in the Thatcher years, the Third Way had imposed a uniform system of state regulation and passive consumerism. Although the idea of active participation in local associations did not command immediate approval, the electorate seemed to endorse the critique of New Labour's record in the election of May, 2010.

Blond's account of how liberal individualism has degenerated into centralised authoritarianism echoes earlier analyses (Wolin, 1960, Spragens, 1981). He advocates the revival of a politics of virtue, the creation of 'moral markets', and the restoration of culture, ritual and tradition as the antidotes to the Third Way (Blond, 2010, pp131-2). Although it is easy to deride these aspects of his proposals as backward-looking, the central insight – that all sustainable forms of social order have to be rooted in cultures and practices, not abstract ethical principles – cannot be dismissed. The left needs to re-engage with its history and traditions to address this challenge.

Meanwhile, the failures of the Third Way, especially in the economic sphere, have already demanded a shift away from contractual and towards moral and social regulation. This was evident in 2008-09, when there was a stream of appeals from government in the UK and US for 'culture shifts' – among bankers, borrowers, civil servants and MPs, for example – towards more prudent, frugal, honest and open behaviour. As governments sought means to curb what Gordon Brown called 'the culture of excess' over the payment of bonuses by banks (BBC Radio 4, 'News', 7 December 2009), there was a tacit recognition that external regulation through rules and taxes could not alone bring about the changes necessary for the public good; bankers had to develop new habits and standards.

But there was already also some evidence that the change in the collective moods of US and UK societies was exerting an influence on the banks. A few days later, Goldman Sachs announced that it would be paying all its 2009 bonuses in shares, which could not be sold for five years. It also said that its shareholders could be expected to influence the decision about the overall size of these bonuses, relative to dividends and its capital ratio. In other words, it was accepting that society's expectations following the financial crash were of sobriety and modesty; the public and shareholders were able to exercise a moral influence on Goldman Sachs' behaviour. But Goldman Sachs did not escape retrospective retribution for its part in the crash, when in April 2010 it faced court action for fraud over betting against the packages of mortgage-backed securities it had been selling to clients.

The balance between external and internal regulation of the economy and society is an art rather than a science. Third Way economic theory (for example, Stiglitz, 2001, 2002) provided a model under which contracts, information and incentives were supposed to give stability with growth, but the crash has shattered this illusion. In the post-crash world, measures such as super-taxes on bonuses and Tobin taxes on transactions introduce a new approach to financial regulation; the IMF also weighed in with both a financial stability charge and a financial activity tax, the first to supply funds for future bail-outs, and the second to be levied on profits and pay (Treanor and Elliott, 2010). But this approach can really only be effective in blocking further high-risk gambles and asset bubbles if there is also a cultural change in that sector's self-regulation. The widely held view in 2009 that bankers still did not 'get it' referred to the evidence that they were impervious to public outrage about their responsibility for the crash, and about the speed with which they restored their expectation of high rewards.

In the UK, the voices of the head of the FSA, the governor of the Bank of England and the Minister for the City were raised against the easy assumption that the good times had returned. This indicated political and moral leadership reinforcing public opinion, in an effort to bring about a culture shift. Phrases like 'socially useless activities' and 'unfairness' (see pp 32–3) indicated a new moral climate among regulators, central bankers and the government in relation to the financial sector.

If politicians and high officials can give a lead in setting the moral tone of economy and society, conversely the scope for changing behaviour through laws and penalties alone is limited. Within a year of the use of hand-held mobile telephones by drivers being made illegal for the UK, their use – which at first fell by half – had risen to above its level before the ban (BBC Radio 4, 'News', 11 December 2009). Mobile phones had become a central part of interpersonal relationships, as had cars; the habit of talking while driving was established as one of the ways in which business was done, love affairs conducted and family ties maintained. In these circumstances, only a moral force (such as a collective movement) of equal strength to the force of habit could be expected to transform the culture of talking while driving, despite the accidents it causes.

Government is certainly not the only, or always the main, contributor towards the development of the 'collective conscience'. One of the failures of the Third Way was that its approach to morality largely denied the existence of such an entity. Being convinced that reflexive, self-responsible individuals were morally sovereign, and should aim to rise above tradition and custom, it failed to recognise that the collective life of the affluent Anglophone countries was becoming drained of moral leadership. Rejecting ritual as backward-looking, and seeing symbols in terms of branding and marketing, it feared collective action and the emotions it engendered.

There are reasons for worrying about the effects of waves of moral indignation or enthusiasm, but Third Way regimes were certainly not reliable bulwarks against such moral panics. Instead they were often compliant or opportunistic in the face of media-manipulated outbursts, for instance over asylum seekers in the UK. New Labour courted the popular press, and cultivated a tough image over crime, drugs and immigration, often at the expense of the kind of leadership and engagement which might have made a real difference in those communities where there were real problems and tensions.

Disillusion with politics in general, and the Third Way in particular, has arisen from revelations that practices which were accepted as routine – whether in Wall Street and the City of London, or in Washington and Westminster – reflected uncriticised assumptions about the entitlements of wealth and power, and a culture of arrogance and impunity. Moral and cultural regulation are not immune to such forms of corruption; the only effective antidote is openness to public scrutiny and the engagement of citizens in every sphere of social interaction. Contractual and moral regulation should be balanced by each other, and above all the exercise of authority should not be protected from citizen involvement and public debate.

In the next chapter I consider the question of how a society whose collective conscience is constructed in the ways discussed above might be judged to have right standards in its social relations, and how we might move from an individualistic and unequal set of relationships to one in which greater social justice is available to all.

In search of a moral compass

In the previous chapter I argued that the Third Way misunderstood the nature of moral regulation in social life, and underestimated its scope. But it could be countered that this was not so much a failure of the Third Way as a problem for all large, diverse, modern societies. After all, Third Way theorists and politicians emphasised the importance of 'community' and 'responsibility'; they also tried to find a basis for political life in human rights and moral values. It is in the link between the everyday world of social relationships, and the more abstract and institutional sphere of general principles, that the problem lies – and this is not only a difficulty for the Third Way.

The problem of this link can be recognised, whether starting with rules for an ideal set of arrangements for human societies or with the specifics of relations between interdependent members. In the former approach, as we have seen, moral regulation relies on an unrealistic version of individual choice by atomistic agents who lack a context for their decisions; in the latter, people share experiences, interpretations and beliefs, but there seems to be no way of judging whether their interactions give rise to right standards or a 'good society'.

At the time when the ideas which made up the Third Way were being developed (the early 1990s), these dilemmas were being disputed between followers of the liberal tradition of John Rawls (1971), along with the libertarian tradition of Robert Nozick (1974), and those who had challenged them in the name of 'communitarianism' (MacIntyre, 1981; Sandel, 1982; Walzer, 1983; Taylor, 1989). As well as trying to bridge the left and the right in politics, the Third Way was attempting to reconcile liberalism and communitarianism in moral and political thought.

While basing its approach on the moral sovereignty, autonomy and choice of individuals, the Third Way claimed to balance rights with responsibilities, and modernisation with concern about 'family life, crime and the decay of community' (Giddens, 2001, p 4). This acknowledged a debt to communitarian thinking, especially the socially conservative version of Etzioni (1994), blaming the narrow focus on market economics for social disintegration in the 1980s. But it relied on civil society and the strength of the voluntary sector as its foundations, rather than trusting to grass-roots forces which could become divisive or exclusive if communities were 'too strong' (Giddens, 2001, p 63). By the end of the 1990s, this combination was claimed to have been adopted, not only by the New Democrats in the US but also by the Social Democrats in Germany, Italy and the Netherlands (Giddens, 2001, pp 4–5). In social policy, scholarly analysis identified a 'liberal-communitarian' consensus in Europe, as well as the Anglophone countries (Seeleib-Kaiser et al, 2005).

There were, of course, several variations between the elements of this model (White, 1998). In the UK, New Labour tended to be more liberal in relation to the mainstream, but justified its stance on issues such as welfare-to-work enforcement by reference to responsibilities within a community. Policies for crime, truancy and the family, along with measures for social cohesion, were focused on deprived districts, in the name of traditional communal values (Driver and Martell, 2001).

In this chapter I argue that the Third Way confined its conception of moral regulation through community to this limited field – the attempt to restore order and cohesion in areas devastated by the market-friendly policies of the Reagan-Thatcher years. It failed to recognise that the individualistic basis of the mainstream social order concealed a wide range of injustices and exploitations which have become apparent in the economic crash. Once its economic model failed, the questions begged by its 'social contract' demanded to be answered.

How might these questions now best be addressed? During the period when economics was the dominant social science, theories of justice looked for principles justifying a structure of society which would give fair outcomes for all. The idea of a contract between the members of a society (which went back to Hobbes, Locke and Rousseau) was revived by Rawls (1971) in the form of an agreement between individuals who were supposed not to know what their endowments of talents and material wealth would turn out to be. This formed the basis of the approach to welfare economics adopted in the 1980s; equity as well as efficiency were best served when citizens could be assumed to have consented to a social contract, embodying equal liberty for all, equal distribution of opportunity, income, wealth and self-respect, unless an unequal distribution of any one of these was to everyone's advantage, including the worst off (Rawls's principles). This was then taken to correspond to the Pareto criterion, that any further redistribution could not make one person better off without making another worse off (Buchanan, 1967; Tullock, 1967; Mueller, 1979, Chapters 1 and 2).

The Third Way implicitly adopted this approach. Its emphasis on self-responsibility implied that individuals were supposed to make the best of the opportunities afforded by its (updated) version of their society's institutional arrangements. Collective action was encouraged mainly to secure the reintegration of deviant individuals into an orderly community, not to press for different arrangements or greater shares.

Both the philosophical approach to justice (discovering the principles which would provide fairness for all members of society) and the idea of a contract between individuals to agree on these principles, have now come under criticism. In his book *The idea of justice*, Amartya Sen (2009) argues for a return to a different philosophical tradition, that of the Marquis de Condorcet, Adam Smith, Karl Marx and John Stuart Mill among others, which looks for ways in which justice can be advanced and improved in a step-by-step process. Instead of trying to discover an ideal set of arrangements to which people might notionally subscribe, this approach focuses on ways in which people can realise their hopes for greater justice in the lives they actually lead (Sen, 2009, pp 9-10).

There are some echoes of this way of analysing and evaluating social relations in the work of Axel Honneth (1995a, 1995b). His central criticism of the 'process of institutionalized individualization' by which commercial and state organisations undermine collective consciousness of injustice (Honneth, 1995a, p 214) is that these processes obscure factors like class at the root of moral issues, and substitute a morality in which individual aspiration and achievement become the basis for moral self-evaluation. They reduce the possibility of people collectively experiencing and communicating the sense of injustice, and getting together to do something about it.

Where Honneth's analysis connects with the argument of the previous chapter is in his insistence that the social order is also a moral order of interdependent members giving each other mutual recognition (1995b). Rights are part of this order, but so are love and solidarity, through which we negotiate our intimate relationships of dependency, and respect each other's vulnerabilities and our responsibilities towards strangers. Rights, recognition and respect all involve *social value* (as argued in the previous chapter) which is generated within a community, with a cultural interpretation of personal self-realisation and the collective good (Honneth, 1995a, pp 227-8).

If this represents the basis of the moral order – an approach which Honneth links with those of Hegel and Marx – then this is to be found in ordinary people's sense of injustice and exploitation, and not in the attempts of the elite to legitimate current arrangements. Although individualisation and fragmentation have weakened any collective expression of this consciousness, it still exists. It was never a coherent, organised set of principles (as the ideology of rulers attempts to be), but it is a more reliable source for the moral intuitions on which advances in justice can be based (Honneth, 1995a, Chapters 12-14).

In this chapter I argue that the post-crash situation offers an opportunity to develop the programme for justice outlined by Sen and Honneth, because the legitimacy of the Third Way has collapsed. Instead of approaching these issues from the perspective of a systematic, abstract justification of the arrangements supposed to create conditions for justice, it builds on the sense of injustice among ordinary people for its moral intuitions.

Liberalism, community and the Third Way

In the liberal political and moral tradition, there has been a separation between the public sphere of political authority and economic organisation, and the private sphere's informal code. The latter was seen as exercised through love, loyalty and belief on the one hand, and hatred, exclusion and bigotry on the other – the 'blood-and-guts code' of sex, power and religious faith (Jordan with Jordan, 2000, pp 54-7). Although these spheres were linked by occupations such as teaching, psychiatry and social work, the liberal social order relied on their separation and these formal processes of bridging, rather than attempting to mix them together.

The importance of this separation was confirmed in the first half of the 20th century by the experiences of fascism and communism, both of which were repugnant to ethical liberals. In mobilising the demons of racism, patriotism and patriarchy, fascism released the violence, domination and war-lust which smashed the fragile structures of liberal democracy. In suppressing the sentiments attached to family and community, Soviet-style communism imposed a political and economic rationale on civil society, engineering the private and associational lives of citizens as well as their work and consumption. All this seemed to reinforce the need to protect the formal order of individual liberty, efficiency through markets and the neutrality of the law from the passions derived from 'race', blood and soil. In the UK daily reminders of these lessons came from Northern Ireland for 30 years, as the Troubles demonstrated the enduring force of tribal and religious hatreds.

So the Third Way was innovative in attempting to ride and steer some elements of the 'blood-and-guts code' in its policies on immigration, crime, disorder, drugs and truancy, as well as on the 'passive claimant culture' and benefits fraud. Although there had always been elements of this populism in the Democratic tradition in the US, especially in the South, for New Labour in the UK it was a new strategy, with considerable risks, to appeal directly to the electorate on these issues, over the heads of professionals like psychiatrists, psychologists, welfare rights and immigration lawyers, teachers and social workers.

In the UK, one part of this strategy attempted to involve the private sector in initiatives to regenerate deprived districts, and provide employment in areas where there were concentrations of benefits claimants of working age (Jordan with Jordan, 2000, pp 183-91). Other programmes, such as the New Deal for Communities, and the Social Exclusion Unit attempted to mobilise more stable and committed groups of residents, in partnership with firms and local governments, to take part in projects in relation to problems of homelessness, drug abuse, prostitution, begging and truancy (Jordan with Jordan, 2000, pp 110-15).

The other part of the strategy involved creating new agencies and forming new professional groupings to carry out the tasks associated with the improvement of the capacities of people in deprived districts, and the enforcement of new controls on those seen as failing to exercise their responsibilities, or as potentially subversive of community building. The Sure Start programme for pre-school children was the flagship of the former initiatives, and it recruited teachers, nursery nurses and social workers into a new service, focused on child development, in an attempt to offset the disadvantages associated with poverty, lone parenthood and social exclusion.

Personal advisers to claimants under the various New Deals – the civil service antecedents to Hayley Taylor of 'The benefits busters' (see pp 14-15) – and Home Office support workers under the schemes to disperse asylum seekers introduced in 1998 and 2002, were the main examples of the second kinds of new professional teams, essentially concerned with the enforcement of government policy goals (Jordan with Jordan, 2000, Chapters 1 and 2).

Seen from the post-crash perspective, the communitarian parts of the Third Way programme have had limited success. Not only has material inequality continued to increase in the UK, and social mobility to diminish when the recession caused unemployment to rise in 2008-09, its most concentrated increases were in exactly the same districts as they had been in the 1980s and early 1990s (Dorling, 2009). Community initiatives did not reduce the need for such heavy-end interventions in the lives of residents of deprived districts as the compulsory removal of children from parents (which rose dramatically after the Baby Peter case in Haringey), or the imprisonment of young people and adults (at record levels by 2009).

Perhaps even more disturbingly, disadvantaged communities in the UK became more polarised along racial and religious lines under New Labour, first with the riots in northern English towns in 2001, and subsequently with the rise (and some electoral success) of the British National Party (BNP) in the second half of the decade. All this was in spite of post-2001 attempts to combat such conflicts in the name of 'community cohesion' (Blunkett, 2003, 2004). Even if the BNP's success in North West England in gaining two seats in the European Parliament in the summer of 2009 was as much about revulsion against the MPs' expenses scandal as about their campaign, the mobilisation of white working-class grievances against Third Way politics showed how far short of its objectives New Labour's communitarianism had fallen.

Part of this failure was, as I have already indicated, that the elements of Third Way policy derived from the notion of community were focused on deprivation but did little to address the economic causes of disadvantage, poverty and exclusion. Initiatives intended to strengthen bonds between residents ('building social capital') were often divisive, because they were perceived as favouring one group over another. When 'community cohesion' aimed at making bridges across these divides, it did so against a background of resentment, fuelled by the fears about Islamic fundamentalism on the one hand, and suspicious over the infiltration of Muslim communities for the sake of security concerns on the other.

But the deeper moral failure of these initiatives lay in their incoherence in relation to wider issues in social relations. The strength of the local and everyday moral order is its sense of injustice over the particular and situational, and its ability to apply emotional, relational and group responses to such issues. But it seldom pretends or claims to construct a general, overall rationale for the social and political order; it relies on leadership from those with a wider vision of society, and the outside world to do this (Honneth, 1995a, p 210). Such a vision was missing from the Third Way's approach.

Instead, it attempted to borrow concepts from the codes of communities which were appropriate at the level of families, kinship networks, associations or districts, and apply them to complex issues like the conditions for benefits eligibility, the control of immigration and parental responsibilities. For instance, the notion of 'reciprocity' – something for something, the mutuality of obligations – is meaningful and valuable at the level where interpersonal cooperation can be constantly monitored, and any failure to fulfil one's obligations to others corrected with a humorous admonition or the raising of an eyebrow.

Indeed, this is exactly how the moral order is sustained at that level (Jordan with Jordan, 2000; Bowles and Gintis, 2002). But this cannot be literally translated into large-scale systems in which benefits claimants are required to fulfil conditions for receiving payments, because of the power exercised (whether by public 'personal advisers', or by commercial 'counsellors' like Hayley Taylor), and the stigma created through official systems of selective poverty relief (Jordan, 1998, Chapter 3).

Finally, Third Way attempts to use popular moral intuitions as guides to public policy misfired because government interpretations were often clumsy and crude. In the UK in the summer of 2009, the Home Office was forced into a humiliating climb-down over its attempts to restrict the immigration of Ghurkha ex-servicemen and their families. Here the application of rules limiting their numbers was made to look mean and unfair by a campaign led by the actress Joanna Lumley, whose father's life had been saved by a Ghurkha soldier when he was an army officer. Mistaking the mood of the country as generally against immigration from outside the EU during a period of recession, the government took no account of the public's ability to recognise a specific injustice against a group of people who had given exceptional service to the state.

Moral foundations

For all these reasons, the Third Way derived little moral energy or purchase from its version of communitarianism. Its dominant themes – individual moral sovereignty, choice and economic efficiency – had much more influence on its policy decisions; ideas about community responsibility and participation were presented in justification for parts of its programme which affected (and sought to control) those outside the mainstream. In this section I argue that this meant that the Third Way lacked a coherent moral basis for its approach to policy issues, other than the utilitarian principle of seeking to maximise the sum total of individual welfare, using cost-benefit analyses, but that such a basis could be available to its successors, despite the socially fragmentary tendencies in affluent societies.

The significance of the analysis of the interpersonal nature of the moral order outlined in the previous chapter is that it shows not only how people construct such an order whenever they communicate, but also that their lives together are a constant search for *recognition* through gaining love, respect, esteem and the sense of belonging (that is, forms of social value). In the process of seeking recognition in their interactions, they potentially provide an ethical basis for society, and hence for government policy. This is the approach to a moral theory of society and politics advocated by Axel Honneth (1995a, 1995b).

In the situation inherited by the Third Way in the 1990s, after a decade of neo-liberal regimes in the affluent Anglophone countries, many of the institutional bases for social recognition among the wider populations of these societies had been undermined. In so far as working-class people relied on social value from interactions in workplaces and neighbourhoods where respect for skill, endurance, strength (of physique and personality), humour in adversity, solidarity and mutual support were the dominant features of the cultures of employment and family life, these sources had been largely destroyed by industrial restructuring and redundancy, and then replaced by service occupations and lifestyles of private consumption (Honneth, 1995a, pp 227-9).

Given that people's need for social recognition was as great as before, they sought it in the forms of interaction prescribed by the commercial media – mass entertainment, shopping, the internet and so on – or in activities which expressed their resistance against their marginalisation and exclusion from the mainstream. This combination of responses was well captured in the genre of films and television dramas which emerged in the later 1980s and early 1990s, such as 'AufWiedersehen pet', 'The full monty', 'Brassed off', 'Common as muck', 'Billy Elliot' and 'The boys from the black stuff', in which redundant workers and their families tried to find new roles and new sources of social value in post-industrial landscapes.

As we have seen (p 109), these processes have been hailed by some Third Way theorists as liberating individuals from the prescriptive and stereotyping constraints of class and gender roles (Giddens, 1991, 1992; Beck and Beck-Gernsheim, 1995, 2002). Post-traditional 'individualisation' allowed greater scope for the achievement of autonomous self-development and a wider diversity of 'projects of self' (Rose, 1996). For the mainstream, therefore, the Third Way celebrated this release from the limitations of family and community life in earlier periods, even if it attempted to restore these traditional controls on the problematic behaviour of deviant individuals in deprived communities.

Because it focused on processes of self-construction through narratives of personal fulfilment (in many cases derived from psychotherapeutic literature), this approach devoted little attention to the significance of social recognition in theories like those of Axel Honneth, Ernst Bloch (1961) and Karl-Otto Apel (1980), derived from Marx and Hegel. Above all, it paid little attention to the ways in which the quest for recognition could produce social value for members of wider communities and societies, and create a moral order, or to how the absence of institutions allowing people to receive this broader social recognition and respect (as a source of identity and self-esteem) could give rise to a sense of disrespect, degradation or insult among large sections of a population (Honneth, 1995a, Chapter 15).

What it did instead was to give rise to a notion of 'pure relationships' (Giddens, 1992; Bauman, 2003), uncontaminated by traditional roles and norms, which allowed the negotiation of intimate partnerships of democratic equality, presumed to be the basic units of a new form of social order. This in turn led to the development of 'intimacy theory', the analysis of close relationships among partners, family members and friends within the more fluid and flexible set of economic and social arrangements which characterised post-industrial societies (Jamieson, 1998).

The important question here is whether increased individualisation can sustain a moral order of civility, respect and solidarity outside the confines of these forms of intimacy in small-scale, personal realisation. Santore (2008) has pointed out that there are similarities between the processes by which analyses of intimacy saw interpersonal bonds of sex and romance between partners creating a 'solidarity' between couples in which each partner achieved 'the development of their own sense of self and the expression of their feelings' (Cherlin, 2004, p 852), and Durkheim's account of how the individualism emerging in the professional classes at the end of the 19th century could give rise to a new kind of social solidarity and moral order. Durkheim postulated that, under this new division of labour, each person's identity as a self-realising individual relied on others' similar self-awareness and exercise of their responsibilities within an interdependent community, with a sophisticated set of specialised roles, involving mutual reliance (Durkheim, [1893] 1933, pp 122, 332).

However, Durkheim was here describing what he conceived as a new type of moral consciousness, sustained by a shared commitment to the cult of the individual, but achieved through the interdependence of such individuals within the division of labour. In this new form of collective cultural consciousness individualism promoted the sense of membership and of obligations towards others (Marske, 1987, p 11); moral consensus about the sanctity of the individual would allow fuller recognition of mutual interdependence and hence stronger social solidarity, in spite of greater diversity of roles and tasks – a recognition of the equal value of all members of society.

> In reality, the duties of the individual to himself are duties
> to society.... [T]oday there is in every healthy consciousness
> a very active feeling of respect for human dignity, to which
> we are obliged to make our behaviour conform both in our
> relationships with ourselves and in our relationships with
> others – this is indeed all that is essential in the kind of
> morality termed individual. (Durkheim, [1893] 1933, p 332)

It is not at all clear that the kind of intimacy analysed in the accounts
derived from Third Way theories of individualisation constructs this sort
of wider moral consciousness and solidarity. Indeed, Beck and Beck-
Gernsheim (1995, 2002, pp xxii-iii) acknowledged that close personal
relationships of this kind were to some extent retreats into negotiable
'ports in the storm' of an increasingly fragmented and insecure social
order, while Giddens (1992) recognised that 'pure relationships' were
themselves subject to massive stress by the demands of late modern
economic and social life, and hence suffered high rates of breakdown.
In other words, far from being the bases for a strengthened collective
conscience, as in Durkheim, recent forms of individualisation and
intimacy reflected the retreat of institutions for wider social recognition
and value, both in labour markets and in government agencies (such as
social insurance, social housing and the public infrastructure generally).

Furthermore, evidence of a deterioration in the public culture of
civility and consideration, of petty crime, squalor and disorder in
urban life (Bunting, 2008) and of the clustering of households into
residential districts with similar profiles in terms of age, income and
lifestyles (Dorling and Thomas, 2003), all indicate that such solidarity
as is associated with this form of individualism is not an adequate
basis for the moral order. The Third Way's policies towards mainstream
economic and social relations consolidated these trends, rather than
challenging them, by favouring choice and autonomy over collective
elements in public culture.

Finally, the Third Way colluded with the tendency of individualistic
commercial relations to obscure 'the hidden injuries of class' (Sennett
and Cobb, 1973), the exclusions of poverty and the degradations
of powerlessness (Honneth, 1995a, Chapter 15). A combination
of irregular, part-time and low-paid service work, under stressful
and exploitative conditions (Abrams, 2002; Ehrenreich, 2002), and
increasingly conditional, means-tested benefits which enforce such
work (Jordan, 1998), denied less skilled workers the conditions for
recognition as socially valuable citizens, and hence the basis for identity
and self-esteem as members of society (Honneth, 1995a, pp 251-6).

Yet the culture of individualism makes it difficult for such people to articulate a sense of collective wrong and harm, because of:

> ... a policy of individualisation the aim of which is to control the consciousness of social injustice. By individualising the experiences of social living, these politics make the communicative identification of social injustice difficult. (Honneth, 1995a, p 214)

This is borne out by comparisons between people born into Class V in the UK in 1946 and 1970. Surveyed aged 26, 58 per cent of men in this category in the former cohort belonged to organisations (mostly trade unions) and 37 per cent of women. Among the later cohort, surveyed aged 30, these figures had fallen to two per cent for men and six per cent for women (Bynner and Parsons, 2003, p 267, figure 10.19). In other words, they lacked any organisational support for the expression and communication of common grievances or purposes. Furthermore, among a cohort born in 1958, only 15 per cent of men with no educational qualifications had experienced being arrested by the time they were 30; among the comparable cohort born in 1970, and reaching young adulthood under New Labour, 46 per cent of those with no qualifications had been arrested by the time they were 30 (Bynner and Parsons, 2003, p 290, figure 10.9). They were expressing their sense of exclusion from the mainstream by individual or gang action against fellow citizens, rather than by collective economic or political organisation, or community activism.

Much the same patterns can be seen across other age groups in districts with concentrations of poverty. A research report commissioned by the Conservative Party in 2009 found that pupils from the poorest 10 per cent of homes were more than five times as likely to be persistent absentees from school as those from the best-off 10 per cent of families (Shepherd, 2009). This was despite the New Labour government's attempts to tackle truancy, by making parents liable to imprisonment if their children persistently missed school, and signing parental contracts to ensure school attendance. Unauthorised absence from school had increased by a third between 1997 and 2009.

In general terms, environments which do not allow participants to feel that they are valued are resisted and avoided, even when people are placed under a legal obligation to attend – as with schools for poor pupils in this example. Similarly, resistance (including violence) is provoked by experiences of humiliation and scorn, as seems to have been the case with the origins of Islamic fundamentalism and movements like Al Qa'ida, which specifically reject individualisation, self-development and consumerism.

Human rights and global moral development

The Third Way's leadership aimed to extend its values from the domestic to the international sphere, through ethical foreign policies and human rights as well as through support for the World Bank's attack on world poverty (World Bank, 2001) and its global economic development programme. In many ways, this was the most ambitious set of moral goals of its political philosophy; in unashamedly supporting the integration of the world economy, writers like Giddens (2000, Chapter 5) argued for strengthening global institutions for its governance, regulating corporate power, controlling conflicts, fostering transnational democracy and managing the global environment.

It is beyond the scope of this book to examine Third Way foreign policy. Many critics would see Tony Blair's involvement in the US-led invasion of Iraq as the greatest moral failure of his period in office; it certainly provoked the largest protest by those who considered that the coalition lacked the legal and ethical justifications for their actions. However, my purpose in this section is to consider the positive potential of the human rights rhetoric which was favoured by the Third Way, as the basis for a global moral order. Can human rights provide the evaluative criteria by which societies might be assessed – universal standards which cannot be generated by the specific interactions within communities which supply the everyday moral order of cultures?

In his analysis of justice as the pursuit of greater opportunities for the realisation of human capabilities through the correction of injustice, Amartya Sen (2009) argues that human rights represent aspirations for ethical improvements. This was certainly the case with the United Nations (UN) Universal Declaration of Human Rights in 1948, when the new international body gave expression to the hopes of the post-war period for democratic freedoms worldwide. Furthermore, under the influence of Eleanor Roosevelt (Glendon, 2001), the Declaration included economic and social rights, reminiscent of those enshrined in the New Deal and in welfare states, such as entitlements to work, education, protection against unemployment and poverty, the right to join trade unions and the right to fair pay. In the context of the 1940s, with most of the world economy still given over to peasant agriculture, and much of its territory still under colonial rule, this was a set of ambitions rather than a statement of immediate claims on behalf of every member of the human race.

Sen argues that those who dismiss these rights as lacking an institutional basis – such as O'Neill (1996) – or as lacking feasibility in poor countries – such as Cranston (1983) – miss the point that they provide a focus for political mobilisations and reforms, around the goal of their realisation (Sen, 2009, pp 382-3). In this sense, they supply the ethical basis for claims about institutional changes required by social justice.

> Just as utilitarians want to pursue maximisation of utilities and the viability of that approach is not compromised by the fact that there always remains scope for further improvements in utility achievements, human rights advocates want the *recognised* human rights to be maximally *realised*. The viability of this approach does not crumble merely because further social changes may be needed at any point of time to make more and more of these acknowledged rights fully realisable and actually realised. (Sen, 2009, p 384)

For these reasons, Sen argues that the literature on human rights should be read in much the same way as Paine's claims for the rights of man ([1791] 1906) and on the rights of woman by Wollstonecraft ([1796] 1995) – ethical analyses and political claims for rights and corresponding obligations, based on critiques of current institutional arrangements and social relationships. Moral and political progress has relied on such critiques of slavery, patriarchy, the rights of black people in the US, the situations of gay people, disabled people and so on. It is in this spirit, he argues, that we should also consider issues of global distributive justice, such as those of Pogge (2002) and Crocker (2008), for a single standard of adequacy of income and capabilities for agency to be applied to every person in the world.

This is a rather different approach to the ethical issues of the international context from the one taken by the leading theorists of the Third Way. Giddens argued that '[a]s a globalising political philosophy, Third Way politics should look to promote further global integration, in full cognizance of how difficult this may be...' (2001, p 122). He went on to base his proposals for institutional reforms and regulatory extensions on the economic changes which accompanied globalisation:

> We do not have an effective balance of the moment. The global economy, and the accompanying processes of technological changes, are swamping nascent forms of governance, which need to be much strengthened.... If we

> take globalisation seriously, as certainly we must, national
> policies have to become more thoroughly integrated with
> global perspectives. (Giddens, 2001, p 124)

In other words, his arguments were directed primarily at economic development and international security rather than universal human rights. In Sen's approach, the aim is to apply 'open impartiality' to ethical evaluations, in which a variety of moral arguments can be advanced in relation to issues, and to the ordering of priorities in the correction of injustices.

The problem, of course, is that there is no global forum in which such deliberations can take place. The literature on 'deliberative democracy', leading ultimately to a 'cosmopolitan constitution' and 'world citizenship', and founded on a 'cosmopolitan matrix of communication', owes much to the work of Habermas (1987, 1996, p 574). This postulates a 'global public sphere' (Bohman, 1996, p 191) for communicative deliberation between stakeholders, rather than instrumental negotiation between representatives of interest groups (Dryzek, 1990, 1999). Other theorists have explored how a cosmopolitan cultural community could give rise to a form of global, inclusive society and 'a pluralistic world of political communities', avoiding the pitfalls of both liberalism and communitarianism (Delanty, 2000, p145).

One way to consider the practical feasibility of these approaches is to try to evaluate the Copenhagen Climate Change Conference of December 2009. The attempt to reach legally binding targets for limiting carbon emissions and to set goals for future temperature rises was well beyond the delegates on this occasion; instead, an instrumental deal between the US, China, Brazil and South Africa allowed a non-binding deal to be agreed, to the disappointment of most other participants. The conference was chaotic because the largest emitter of carbon dioxide per head of population, the US, had stayed outside the UN's Kyoto agreement, and hence a twin-track process of negotiation of any new treaty was required. But it was also greatly complicated by the fact that those most at jeopardy from rising sea levels, Bangladesh and many small island states, were desperately weak politically, having no threat power. So their ethical arguments were pitted against the economic interests of larger and richer states, and they eventually were the losers.

This experience indicates how difficult it is to address global ethical issues in what is still a Hobbesian world of international relations – a context in which power and material advantage are still the most potent forces in determining outcomes. Perhaps the most encouraging aspect of the conference was the fact that this was obvious to all participants and observers. The ethical arguments of the smaller and weaker nations were not defeated, nor was the eventual deal justified in pseudo-moral mystifications. Instead, it was recognised as an inadequate, partial and even cynical compromise, at best a necessary first step in a process which needed to be progressed very urgently. So it was not that evaluation of the agreement was impossible, because of the complex rival moral arguments, but rather that the conflicts of material interests over future economic growth and environmental restraints could not be resolved.

Conclusions

The Third Way's approach to government was forged at a time when there was something of a stalemate between liberal and communitarian principles in political and moral philosophy. Liberalism had been justifiably criticised for its reliance on attempts to design institutions for perfect justice, based on contracts between individuals, abstracted from their social context. But when Rawls (1985) conceded that his conception of equal rights required some such contextualisation, communitarians had been unable to meet the counter challenge that they lacked general ethical criteria by which to evaluate any claims that particular communities achieved the characteristics of a 'good society' (Honneth, 1995a, Chapter 14).

The Third Way's attempt to combine liberal and communitarian elements in its approach to government was something of a fudge. As I have shown, its communitarian features were largely focused on the control of social deviance and disorder in deprived districts, and in justifying the use of conditionality and compulsion in relation to welfare-to-work measures. It did not develop a coherent account of how individual freedoms required the balance of obligations to wider society, or to disadvantaged groups, which applied to mainstream citizens, and its ideas on global responsibilities, although ambitious, were grounded in economic theories about globalisation rather than a convincing version of the duties owed by each to all other human beings.

Above all, the Third Way's central weakness was its lack of a persuasive moral intuition on which to base its programme. Despite its claims to modernise and update socialist values in the new global economic context, it really abandoned the main thrust of socialist principles, which had relied on the sense of injustice in capitalist relations. It turned its back on the moral intuition that the majority were somehow disadvantaged and exploited under capitalism, and endorsed an approach in which individuals were encouraged to feel responsible for their own destinies, including their labour market insecurity, their low wages and their social marginalisation. In this way, it accelerated processes in which many, if not most, were denied the social value which comes from the recognition of their abilities, contributions and characters.

This weakness was all the more obvious because the Third Way followed on from a momentous period in world history, when the state socialism of the Soviet model had been defeated by liberalism, democracy and markets. But this had in many respects been a moral victory, because politicians like Margaret Thatcher and Ronald Reagan had attacked what they saw as the central injustice of this form of socialism, that it denied its subjects individual freedom. By focusing on this feature of the over-controlled and over-administrated regimes of the Soviet Bloc they discredited these systems in the eyes of their citizens, and the people of Central and Eastern Europe eventually reclaimed these freedoms in 1989, as their economies and their governments weakened.

There were many ironies in this process. After all, Margaret Thatcher in many ways consolidated the power of the central state in the UK, and particularly the power of the police and the security forces, yet she was hailed as a liberator in East Germany and the Czech Republic. She smashed the British trade unions in the printers' and miners' disputes, yet she praised - and was praised by – the Polish union, Solidarnosc (Solidarity), for its leading role in opposing the rule of the Communist Party. And indeed there was something heroic about her championing of the liberty of individuals and free associations because it offered moral force to the collective movements which opposed these authoritarian and arbitrary administrations.

By contrast, both Bill Clinton and Tony Blair were – in their different ways – charismatic leaders, but they lacked a fundamental moral intuition and vision. And it was for this reason that the Third Way lost its momentum as a political creed in the US and Australia, and was found wanting by a series of crises in the UK. Indeed, the moral failures of the Third Way became clearest in the UK because New Labour remained in office from 1997. By 2009, the government had been forced to reverse many of its economic policies, and suspend its programme for reforming public services.

Above all, it had been required to tax, regulate and express moral disapproval of the financial sector's activities. All this was in marked contrast with the previous 10 years during which it had heaped peerages and knighthoods on leading bankers, praised their contribution to economic growth and boasted of the City of London's pre-eminence in world financial markets. The New Labour leadership finally had to recognise and respond to public outrage about the banks' part in the crash, and acknowledge that statements like Peter Mandelson's, that he was intensely relaxed about the fact that some people in Britain were filthy rich, had become unacceptable.

This was therefore a shift away from the Third Way's approach to the justification of its guiding philosophy, in which it announced the inevitability (and beneficial effects) of global economic integration through market forces, yet also proclaimed its commitment to the values of social justice, equality of opportunity and community. It marked the end of its capacity to obscure a whole range of moral and political issues about how wealth and income were shared, about how power was deployed, about work obligations and the state's enforcement of them and about the division of labour between paid and unpaid activities (see pp 15-16).

For example, did it really make sense for the UK economy to depend on attracting the most risky and speculative elements in investment banking, currency trading and hedge fund management to the City, and for the government to rely so heavily on them for its tax revenues? In the medium term, did it make sense for government revenues to depend to an even larger extent on taxes on the (depletable) oil and gas extraction industries (BBC Radio 4, 'Today', 31 December 2009)? What possible logic, in terms of efficiency and gains in economic value, justified the most exuberant and bombastic mergers and acquisitions of large corporations, such as the RBS's purchase of ABN Amro just before the crash? Were these not rather expressions of the inflated egos of chief executives? Why were more people employed in retailing in the UK than in manufacturing (BBC Radio 4, 'Today', 31 December 2009)? What sense did it make for the government to be enforcing such employment on less skilled citizens, when it largely involved the sales of Chinese-made goods that our economy had got into debt to import?

But it was not only government policy which had come to lack a moral compass. Under the terms of the ruling economic orthodoxy, every organisation was encouraged to seek the best financial returns on its assets, without regard to the sources of these gains. Within the collective landscape, there was no institutional counterweight to the banks, the insurance companies and the hedge funds, because every pension fund, educational endowment, charity and sovereign wealth fund had come to share in the hunt for quick gains. All these snapped up the mortgage-backed securities made available to them in the original asset bubble, and they are still investing in bonds and private equity now the property boom has ended.

> A recent report on hedge funds said they were on their way back to accumulating $2 trillion (£1.31 trillion) in investments by the end of the year and would soon regain the $2.7 trillion they amassed just before the crash. Private equity, which was equally badly hit by the flight of investors during the crash in 2008, is enjoying an influx of funds. Bond funds have also swelled, not as a safe haven, as in the past, but for many a route to riches. (Inman, 2010, p 30)

A future which is more secure and reliable, and which protects vulnerable individuals from sudden catastrophic loss, requires institutions like pension funds, sovereign wealth funds and insurance companies to follow principles which are different from those of financial intermediaries. They should be part of the process of pooling risks among citizens (that is, buying government debt) or sharing costs of future development, not creating asset bubbles.

As Sen points out in the final chapter of *The idea of justice* (2009), from the earliest political economists who adopted a mechanical or 'scientific' view of the operation of market forces, the inevitability of certain outcomes on human life has been asserted. In the drought-ridden summer of 1816, James Mill and David Ricardo discussed the unavoidable deaths of the poorest third of the country's population. Ricardo railed against the 'agitators' who had roused the people into demands that the government did something to mitigate the effects of impending starvation (Sen, 2009, pp 388-90). Claims about the iron laws of market economics have similarly been urged on governments in every subsequent age, and especially by the IMF on developing countries during the Washington Consensus of 1980-95. Similar claims are now being made about the need for public spending cuts in those countries with large ratios of government debt to national income.

The Third Way was far more optimistic about the beneficial effects of global market forces than Mill and Ricardo had been about sustainable population levels, or the IMF about the potential of developing economies. It put a positive spin on globalisation, and used this as a smokescreen for the underlying problems of social relations in the affluent Anglophone countries, which it had no desire to address. By the end of 2009, in the UK New Labour still had no agenda for issues of redistribution of wealth, income and power, or a rebalancing of economic activity.

This lack of a moral compass in the post-crash situation was symbolised in an advertisement, shown on television during the final weeks of 2009, for the NatWest Bank, part of the RBS, by then 80 per cent owned by the taxpayers. In this, without a trace of irony or shame, the staff of an organisation which had had to be bailed out to the tune of tens of billions of pounds, were seen in the classrooms of state schools, teaching children about how to manage their money. In much the same way, the New Labour government, driven into desperate measures of crisis damage limitation, entered an election year proclaiming that it offered the best prospects for an economic revival, but advancing no vision of a shift in direction or purpose.

This allowed the Conservatives to set the agenda with their Big Society plea for participation and civic virtue. Whatever the limitations of the analysis on which this was based, it is now theorists like Blond (2010) who are defining the terms of the political debate, and doing so in ways which challenge the left to discover a new moral vision. By locating Conservatism in a wide range of cultural traditions, including working-class associations and co-operatives, Blond and Cameron have constructed a narrative that captures the ground surrendered by the Third Way's individualism and authoritarianism.

In the final part of this book I consider some of the few new moral intuitions which address the issues concealed by the Third Way approach to public policy, and some practical proposals for how these might be implemented.

Part III
The policy response

Sharing wealth, income and work

If the Third Way's failure has ultimately been a moral one, and the evidence of this lies in its incoherence in the face of the global economic crash, what might be a morally persuasive policy response to this new situation? In the final part of this book I turn from analysing the shortcomings of the Third Way to proposing alternative approaches.

The ideas to be discussed in this and the next two chapters are a mixture of general principles which have been around for many years, and whose moment may finally have come in the present crisis, and specific proposals by politicians and think-tanks, which recommend immediate steps to address current issues. In this chapter I aim to show how a set of recommendations for reorientating the tax-benefit system, in order to correct specific failures and unintended consequences, might be a first step towards a long-term shift in the way public institutions shape the distribution of wealth, income and work, as well as deploy state power in relation to citizens.

Interviewed in the *New Statesman* magazine on 29 October 2009, the controversial and high-profile Slovenian philosopher Slavoj Žižek talked about the response to the crash as follows:

> The only serious, true serious, proposal that we know about is on the one hand this Krugman-Stiglitz leftist Keynesianism, and on the other this idea, popularised in Europe and Latin America, of basic income. I like it as an idea, but I think it's too much of an ideological utopia. For structural reasons, it can't work. It's the last desperate attempt to make capitalism work for socialist ends. The guy who developed it, Robert [he meant Philippe] Van Parijs, openly says that it is the only way to legitimise capitalism. Apart from these two, I don't see anything else. (Žižek, 2009a)

In the first two parts of this book I argued that the Keynesian response to the crisis has been a desperate attempt at damage limitation, by both neo-liberal governments (for example, George W. Bush's administration in the US) and Third Way and Christian Democratic ones in Europe and the other affluent countries. I therefore propose to focus on the second proposal, a basic (or citizen's) income – the idea that each individual person should be entitled to an unconditional income, without means test or work requirement.

I have been associated with this idea for almost 40 years (Jordan, 1973, 1985, 1987, 1998, 2006a, 2008). It has been advocated from a number of different political and moral perspectives (Fitzpatrick, 1999), and one of its attractions is that it seems capable of reconciling several different ethical objectives and implementing several improvements in equality and justice. But Žižek is right to claim that the best-known philosophical arguments for basic income have been advanced by Philippe Van Parijs (1992, 1995), and that his analysis takes the form of a search for abstract principles of justice, based on a contract between people with only very schematic abilities and characteristics, of the kind criticised by Sen (2009). Hence the most fully developed justifications for basic income as the fundamental institution for ethical relations between members of an ideal society do indeed take the form of a utopian blueprint in the Rawlsian tradition; and it is also true that Van Parijs's claims that such institutional arrangements would simultaneously justify capitalism.

Against this, I argue that there are steps towards the integration of tax-benefits systems which would increase social justice and address felt injustices, therefore allowing a policy shift in a direction which responds to a moral intuition about present inequities. The arguments for these steps are not necessarily utopian, individualistic or pro-capitalist; nor do they necessarily involve a counterfactual 'original position' and social contract. Indeed, the principle of a basic income is being tried out in pilot projects in societies as diverse as Brazil, Namibia, Mongolia and Alaska, and in very different institutional forms. And – although this is not acknowledged by the authors in their report – it is also a direction taken by the CSJ (2009), a think-tank linked with the UK Conservative Party, in their proposals for the reform of the tax-benefit system.

The central moral thrust of the basic income proposal is that every individual needs some kind of material security on which to build his or her realisation of capabilities, and to form relationships with others. It first occurred to those who argued for the rights of man and woman in the revolutionary context of the foundation of the US. Jefferson ([1784] 1903) and Paine ([1791] 1906) argued that shares of land could supply this basis for independence *and* membership of the new society of free and equal citizens. In the following century, others such as Fourier ([1836] 1967) argued for a share of income for each in the changing context of an industrialising economy. And in the 20th century, the Great Depression sparked a series of proposals for 'social credit' or a 'national dividend' (Douglas, [1930] 1951, 1934), including ones from leading economists of the day, such as G.D.H. Cole (1929, 1935) and James Meade (1938).

The re-emergence of the proposal towards the end of the century addressed the recognition that a new, more fragmented and dispersed form of capitalism, in which affluent economies relied mainly on service employment, much of which was low paid and insecure, had, if anything, enhanced the case for a regular and reliable source of income for all. Political philosophers (Barry, 1997; Wright, 2004), including feminists (Pateman, 2004), began to argue that a basic income could protect against exploitation and enable new forms of cooperation, as well as allowing women to negotiate for equality in the labour market and the domestic sphere. Finally, the crash of 2008-09 made a link between the case for a basic income and the supply of credit, which had been part of the debate in the 1920s and 1930s (Jordan, 2010).

The basic income proposal is sometimes distinguished from that of the social dividend or demogrant (Ackerman and Alstott, 1999; Nissan and Le Grand, 2000), in which citizens or residents are given a lump sum, either annually or at a certain age. But essentially they represent the same principle, of an equal, universal and unconditional redistribution, which can be used either as wealth or as income. Of the existing schemes in the world, Alaska pays an annual dividend of US$1,300 from its oil wealth to all its citizens, and a similar scheme is proposed for Mongolia. Brazil and Namibia have local versions paying weekly incomes. The UK's Child Trust Funds were small sums paid to all children at birth, to be saved or invested for use when they reach adulthood.

On the face of it, the basic income proposal is highly individualistic, and it seems to be aimed at giving each recipient autonomy. This has been part of the philosophical justification of the principle, and it has some intuitive appeal to libertarians and feminists on this basis. But others argue that it can equally well be seen as the basis for free cooperation between people who enjoy a fundamental equality through its provision, and an escape from exploitation by both the owners of productive resources and the agents of the state.

Furthermore, it can allow changes in government priorities and in lifestyles in line with the requirements of the environment. If people can choose to live modestly on their basic incomes, this can reduce emissions and the use of depletable resources.

In this chapter I focus on those arguments for a basic income which see it as a potential contribution to the rebalancing of economic activity between paid and unpaid work, and between production and conservation. Market economics has followed a logic of growth and the intensification of work effort; the Third Way approach to government has reinforced these tendencies, and made individuals responsible for their security and self-development in the economy. I argue that the basic income principle could allow people to make a more balanced choice of combinations of employment, self-employment and unpaid work, both individual and collective. It could also allow them to devote more time and energy to relationships with others, which would improve their well-being (Jordan, 2008).

But a basic income for all would also allow a higher priority for collective activities of many kinds, from environmental and recreational projects to cultural endeavours and democratic participation. It would take away the state's power to coerce citizens into meaningless and often counterproductive employment, and allow a more rational allocation of resources in the economy. Far from being utopian, as Žižek argues, I suggest that it is now a practical policy proposal, but that the first steps in this direction will look modest, and benefit only the poorest members of society.

Social credit and the crash

From a policy perspective, the first reason why the basic income proposal is not utopian is that it directly addresses many of the issues raised by the crash of 2008-09. Indeed, in October 2008, when bank credit dried up worldwide almost overnight following the collapse of Lehman Brothers in the US, both the Bush administration and the Australian government distributed fairly substantial unconditional sums to all their citizens, as part of their response to that crisis. The Japanese government followed suit some months later. And a series of commentators urged the UK government to do the same, rather than to bail out the banks in the hope that they would begin to lend to their customers (Jenkins, 2008; Monbiot, 2009).

These initiatives and urgings echoed proposals which commanded widespread support, and motivated an impressive political mobilisation, following the stock exchange crash of 1929. The leaders of this movement argued that the whole system of banking and credit should be replaced, in favour of a scheme for 'social credit', which would include a 'national dividend' for all citizens.

During the First World War, many had been struck by the fact that governments were able to spend huge sums on armaments and munitions, that new technology and productive capacity had enabled massive increases in output and that working-class living standards had shot up. The challenge of post-war reconstruction was to sustain productivity, incomes and social harmony, and in 1918 there were two schemes proposed for new forms of government credit to achieve these ends (van Trier, 1995).

The first of these was for a 'state bonus' for each citizen, financed by a universal 20 per cent tax on incomes of all kinds, by a Quaker, Dennis Milner (1919, 1920). The second was for an agency to supply credit for production and to increase consumer purchasing power by Major C.H. Douglas (1918, 1919, [1920] 1974). Douglas's proposals were taken up by the editor of the Guild Socialist *New Age*, A.R. Orage; they included an unconditional national dividend for each citizen, and were derived from a critical analysis of the roles of banks in the creation of credit and the power they wielded over the productive economy because they could create or refuse to create money.

Although the Douglas/*New Age* analysis was rejected by the Labour Party, it attracted a considerable following in Canada and New Zealand (where Social Credit Parties still exist), in Australia and Norway, as well as in the UK. These ideas and organisations were therefore ready to explain the 1929 crash, and bring forward alternative proposals for the recovery. Douglas pointed out that in the Wall Street bubble 'financial credit' had become disconnected from 'real credit' (the true value of the means of production, including human expertise); he also pointed out that the government's own borrowing, the national debt, allowed the banks to hold it to ransom. This, of course, is paralleled today; not only do some countries like China, Norway and some oil-rich Gulf states have sovereign wealth funds, but others, like Japan, are able to run a level of public borrowing almost twice as high as the UK's, because its national debt is owned by Japanese savers, mostly pensioners, not international banks. In other words, citizens provide a source for national *credit*.

Milner, Douglas and the others who first presented the case for universal, unconditional distributions of income made it clear that these were shares in the value of national physical and human resources – the wealth of the whole community. In the Douglas/*New Age* proposal, the rejection of finance capitalism and its replacement by social credit (with elements of guild socialism) represented a new direction in human development. The original version, written in the 1920s, was very critical of the 'superproduction' driven by bank credit and debt, and argued for a level of output geared to 'sufficiency' – a kind of anticipation of the notion of sustainability. Douglas specifically suggested that production should promote 'well-being', and thought that this could be achieved with less working time than was used in capitalist industry (Douglas, 1919, pp 79, 104–5). His proposed national dividends were meant to free people for more constructive activities, ending wage slavery, through a share in commonly owned assets.

So the moral impetus for this justification of the basic income principle was in the direction of a more communal society, in which credit based on collective resources would be used to improve quality of life, not economic growth. The critique of bank credit was that it tied both firms and workers into perpetually increasing output and productivity, in order to pay the interest on loans.

Of course, Douglas and Milner were writing long before the enormous expansion of private credit for mortgages and consumption (credit cards), and before the internationalisation of money markets, which allowed these to be financed out of borrowing from China, Japan and the Middle East at the start of this century. Since it was this form of credit, rather than excessive borrowing by manufacturers or stock market speculators, which caused the crash of 2008-09, the case for some new form of social credit, and against bank credit, is much stronger than it was in the 1920s. Indeed, it is also strengthened by the fact that the governments of the UK and US had made bank credit the centrepiece of its policies on citizens' self-reliance and self-realisation (see pp 109-10), and banks so fundamental to its model of economic stability and growth (see pp 30-1).

In fact, the crash did usher in a period in which new forms of social credit were improvised – firms lending money to their suppliers and customers, districts launching or expanding credit unions, local authorities lending money to entrepreneurs and established businesses, the post office expanding its banking operations and governments issuing bonds and making payments to citizens. All this was done in an ad hoc way, to deal with the immediate consequences of the withdrawal of bank credit, rather than as a concerted set of policies, based on a coherent theory. But – taken together with the revulsion against bankers' greed and recklessness – it represented something like a revival of the Douglas/*New Age* movement against the power and presumption of finance capitalism, driven by very similar moral intuition and indignation.

'Real freedom for all'

This justification for the basic income principle can be contrasted with the one provided by Philippe Van Parijs (1995), which is derived from a hypothetical contract between the individuals who make up an imaginary society, and is aimed at giving 'real freedom for all' – the opportunity for each to live as he or she might like to live (to do whatever he or she might want to do). Since these individuals are assumed to be diverse in their tastes and aptitudes, markets and flexible employment contracts generate the best outcomes towards that 'real libertarian' goal, and any 'particular substantive conception of a good life' (p 28) is rejected as 'perfectionist'.

This was an individualistic justification for the basic income principle, and Van Parijs adopted a methodologically individualist argument throughout the text, only as an afterthought conceding that the 'emotional basis' for redistributions among populations might have to be fostered by institutions (if necessary with compulsory powers) to achieve a 'sufficient level of social cohesion' (pp 230-2). In other words, the freedoms to choose the life of a beach bum or a manic entrepreneur were the primary considerations, and the underpinning solidarities to enable this were secondary.

Although this differed greatly from the New Labour government's *New ambitions for our country: A new contract for welfare* (DSS, 1998), rejecting the latter's conditionality and stigma attached to the benefits, it did share its individualistic and contractarian basis for social justice; both relied on a largely commercial logic for the activities within which individuals interact, and on contract as the defining relationships between them. Because markets create the fewest obligations, and allow the greatest scope for the pursuit of diverse projects for self-development, they were favoured by both models. One might even say that Van Parijs's and New Labour's were the libertarian and authoritarian variants of the model of a contract-based society.

The trouble is that the economic crash has (literally) discredited this sort of society. Van Parijs argued against the kinds of labour market regulation prevalent in the Scandinavian countries, and in favour of 'flexibility' (1995, pp 222-3). He favoured global economic integration over any traditional social groupings, such as kinship networks, crafts and communities, in the process of development, and applied the principles of individual sovereignty, of self-fulfilment through choice, of easy access to and exit from all collective units and free mobility of the factors of production to every society. In arguing that these principles – in line with the World Bank's model for global development – would enable the maximum sustainable basic income to be paid to populations in poor countries, he relied on processes of 'creative destruction' of those social units (based in emotion, faith and solidarity) which acted as barriers to the free play of market forces and the contractual relationships between utility-maximising individuals (pp 214-19).

However, Van Parijs concluded the book with suggestions for how an integrated world economy might avoid a 'race to the bottom' in which welfare states were dismantled and poverty relief made meaner and more conditional, under pressure of competition for capital and skilled labour between political communities. Here he departed from the methodological individualism and the libertarian principles of the previous analysis, arguing that the media and international NGOs should provide the resources for the 'emotional cohesion' required for new global redistributive systems (p 228). He hoped that 'solidaristic patriotism' in those countries with welfare state traditions would contribute to pride in collective projects guarding against levelling down through competitive pressures.

> One can hardly expect the required dispositions to flourish as a spontaneous expression of universal human nature.They will have to be nurtured, preserved, encouraged, engineered into existence by specific social conditions, specific ways of organising social life. (Van Parijs, 1995, p 231)

The trouble here is that the kind of contractual relationship between individuals advocated by Van Parijs (and both the Third Way and post-Washington Consensus) has shown itself to generate no such conditions or dispositions. Instead, it promotes ones of self-interest, social fragmentation into groups with similar incomes and lifestyles and the exclusion of poor and disadvantaged people from mainstream activities (Maurin, 2004; Seldon, 2009). So, when van Parijs attempted to ground his sense of solidarity and emotional cohesion in the fact that 'people of all social groups have no option but to grow up (if not at home) in the same crèches and the same schools or to be born and die (if not at home) in the same hospitals' (p 231), he was describing a situation which has long since ceased to exist in the affluent Anglophone countries, and whose demise has been accelerated by Third Way policies. As a slightly desperate afterthought, Van Parijs added, 'Perhaps one should even introduce compulsory public service whose explicit purpose may be, say, to look after the environment' (p 231).

My analysis in this book suggests that the moral requirements for solidarity and mutual support lie not in such special measures (which go against everything else in his approach), but in enabling everyday processes of communication between people with different ideas, abilities and commitments, which create mutual recognition, social value and a moral order.

In the next chapter I develop the policy implications of my analysis of the foundations of this moral order, with reference to the earlier account of the neurophysiological basis of emotional connectedness

(McGilchrist, 2009) and the contextual conditions for enabling the development of the 'social brain' (Grist, 2009b).

Van Parijs's argumentation was slightly similar to the Third Way in seeking to find some sort of communitarian basis as an afterthought to a market-orientated justification for his central policy proposal. This seems to me to be misguided, and to give ammunition to those who (like Žižek) are rightly suspicious of programmes for fundamental redistributions which are embedded in ethical legitimations of capitalist social relations. If a basic income really will share power, wealth and income more fairly, as well as end exploitation and give real freedom to all, then we would be more convinced by arguments which locate its justification in the everyday morality of love, respect and membership.

How could the basic income achieve its ethical goals?

In order to overcome Žižek's doubts, basic income advocates need to show that it could feasibly improve social and economic relations in respect of felt injustices and inequalities, and that we could move from where we are now towards such an arrangement in a politically feasible way. Many claims have been made about the changes in society which a basic income might enable; in this section I consider which of these are desirable and practicable.

In addition to the claims made for the proposal in relation to justice between citizens, some theorists have argued that it would allow changes analogous to those sought by socialists and feminists to come about. This amounts to a claim that the terms on which modern individuals were defined and government justified (for instance by John Locke ([1698] 1976) at the time of Britain's Glorious Revolution, or by Jefferson and his colleagues in the American Constitution, missed out one or more dimensions of the freedom people needed to realise their ends as social beings, and the security they required for uncoerced cooperation. Locke's justifications of property and the authority of governments, which in turn underpinned the institutions of the US, still allowed the exploitation of those who had to accept employment for their subsistence incomes, and the basic income would put this right. As Brian Barry put it:

> Provided that the basic income is genuinely adequate, we can say that nobody is exploited, however low the pay. For the job is freely chosen in preference to an acceptable alternative of not having a job. (Barry, 1997, p 167)

This in turn, he argued, would allow the reorganisation of socially desirable work, such as the maintenance of transport systems, health and social care tasks, urban environmental conservation, education and training. But it was still unclear from this how these kinds of employment, seen as onerous, unpleasant or demanding by the citizens of affluent countries, and often actually performed by immigrants from poor ones, could best be done, in ways which would enhance well-being through the production of social value and the recognition of fellow members as worthy of esteem and respect. Barry seemed to be hinting at expanded state agencies for those tasks, but why should this approach, discredited by state socialism, be more desirable just because people would not be driven by destitution to accept them? For instance, would the quality of care in hospitals and old people's homes be improved under such a regime?

Similar questions arise about the justifications of a basic income advanced by Erik Olin Wright, who considered that a basic income would alter the balance of power between the classes, reducing workers' dependence on capitalists and enabling more voluntary cooperation (Wright, 2004, p 79). Again, although some of the arts continue to attract willing participants, both paid and unpaid, the other 'socially productive' practices (such as caregiving and politics) listed by Wright do not motivate a majority of people to involvement on a collective basis. They are undertaken either within a set of family relationships (caregiving) or as aspects of a career or a group project for achieving power (politics). For a transformation that would induce mainstream citizens to undertake them voluntarily on a widespread basis, there would have to be a shift away from the pursuit of rational utility-maximisation under markets and contracts, towards one in which mutual recognition and negotiated common purposes were more overtly enabled. If not, why would a basic income not be seen simply as an individual right, enabling each self-developing person to fulfil his or her 'project of self' (Rose, 1996) more fully (and perhaps more selfishly)? Might it not merely consolidate choice and contract at the heart of social relations, rather than promote greater consciousness of social and political needs?

It is perhaps not surprising that these issues are more directly addressed by a feminist advocate of basic income, who has written extensively about the contractarian origins of Enlightenment modernity and the interpersonal power they enable. Carole Pateman (1988) had shown how women were subordinated under the 'fraternal' contract by which theorists like Locke ([1698] 1976) overthrew the paternal absolutism of divine right, and substituted the limited authority of government by the consent of men as property owners and heads of households. Her support for a basic income rests on it providing the missing element in the freedom conferred on such citizens by that version of justice because it allows democratic self-government by members who are truly autonomous. This should include, she argues, the workplace and the household (Pateman, 2004, pp 90-1).

Although she emphasises autonomy and self-government, this view is consistent with the account given of the moral order in Chapters Five and Six earlier in this book. Pateman emphasises that the transformation which could be brought about by a basic income requires people to *create* a new, democratic order in their everyday interactions. It will not stem from government initiatives for employment creation, or from commercial opportunities to pay low wages for demanding or dreary tasks. This implies that other structural reforms will be needed, but that these are likely to result in improvements in well-being only if they allow people to organise themselves in new ways. She writes of the need to have discussions in workplaces and households in which 'feminist arguments are taken seriously' (2004, p 97), and that the sphere of social reproduction should be one focus of reform, addressing 'social relations and institutions, rather than atomistic individuals' (p 101).

This implies a re-evaluation of all the tasks undertaken through formal and informal work, including those given little recognition or reward under present conditions. Through democratic negotiation and collective action, a higher value could be placed on things that women have done on an unpaid basis, and tasks of care and nurture could be given a higher priority in public policy and voluntary action.

In the post-crash economy, this makes good sense, because of the conflicting demands of mounting public debt on the one hand, and unemployment (or falling real wages) on the other. For example, in the US President Obama is under increasing pressure to focus on job creation, but government borrowing has expanded enormously in his first year in office. There were fewer people employed in the US private sector at the end of 2009 than at the beginning of 2000, and the unemployment rate stood at over 10 per cent (BBC Radio 4, 'Correspondents look ahead', 2 January 2010).

Part of the rationale for a basic income might be that it would allow tasks of healthcare and ecological conservation to be organised by communities themselves, and enable individuals to balance paid work with participation in such projects. This is discussed in the next chapter.

What would be the first step towards a basic income?

On the face of it, the Third Way has taken public policy in the affluent Anglophone countries in the opposite direction from a basic income, towards more conditional and restrictive benefits administration, and more intrusive intervention in the decision making of claimants over how to balance paid work with their family and social responsibilities, as in 'The benefits busters' programme (pp 14-15). Continental European countries have followed suit in implementing programmes of 'activation' (Cox, 1998), finally including Germany, the country where 'work sets you free' ('Arbeit macht frei') was recognised as being a slogan not of the Third Way, but of rather something else.

But in the US first, and then in the UK and – with variations – more widely, the attempt to ease the transition from claiming into employment which is usually low paid and insecure, and also often part time, has spawned schemes which attempt to give more incentives and reduce hardships. In the US and UK, tax credits have grown rapidly into a major feature of the system for sustaining the incomes of those in the lower-paid half of the labour market (Newman, 2002). As a result, the combination of welfare-to-work enforcement and tax credit subsidisation of low-paid and fragmented employment has come to be the standard model of liberal-communitarian social policy.

This model has obvious weaknesses in the post-crash situation, where young people, including graduates, are finding it very difficult to enter the labour market. For many years, critics in the UK have drawn attention to the gap to be straddled between the level of out-of-work benefits (themselves complex and means-tested, with a range of rates and entitlements) and the 16 hours a week of employment required to qualify for tax credits. This means that people who do less than 16 hours of work are not better-off because their pay is confiscated by the benefits authorities, and they risk losing their entitlement altogether (Jordan et al, 2000). It leads to a situation in which large numbers of claimants are doing expensive training courses or motivational programmes of dubious value and questionable ethical justification (as shown in 'The benefits busters'), because neither commercial firms nor voluntary bodies can offer them entry opportunities with fewer hours.

Even in 2000, in the early days of New Labour's welfare reforms, colleagues and I argued that the direction taken by the government's attempt to 'make work pay' was already leading towards the first step on the road to a basic income (Jordan et al, 2000) – a 'labour market participation income' (Atkinson, 1995). Research had shown that unemployed people and lone parents often used means-tested social assistance benefits as a kind of unofficial basic income, and did not declare occasional or modest regular earnings to the authorities (Evason and Woods, 1995; Rowlingson et al, 1997; Jordan et al, 1992).

What we then proposed was a scheme which regularised this practice, by introducing a far gentler taper on the withdrawal of benefits for earnings related to work up to 16 hours a week (Jordan et al, 2000, p 55). Taken together with a small increase in the allowance for tax-free earnings, this could have provided a tax-benefit system with simple and consistent incentives to work, and could lead to a further step-by-step integration of tax allowances, tax credits and benefits, to include similar entitlements for students, carers and volunteers, a 'social and economic participation income'.

As we were advocates of the basic income, we were open about the direction in which we thought these pragmatic steps should lead. But a remarkably similar set of proposals emerged in the UK from a very different source, The Centre for Social Justice, a think-tank founded by the former leader of the Conservative Party and (since the election of May 2010) now the UK Secretary of State for Work and Pensions, Iain Duncan Smith. Although its rationale on incentives was the same as ours, its advocacy of tax-benefit integration was for the sake of 'welfare that works', and did not claim basic income as an ultimate destination of reform.

The CSJ's report formed part of an attempt to shift Conservative Party policies in the direction of a programme to reduce poverty and social exclusion, championing the worst-off and criticising New Labour's failures to reduce deprivation and inequality. In an echo of the then government's own critique of its Conservative predecessors (DSS, 1998), it pointed out that one in seven working-age households still relied on benefits for more than half their incomes, including more than half of all lone parents.

Including those on disability benefits, there were 10.4 million non-working members of the population of working age outside the labour market, around 5.5 million of whom had been out of work for 10 years; 1.6 million children lived with a non-working lone parent. Despite £2 billion spent on the New Deal for Young People by New Labour, the proportion of such NEET (not in employment, education or training) citizens had grown from 18.8 per cent in 1997 to 18.9 per cent in 2006, and the number was increasing to a million by the end of 2009 (CSJ, 2009, pp 15-16).

The starting point of the CSJ report was that all the welfare reforms since Margaret Thatcher came to power had failed to stem the inexorable rise in the costs of benefits for claimants of working age and their children, standing at £74.4 billion in 2009. It concluded that the structure was at fault, because it penalised work and earnings, discouraged marriage and savings and was complex and costly to administer.

For the first time, a document from a centre associated with the Conservative Party recognised that the problem originated in the interaction between several means-tested benefit schemes and an income tax system impacting at a low level of earnings. The loss of all benefits relating to unemployment and lone parenthood on entry to work, and the withdrawal of benefits relating to the costs of rents and council taxes, and then of tax credits as earnings increased together with income taxation, led to two million claimants facing effective marginal tax rates of more than 60 per cent, and some of more than 90 per cent. Thus '[t]he security of keeping what a claimant already has often trumps the potential gain from work' (CSJ, 2009, p 18); only 25 per cent of claimants thought they would be better off working and 39 per cent thought they would be worse off (p 19).

The report compared these features unfavourably with the situation in other OECD (Organisation for Economic Co-operation and Development) countries. It found that 1.8 million low earners were worse off living together by an average of £1,000 a year than staying separate, and they also faced disincentives to home ownership and savings from the means-tested benefit schemes' eligibility criteria (CSJ, 2009, p 20). All this was before considering travel-to-work and childcare costs, while the complexity of a system with 51 different benefits meant that people were afraid to change their situation, and deterred by the separate forms, assessment processes and agencies required by changes in their work status.

What the report proposed was that employment incentives should be improved (to an extent that would make the reforms self-financing) through increasing the rewards for those taking a small number of hours of employment. This would be achieved by generous disregards of earnings – effectively claimants would keep their benefits for the first few hours of weekly work they undertook. The aim would be to achieve an even 55 per cent withdrawal rate (across the board, post-tax), and to reduce the penalties for couples, mortgage holders and low-income savers (CSJ, 2009, p 25).

The proposed tax-benefit integration would reduce the assessment process to two elements. Eligibility for 'universal work credits' (which would replace Jobseeker's Allowance, Income Support, Incapacity Benefit and Employment and Support Allowance), would thus roll up those elements related to being outside the labour market in the present benefits system. 'Universal life credits' would replace Housing Benefit, Council Tax Benefit, Disability Living Allowance, Working Tax Credit and Child Tax Benefit, thus combining all those elements relating to living costs in the present system. The effect would be to create one payment, acting as a combined benefit and tax credit, the first part of which would be withdrawn as people moved from low amounts of work to higher, and the second for those on slightly higher earnings, with the effect of the withdrawal being at the same rate right up the scale.

The authors of the report claimed that it would give five million households an extra £1,000 a year, and take 800,000 of them out of poverty. Employment would increase by 600,000 and gross national product (GNP) rise by £4.7 billion, they calculated. These gainers would justify the main aims of the whole process, since they would be both better off and included in employment, with incentives to form families, to buy houses and to save in the longer term.

Nothing in the report relates these changes to a basic income, yet it is quite similar to the scheme my colleagues and I suggested as a first step in this direction in 2000. In its 2010 election campaign, the Liberal Democrat Party proposed an increase in tax allowances, so that no one earning less than £10,000 a year would be liable. When the Conservative-Liberal Democrat coalition government was formed, this change was adopted as one of its policies. In combination, the two reform programmes would give rise to a roughly equivalent set of policy measures to the one we outlined then. (The Conservative Party's proposal of an additional tax allowance for married couples would not re-enforce this scheme in the same way.)

Up to the time of planning this book there had been few serious attempts to propose costed tax-benefit integration measures of this kind, either by politicians and policy analysts, or by economists and political theorists. For the former, it seemed a far too risky step to depart from the conditionality of benefits, and the apparatus of coercion and 'advice' used to implement this under welfare-to-work programmes. The CSJ says little about this aspect, but one striking feature of its proposals is the absence of all the paraphernalia of enforcement, first introduced by neo-liberal governments in the 1980s, and elaborated under Third Way regimes. It is ironic that right-wing Conservatives welcomed Mr Duncan Smith's appointment to responsibility for work and pensions because they anticipated that he would enforce benefit conditions fiercely. Indeed, his first speech as Secretary of State announced his intention to do so – but as part of a reform package in which he would attempt to implement the principles of the CSJ report.

From the point of view of the moral and political philosophers whose advocacy of a basic income was discussed earlier in this chapter, the reluctance to support such ambiguous measures stems from the fear that, unless the basic income was 'adequate for subsistence', it would not truly end exploitation. The CSJ proposal is more of a negative income tax than a basic income; it assesses households not individuals, and it does not encourage education, caring or voluntary work; for all these reasons, it is not 'pure', and would be seen as a half-measure. However, it is difficult to see how we could get from the present system to the one claimed to achieve social justice except by some such route.

Of course there is a real danger that any attempt to move in this direction which is combined with cuts in other benefits will discredit the whole approach. This would be very much a 'low road' to basic income, with none of the elegant simplicity of principle of the ideal model. But perhaps the most important points are that all benefits would be paid by a single agency, regardless of whether someone is in work or not, and withdrawn through the Pay-As-You-Earn income tax system; and that application for the award and income disregard would have nothing to do with how much someone earned (CSJ, 2009, p 27). This would break down the Third Way's rigid distinction between in-work credits (seen as mainstream entitlements), and benefits for those outside work (stigmatised and conditional).

What this report indicates is that Žižek's (2009a) scepticism about the feasibility of a basic income was misplaced. The failures of the Third Way approach to issues of work, taxation and benefits listed by the authors demand new policies, and the logic of the systems developed since the 1980s drives these towards tax-benefit integration. Once this is done, rather on the lines proposed, it would be quite a small step to extend it to a social participation income (where students, carers and volunteers qualify for allowances), which would also facilitate the goals of the Big Society programme for active participation in community affairs. From there, it might eventually be both logical and administratively cost saving to convert to a basic income scheme, including all citizens as individually entitled. In this way, opportunities for sharing wealth, income and work more fairly are gradually opened up.

Conclusions

In this chapter, the policy measure claimed by Žižek to be 'the only serious proposal' for an ethical improvement to social relations in the post-crash situation, and advocated as a new basis for social justice by several leading moral and political philosophers, has been shown to be potentially on the agenda of one affluent country, the UK, if only as a pragmatic response to policy failure.

However, there are other routes towards the same outcome, and other pilot projects in very different economies. For instance, in Namibia a coalition of NGOs has implemented a project in the Ot'ivero-Omitara district, where 1,000 residents aged under 60 were provided with a grant of N$100 per person per month for two years. In an economy with an unemployment rate of 36 per cent, and a population in which 44 per cent are under 16 years of age, living predominantly in rural areas like this one, with high inequality of income and wealth, this pilot produced very striking results. Poverty levels and child malnutrition declined dramatically, while school attendance and utilisation of the local clinic improved. Economic activity increased significantly, while crime levels dropped. The basic income allowed people to start small businesses, children to gain education and health to improve – all indications that it was effective in sharing resources and work more fairly, as well as the quality of life within a community to rise (Basic Income Earth Network newsflash, December 2009).

At the same time, the Mongolian government pledged to set up a 'sovereign wealth fund', using royalties from new gold and copper mines, which are expected to begin to generate large revenues within the next three to five years. The fund is planned to distribute part of its revenue as an annual income to every Mongolian. The finance minister commented in an interview that the project (the first national basic income scheme, if it is established) is based on the Alaskan Permanent Fund, which distributes an annual grant of US$1,300 to all residents of that state from its revenues from oil production ('Mongolia fund to manage $30 billion mining jackpot', *Bloomberg News*, 11 September 2009).

Because Mongolia is such a poor country, the annual demogrant is likely to have a far greater impact on the fortunes of its citizens than its Alaskan counterpart. Similar schemes have been proposed for regions of South American oil producing states, such as Bolivia, where President Evo Morales is seeking to give indigenous populations a share of this national wealth (BBC World Service, 'News', 26 January 2009).

There has also been great interest in this proposal in Brazil, where President Lula's government has tried to give income security to the whole population. In the state of São Paolo, a citizen's basic income which corresponds with the requirements of universality, unconditionality and individual entitlement, has been established for a population of over 7,000, in the municipality of Santo Antonio do Pinhal (Basic Income Earth Network newsflash, December 2009).

All this demonstrates that the basic income principle has (in a number of forms) been seen as an approach relevant for social justice in the sharing of wealth, income and power, in very different economic and social conditions, from the highly unequal societies of Namibia and Brazil to the poverty of Mongolia and the affluence of Alaska. It seems to fulfil a similar function to the land redistributions which launched rapid economic development in East and South-East Asia and some Indian states in the 1960s and 1970s (Sen, 1999, pp 41-7), allowing both the security for rural populations to improve their education and health, and the opportunity for younger people to move into cities, where export-orientated manufacturing was expanding – processes which help explain the advance of these economies in comparison with the stagnation of African countries, where no such land redistributions have taken place.

But in affluent societies, the basic income would fulfil a very different function. It would provide the basis for a redistribution of work between formal and informal, commercial and communal work. Here the requirements of social justice point to the inclusion of marginal groups in economic activity of all these kinds, within relations in which they can gain recognition and respect, as well as economic security and the opportunity to realise their potentials.

This would be a major shift away from the approach of the Third Way, which (in the name of a cod communitarianism that tried to mobilise 'partnerships' between commercial interests, local authorities and local residents), used state power to enforce benefit conditions and impose a top-down order. In the next chapter I consider how quite different approaches to the mobilisation of deprived communities under a basic income regime might be far more successful in including marginal individuals and districts in economy and society.

The examples from developing countries show that the basic income proposal does not rely entirely on the leadership of affluent states for the implementation of a global programme to give each citizen of the world this form of freedom and security. Although those poorer nations in which the policy is being pioneered are mainly ones with mineral wealth, the fact that their governments and international NGOs have been able to demonstrate the success of pilot projects is highly significant for the future politics of a basic income. It means that the proposal cannot be dismissed as 'utopian', or associated with a particular set of economic relations. It also means that its justification does not have to depend on the mixture of libertarian and (as an afterthought) communitarian principles found in the work of Van Parijs (1995). Instead, it can be advanced through the approach which addresses specific injustices, and shows how the basic income could significantly improve the quality of life and range of capabilities for populations in a great variety of societies, leading ultimately to a kind of new world moral order.

Sustaining quality of life

At the start of a new century, two issues have challenged public policy, and especially the economic model on which government had come to be based after the momentous geo-political events of 1989. The first was the failure of self-assessed well-being to rise in line with incomes per head in the affluent economies (Kahneman et al, 1999; Frey and Stutzer, 2002; Helliwell, 2003; van Praag and Ferrer-i-Carbonell, 2004; Layard, 2005; Jordan, 2008).

The second was the evidence of accelerated global warming, and the requirement for coordinated action to reduce carbon emissions. Neither of these newly recognised phenomena was susceptible to the policy approaches adopted by the Third Way. The economic crash of 2008-09 signalled the Third Way's failure, even on its own terms, but it also supplied an opportunity to reconsider policy responses to these other two challenges in the light of a new situation.

Ideally, what might emerge from the crash is a realignment of economic activity, in which the moral demands of an ecologically sustainable form of development are reconciled with a set of social relations more conducive for the well-being of populations. The former requirement involves changes in production and consumption, as well as in the use of resources such as fossil fuels; the latter demands that more attention is paid to the creation and exchange of social value in economic as well as recreational and cultural interactions (Jordan, 2008).

In this chapter I argue that these policy goals can be reconciled if a radical new approach is applied to the organisation of *services*, both commercial and public. Services now supply around 70 per cent of employment in advanced economies, and they comprise every aspect of economic activity, from the highly rewarded financial services to domestic and personal services such as hairdressing, social care and cleaning, which are among the lowest-paid occupations.

In principle, it would seem reasonable to suppose that this growth in services, and especially of work in education, healthcare, social and community work, should have contributed to the improvement in rates of self-assessed well-being in these societies. All of these occupational groups, and many others (such as hospitality, tourism, culture and recreation in the commercial sector) claim that their objective is to improve well-being, happiness and quality of life. In so far as they involve frequent interactions with service users and customers, they might also be expected to yield work satisfaction to the employees in these fields. And indeed these intuitions are borne out in the case of Scandinavian countries, where levels of subjective well-being (self-assessed overall happiness) and trust between citizens are among the highest in the world, and where services, especially public services for health, education and social welfare, form among the highest proportions of such employment among the affluent economies.

But elsewhere, and notably in the US and UK, high levels of service employment co-exist with relatively low levels of overall life satisfaction and trust between citizens, and well-being statistics have flat-lined during the long period in which service employment has grown as a proportion of the workforce. Although most of the literature has focused on the failure of subjective well-being to rise with income, its lack of correlation with increased service work and the increased availability of services for consumers' welfare needs is equally paradoxical and puzzling.

This is particularly disappointing for Third Way policies, since they have focused on improving outcomes in health, education and social care, and expanding service employment in sectors like retailing, hospitality and recreation. In this chapter I address the failure of Third Way programmes in these respects, and outline alternative approaches which might contribute more positively to well-being. These would aim to involve people in projects to improve their quality of life and that of their communities.

Part of the disappointment of the Third Way programme for public services has been that they have done so little to reduce inequalities, even in such factors as social mobility and health (Wilkinson and Pickett, 2009), in which the affluent Anglophone countries perform poorly in comparison with European ones, with Japan, and with some less developed countries. Another is that, as we have seen, the approach to service delivery in terms of choice, contract and efficiency, focused on instrumental and technical factors, both in how they were provided and how they were consumed, largely ignored the social value implications of these processes (Jordan, 2008, Chapter 9). But a final factor was that, in line with the analysis of the moral order in communications between members of communities, which enable quality of life to be constructed and interpreted according to cultural standards, services have not improved the culture of public life.

This implies that the way services were reformed and managed under Third Way regimes suffered from the shortcomings of its general approach to government, as outlined in Chapter Two – a concern for abstract, formal and generalised principles of legislation, guidance and regulation, and a lack of empathy, responsiveness and imagination in relation to human communications, the 'left side of the brain syndrome' (McGilchrist, 2009). This in turn meant that the structures and systems it created were unable to mobilise the capacities of employees and citizens to interact in ways which created social value and enhanced well-being.

This critique is now gathering force in the UK. Reporting on a project on how to develop social institutions which realise the potential of the 'social brain', Grist (2009a, 2009b) argues that its development requires arrangements enabling social interactions for sociality to be learned and sustained:

> As we understand more about the brain, we realise that it is designed to develop and function with the aid of culture (ie social practices that are passed on). So, for example, learning self-control seems to depend in large part on practising it in a supportive yet disciplining environment consisting of families, schools and the wider community. Take away or degrade that environment and it is really hard to learn the skill. So social institutions are simply the cultural means by which the norms and techniques are passed on that enable our learning of the skills we value. (Grist, 2009b, p 1)

His work, which echoes that of Offer (2006) on self-control, suggests that the neglect of social institutions and cultures during the past 40 or 50 years has allowed the context on which appreciation of the quality of life depended to be degraded. In many respects, the Third Way accelerated these processes, because it sacrificed the acquisition of communication and cooperation expertise and the sharing of meaningful common experience, for economic efficiency and quantifiable cost-effectiveness in the achievement of target outcomes. By 2010, one in six children were having difficulty learning to talk (excluding those with learning difficulties or autism spectrum conditions), a phenomenon which the YouGov researchers who made this finding attributed simply to the fact that their parents, giving priority to working, earning and spending, found little time to talk, read and recite with them (BBC Radio 4, 'Today', 4 January 2010).

In this chapter I examine policy proposals for strengthening families, neighbourhoods and communities, a notoriously difficult field for government intervention. Among the few original voices in the post-crash political environment has been Phillip Blond, the 'Red Tory' advocate of a radical redistribution of resources and power to local communities (Blond, 2009a, 2009b, 2009c, 2010). Unlike Third Way policies, which retained decision making and authority in central government hands, and devolved only a few initiatives concerned with social control to local communities, he argues that substantial assets, sequestered from the break-up of large banks and business corporations, should be devoted to a whole range of local organisations, to fund mutual societies, cooperatives, social enterprises and community groups. This would represent a very different approach to the issues of social policy, which, under the Third Way, were tackled in terms of services tightly managed under contract to the centre. It would also enable a far greater diversity of formal and informal organisations, and of the terms on which their members worked together in them.

The other big question for this chapter is whether this approach might also offer a better way to tackle issues about environmental conservation, especially in the face of climate change. The first response of governments to the dawning recognition of the threat to quality of life through global warming has been to try to find quasi-market solutions, such as carbon trading, and technical fixes, such as bio-fuels, wind and solar power. But there are equally large gains to be made by changing lifestyles and increasing awareness of waste and over-consumption, and by community projects for recycling, reclamation and regeneration.

A basic income would allow projects of the latter kind to be organised and staffed at the local level by a mixture of volunteers and people working a few paid hours a week. It would enable conservation and energy saving to become part of a local culture, and communities to make themselves responsible for achieving these goals at this level. Already many rural districts are seeing active commitment to small-scale projects for water-powered electricity generation using simple technologies such as Archimedes' screws, and for using food and farm waste for heating and power units (Jordan, 2010, Chapter 1).

The crucial question is whether moral regulation through cultures of social value, nurturing and shaping the 'social brains' of participants, can replace the discredited contractual regulation of Third Way policies on a range of issues in public health, community education and the physical environment. I argue that the crash has already provided evidence that – given a more favourable organisational context and some additional resources – it can.

Role of services in an affluent society

Theories of economic development, from Adam Smith and Karl Marx through to Arthur Lewis (1954) and Charles Kindleberger (1967), have paid relatively little attention to service employment. They have focused primarily on the dynamic interaction between a relatively backward sector (in terms of technology, productivity and wages), and a more advanced one, in which output and wages are constantly being raised through technological innovation.

In all these models, the former has been represented by agriculture, investment in which has allowed increases in production to occur at the same time as workers are leaving it to work in the latter sector, industry, where productivity and incomes as well as output are constantly expanding. In this way, employment is sustained as development occurs, a model still applied to the new industrialising countries of South-East Asia during their rapid emergence as manufacturing exporters in the 1960s and 1970s (Jordan, 1985; Sen, 1999), and now in China (Zhang, 2007).

Hence development economics has traditionally treated services as almost a residual sector. Adam Smith ([1776] 1976, pp 330-1) regarded service workers (including the monarch, judiciary, clergy and military) as 'unproductive labourers', because their outputs could not be stored, reused or traded on. In the 1970s, 'Britain's economic problem' was diagnosed in terms of there being 'too few producers', that is, too many services, and especially public service, workers (Bacon and Eltis, 1976). Yet by the 1990s, policy analysts such as Esping-Andersen (1990, 1996, 1999) and Iversen and Wren (1998) were arguing that the relative success of the Anglo-Saxon economies lay in their ability to create service employment in both their private and public sectors, through flexible employment terms and wage structures which allowed married women and young people to be drawn into the labour market. This was contrasted with the Continental European model, where high minimum wages, redundancy entitlement and social insurance contributions made it expensive to create employment in services, both commercial and public.

But in the post-crash situation, with a need to try to rebalance the economy in the wake of the collapse of the banking system, there are again calls for a relative expansion of manufacturing employment – made more feasible by the effective devaluation of the pound and the dollar – and the containment of public service expansion. In the UK, both major parties, faced with the need to cut the national debt, promised efficiency savings in these services, but a more radical re-evaluation of the nature and scope of future service employment seems now to be required.

It would also be enabled by the adoption of the basic income principle in income maintenance. Much of the rationale of the Third Way's welfare-to-work programme was that it allowed the growth of part-time, low-paid, short-term and irregular hours employment and self-employment, most of which was in the service sector, because tax credits topped this up to a subsistence level; but that benefits claimants needed to be pushed into accepting such jobs. Basic incomes would allow even greater flexibility in the way that hours of paid work were combined with other unpaid activity, but it would dispense with the state's power to enforce such work on benefits claimants. In other words, conditions under which people accepted low-paid employment, and the context in which they worked, would have to attract and motivate them, and sustain this over time.

This means that the role of moral regulation would have to be expanded, at the expense of contractual regulation. People would need to be drawn into employment for the recognition and respect they got from colleagues, consumers and service users, rather than because they were required to do it under a 'contract for welfare' (DSS, 1998), or an agreement with a 'personal adviser'. And they would also need to cultivate ways of working which were more intrinsically rewarding (in terms of social value), and which gave more accessible well-being to those using services.

Not all service work would be susceptible to this kind of transformation. But some of the more routine and laborious tasks, such as those connected with the cleaning up of the environment and the reduction of wasteful energy consumption, might be able to be done on a voluntary basis, if serious attempts were made to engage whole communities in taking a pride in local projects. The same might also be possible in some kinds of social care, which are notoriously labour-intensive, but where collective projects at a local level might greatly improve the quality of life both for those needing care and for family carers.

After all, the history of service employment in economic development has been a paradoxical one. As agricultural societies replaced hunter-gatherer ones, slaves and paid workers began to perform the tasks required by rulers and landlords (ceremonial duties, construction projects and personal services) previously performed communally or through kinship. By Adam Smith's time, it still made sense to see service workers as being either parts of authority systems, or parts of the retinues of lackeys and servants employed by the nobility and gentry.

By the end of the 19th century, with the growth of the industrial and professional middle classes, domestic servants were still the largest category of service workers, and were mainly drawn into cities from the rural regions.

The effect of post-war welfare states seemed to be to replace domestic services by commercial and collectivised ones. The expansion of state health and educational provision, social care and a range of local authority services, and the decently paid employment, often for women, which this created, as well as progressive taxation on higher incomes, meant that there was neither a supply of, nor a demand for, domestic workers; middle-class people got used to using new technology, such as vacuum cleaners, refrigerators and washing machines, for self-provisioning, a trend which continued into the 1980s (Gershuny, 1983).

Neo-liberal restraints on public service growth in that decade, and the decline in wages of unskilled workers, combined de-industrialisation in the affluent economies with globalisation, and led to greater polarisation of incomes in the Anglo-Saxon countries. As a result, there were more poor people willing to take work as cleaners, nannies and care assistants, while better-off households could afford to employ them, as better-educated women found work in high-paid professional and financial sector employment. Low-wage employment, subsidised first by income supplements and then by tax credits, allowed restaurants, pub and recreation facilities to expand, enabling eating out or takeaway food to replace cooking even in lower-income households (Offer, 2006, p 147). More women entered these kinds of work by necessity in unskilled households; more women entered high-skill employment by choice, increasing demand for all these services.

The final phase in this story has been the Third Way's attempt to create this kind of work for its own sake, as a way of sustaining economic growth. In the UK and US, this often meant attracting immigrant workers, most of whom took the new jobs created in service sectors, as a larger proportion of unskilled citizens occupied places on claimant rolls as chronic invalids, disabled or early retired. Indeed, by the time of the crash, policies in the UK over work obligations were full of contradictions, as the same roles and tasks came to be performed partly by immigrants (nominally restricted in access in the case of people from outside the EU), partly by citizens under compulsion, as a condition of benefit receipt when unemployed, and partly by offenders doing community service under court orders (Jordan, 2006a).

So the economic crash provides an overdue opportunity to reassess the role of services in economic development. In particular, it is a chance to analyse how service expansion has failed to raise levels of subjective well-being.

Contribution of services to quality of life

The growth of service employment in the affluent economies, and particularly in the Anglo-Saxon countries, has been part of higher overall rates of labour market participation, especially by women. Third Way policies encouraged this, insisting that employment was not only the most reliable route out of poverty, but also the best way for individuals to develop their potential and to realise their projects for self-fulfilment.

However, those economists who have taken seriously the phenomenon of stalled well-being in affluent states have seen rivalry and insecurity in 'flexible' labour markets as part of the explanation of why overall life satisfaction has flat-lined. For instance, Layard (2005, Chapters 10 and 11, 2006) has argued that inappropriate application of payment by results and performance targeting in public services has increased stress in these jobs, and that a tax on excess work effort is needed to eliminate the effects of competitive pressures to earn and consume under conditions of affluence. This echoes findings by Abrams (2002) and Ehrenreich (2002) that the intensification of work in services like cleaning, table waiting, packing and social care, in search of efficiency gains and through managerial surveillance, makes work in these low-paid services particularly stressful.

The question is whether a quite different rationale for service work (and particularly for the division of labour between paid employment and voluntary communal work or self-provisioning) could make a better contribution to quality of life. I have already argued that this rationale can be found in the attempt to increase social value through interactions between members, rather than to increase overall utility through expanding output and improving efficiency in resource use (Jordan, 2008). If the focus is shifted from the welfare available to individuals through their choice among service options to the intimacy, respect, recognition and sense of belonging they gain (and give) from their communications with service providers, this would justify changes both in practice and in organisational arrangements, as well as the policies regulating services.

Part of the problem of the Third Way approach to services is that it sees them as being 'consumed' by individuals. This is in line with micro-economic theory, but it misses the point that almost all services unavoidably involve interpersonal exchanges, often of emotion and recognition as well as politeness and respect. In economic (and hence Third Way) thinking, the active part of receiving a service lies in the choice among options, whereas in reality how services differ from goods is the fact that they can very seldom be received without engagement with those who give them, and this interaction (often extended communication) is part of the experience of getting a service – in many cases the part which gives most of the value associated with receiving it.

The other way in which my analysis is different from that of Layard (2005, 2006), with many of whose conclusions about how well-being might be improved I agree, concerns the value of therapy. Because Layard is a utilitarian, he sees the goal of reform to address the flat-lining of subjective well-being in conditions of growing affluence as increasing individual happiness, and reducing individual misery. As his own work shows, psychological distress, depression and anxiety have grown markedly in the US and UK among all age groups, especially among the young (Layard and Dunn, 2009). They appear to be related to inequality of incomes (Wilkinson and Pickett, 2009), and Layard recommends income redistribution as one of his policy proposals. But another is a large increase in individual psychotherapy, especially cognitive behavioural therapy, a recommendation he has been able to implement to some extent in his role as 'Happiness Czar' to the New Labour government.

But increases in these kinds of services do not seem to be justified by the evidence on subjective well-being. In both the US and the UK, since the 1980s, the growth of counselling and psychotherapy, mainly by private practitioners, has been spectacular; in the UK, therapists of several kinds were among the fastest-growing occupational groups in recent years. There seems to be no correlation between the availability of these forms of counselling and overall life satisfaction.

On the other hand, research on the factors contributing positively to well-being consistently finds that participation in the community (Argyle, 1999; Helliwell, 2003) and membership of associations (Helliwell and Putnam, 2005) are highly significant. In other words, it is not the passive receipt of services, even skilled and empathetic ones, which improves quality of life, but active involvement in collective affairs, from sport and culture to politics and religion. This would seem to suggest that the services which can contribute most to subjective well-being are those that involve people as activists in various kinds of groups and associations, or at least that engage them with others as participants in some kind of joint activity.

This is consistent with the account of moral regulation and the production of social value given in Chapters Two, Five and Six earlier in this book. People get the sense of intimacy, recognition, respect and belonging from their interpersonal relations with others, and especially from exchanges in which they are recognised as contributing to as well as gaining social value. Indeed, this form of value cannot be 'consumed', unless we count as gains the kinds of routine and impersonal communications contained in words such as 'have a nice day', or the messages in greetings cards.

This has important implications for social policy. In his pamphlet on the 'social brain', Grist (2009b) rehearses many of the findings in neuropsychology discussed in relation to Gladwell's (2006) work in Chapter Two. The brain works through strengthening and proliferating connections between neurons; it responds with largely automatic reactions to social situations, and follows social norms learned in past experiences; it makes decisions largely through these automatic processes; it forms habits, based on these intuitive responses, which are the main influences on behaviour; it is bad at long-term planning and taking account of future circumstances; it gains positive feedback from others' reactions, and from activities which are experienced as intrinsically valuable (pp 38-9). Cognitive and emotional brain processes do not develop properly without the right kind of nurturing and learning; those who do not receive these experiences may grow up to be fearful and aggressive, and to lack empathy with others.

The 'social brain' hypothesis comes from evolutionary anthropology, and claims that the main advantage of large brains in humans is the ability to think about and manage our relationships with others (Dunbar, 2008). As Adam Smith supposed, we are automatically primed to act with others' expectations in mind, and to respond to their actions with mimicry, a process leading to mutual sympathy and benevolence (Ashton-James et al, 2007). In this way, reciprocity becomes an automatic response. Social networks are powerful influences on behaviour, both healthy and benign, and unhealthy and hostile (Christakis and Fowler, 2009). Emotions dispose us to cooperate with others for our own security, and these can be trained and refined to increase our sociability (Damasio, 1995, 2009).

Perhaps the most important evidence of the pro-social tendencies of brain functioning comes from ultimatum games, pointing to an innate sense of fairness. One of two experimental subjects is given a sum of money and invited to make an offer of a share to the second player, who can either accept or reject it. A wholly self-interested outcome would consist in the first making the smallest possible offer, and the second accepting it (something being better than nothing). Yet the experiments show that it is common for offers of 30 per cent or more to be made, and for offers of less to be rejected (Fehr and Schmidt, 1999), subjects offered unfair shares reporting themselves as feeling disgusted at the unfairness. Other experiments have shown that subjects are willing to help each other make gains without expectation of reward (Sanfrey et al, 2003). The fact that primates exhibit similar behaviour patterns suggest that this is related to evolutionary biology, even though it is made habitual through culture in humans.

Other responses by experimental subjects point to brain programming which promotes reciprocity and cooperation, such as the willingness to forego gains in order to ensure that others contribute their share of effort or resources (Fehr and Gächter, 2000, 2002). As Grist (2009b, p 55) points out, the fact that volunteering to help others and participation in community projects leads to higher subjective well-being indicates an emotional benefit from such activities, but the fact that it also produces longer and healthier lives (Haidt, 2007, p 174) suggests an evolutionary benefit.

On the other hand, research suggests that people switch from altruistic and participative strategies to selfish ones if they believe others will not reciprocate, and are seeking to free ride on their efforts. Summed together, these shifts can destroy cooperation. Social networks that sustain norms of reciprocity and giving through culture are the best way of avoiding this outcome (Wilson et al, 2009). But self-control over long-term planning requires specific social institutions – what Offer (2006) calls 'commitment devices' – which enable individuals to overcome impatience and greed.

Grist (2009b) argues that the policy implications of these findings from neuropsychological research point towards supportive collective arrangements and active engagement as the basis for autonomy and responsible individuals. Interdependence requires social justice to sustain it, especially under the conditions of market affluence which undermine both regard for others and self-control (Offer, 2006). Grist quotes an initiative on establishing social support networks for children in deprived districts of New York as an example of the application of this insight (Dobbie and Fryer, 2009). Its results show far better educational outcomes for children than conventional policy responses, such as Early Years learning, smaller class sizes and improved teachers' pay, and this is attributed to involving whole communities in supporting children's learning and socialisation (*New York Times*, 5 August 2009).

So Grist concludes that the shift in policy required to take advantage of the 'social brain' findings, and to overcome the negative effects of market individualism, is to foster the engagement of communities in solving their own problems, to create situations where active trust can be built and to develop autonomy through interdependence. But this can only be achieved through a radical decentralisation of political power, to enable participation, collective responsibility and trust (Grist, 2009b, p 69). This is the subject of the next section.

Devolution to communities

The radical implication of the 'social brain' research is that the whole concept of 'services' is misleading, if policy wishes to address the failure of increased spending on healthcare, education, psychiatry, counselling and social care to improve subjective well-being, and the quality of life in disadvantaged communities. Since active participation on the scale of neighbourhoods, and direct engagement with local problems, seem to be the prerequisites for cultures of interdependence and cooperation, the goal should be to facilitate these forms of involvement. Indeed, the Third Way emphasis on choice, the consumption of services, efficiency in delivery and top-down management were all bound to be counterproductive in the absence of these conditions, according to that research evidence (Grist, 2009b).

Above all, the findings suggest that moral regulation would be a far better approach to the attempt to enable such engagement than contractual regulation. If people are not actively engaged in reciprocity, sharing and negotiation about the quality of their own lives, they will neither produce a culture which reflects their pro-social potentials, nor will they benefit from the social value which is generated by participation in a collective endeavour.

Grist (2009b) argues that these principles can be derived from a kind of collectivist application of Giddens' notion of reflexivity – that people can deliberate together about the shared issues facing them over ecology and social relations. He says that this could constitute a 'new' or 'real' Third Way in politics. But it is difficult to see echoes of this approach in the New Labour leadership's programme for the UK, which seems as rooted as ever in the idea of delivering services efficiently to produce target outcomes. Only Jon Cruddas on the left argues for a complete change of direction, including a basic income and devolution of power to communities (Cruddas and Rutherford, 2009).

So once again it is from the right that the radical new thinking is emerging. The self-proclaimed 'Red Tory', Phillip Blond, was installed in London by David Cameron to address these issues, and has been fearless in attributing the moral failures of the past three decades as much to Margaret Thatcher's neo-liberalism as to New Labour's managerialism. In the name of the one nation conservatism of Edmund

Burke, Thomas Carlyle and Benjamin Disraeli, and of the religiously informed liberalism of Hilaire Belloc and G.K. Chesterton, he criticises both markets and states for enabling power to be concentrated in large, monopoly organisations, at the expense of individuals and communities.

Blond's central thesis is that the civic associations and 'little platoons' of mutuality and cooperation which thrived in 19th-century Britain and the US (de Tocqueville, [1836] 1968) have been subverted, first by bureaucratic state agencies in the post-war settlement, and then by monopoly finance and big business in the 1980s and 1990s. Thatcherism was an attack on monopoly state authority, but it succeeded only in giving similar power to global banks and businesses. Blond sees modernity as atomised individuals, stripped of all control over their fates, and confronted by the overwhelming power of both states and corporations. Worse still, he claims, secular liberalism has destroyed morality in the name of permissiveness, commodified sex and the body, disconnected individuals from the common good and substituted universal self-interest for mutual assistance (Blond, 2009c, 2010).

He compares the UK's welfare state arrangements unfavourably with those of European countries. After the Second World War the requirements of reconstruction in Europe meant that capital and organised labour had to pool their interests with those of the state to rebuild their economies and societies. But in the UK the unions retained their rights to free collective bargaining, and the state regulated industry, so the country remained 'frozen in a state of unresolved class conflict', with low rates of investment and no sense of the shared national interest.

So the Thatcher revolution was essentially a war on the trade unions and the state bureaucracy, waged in favour of the entrepreneur, but ultimately giving gains only to the rich, with the middle class sinking into debt, and the poor further impoverished and marginalised. In short, Britain remains stuck within a contested, class-based capitalism that has done great damage to British life (Blond, 2009c, p 3). Monopoly power has extended, culminating in the crash, brought about by a 'modal monopoly – a way of doing business which constituted a cartel' – among the firms in the financial sector, creating asset bubbles and trying to exit before they burst.

> For example, the great housing crash is primarily the result of the absorption of all local, regional and national systems of credit into one form of global credit.... This strategy of market manipulation deployed enormous amounts of capital

> in speculative arbitrage (just five US banks had control over
> $4 trillion of assets in 2007). (Blond, 2009c, p 3)

It is certainly striking and refreshing to read a Conservative commentator who asserts that markets have been as socially damaging as statism. But Blond's policy recommendation is not another attempt to rebalance these two forces, but a new localism which re-empowers communities, including a transfer of wealth from global and national concentrations in business and banking centres to the economic periphery. At the heart of his proposed programme is the notion of relocalising the banking system and developing local capital, giving people new assets through breaking up big business monopolies.

Blond recommends a whole series of innovations for a 'parallel banking system' in the wake of the credit crisis. These include a strengthened post office bank, quantitative easing to underwrite both business and mortgage credit and a local investment bank. He also proposes the establishment of local investment trusts as centres for local finance, with local authorities compelled to deposit funds in them (rather than Icelandic banks). These should fund new cooperatives and guilds, giving rise to a 'conservative cooperative movement'. Local government procurement should be devolved to local bodies, Blond quoting a finding by the New Economic Foundation in 2005 that every pound spent with a local supplier generated £1.76 in the local economy, whereas every pound spent outside it generated only 36p; a 10 per cent increase in local spending would generate £5.6 billion nationally. Local bonds should also be issued by these investment trusts.

Finally, Blond advocates a reversal of the politics of class through the sharing of capital with workers. The proportion of wealth (excluding housing) held by the bottom 50 per cent of owners fell from 12 per cent in 1976 to one per cent in 2007. Blond recommends an end of a meritocracy which, under New Labour, has given security of living standards to only 10 to 15 per cent of the population, in favour of new social relations in which all citizens are given value, merit, security and a share of wealth.

Aiming to reclaim the radicalism of William Cobbett, John Ruskin and R.H. Tawney as well as the one nation Tories of the 19th century and new Liberals of the early 20th, Blond reels off a set of new institutions and policies to enable this transformation (Blond, 2010, Chapter 9). There should be employee share ownership in firms, workers' buy-outs, equity and guilds and asset cooperatives. Conservatism should break with big business and cartels, championing the many, and making markets work for them, not the plutocratic few – a capitalism that benefits the poor. It should use the opportunity of the selling off of the nationalised banks – which should realise £50 billion – to lower the tax burden on the lowest paid, and exempt savings from taxation (Blond, 2009a). But it should also distribute investment vouchers, which could only be activated in conjunction with others, thus creating an associative investment pool among the poorest citizens, to be invested in social enterprises, local shops and other business ventures.

This last proposal illustrates the central weakness of Blond's recommendations. The idea that poor people can be turned into 'dragons' – in Blond's (2009a) own term – invites scepticism. Even under his associative proposal, there would be a high risk that many of these assets would either be lost in failed business projects or end up in the hands of wealthy opportunists, as in the case of 'voucher capitalism' in the Czech Republic after the break-up of state enterprises in the early 1990s. Blond is also less than specific about how his many new mutual and cooperative organisations and investment funds would be accountable to their communities and stakeholders. There is a danger that they would fall under the control of incompetents or the local mafia, unless a great deal of attention was paid to this aspect.

The important point, however, is that Blond's ideas could supply principles of redistribution of wealth to local communities, both as a counterpart to the basic income proposal in respect of individuals, and as a way of funding the institutions corresponding to the 'social brain' hypothesis. If Blond's attempt to remoralise politics and society is anchored in 19th-century romanticism and theology rather than evolutionary biology, Grist's account of the associative and cooperative potential of the human brain lacks any convincing material basis. An open attack on the monopolistic origins of corporate wealth provides the missing link in the case for devolution of resources to communities, without which the proposals are idealistic. It is ironic that this is supplied by a Conservative thinker, and not someone from the Third Way, old or new.

Interest in Blond's ideas has intensified because of David Cameron's acknowledged debt to them for his 'Big Society' theme in the UK General Election of May 2010. Insisting that the Conservatives were now the radical force in British politics, Cameron urged people to take collective action to run their communities and services:

> So if parents want new schools in areas where their children
> are being failed, we will empower them. If social workers or
> job centre staff want to join together in co-operatives to run
> their services, we will encourage them. The same principles

> extend to welfare, to prisons, to drug rehabilitation, to early
> years support. We will tear up the tangle of public sector
> targets that trap public sector workers. (Cameron, 2010,
> p 34)

But equally significantly, Cameron said nothing to endorse Blond's ideas about the massive redistribution of resources from the commercial sector needed to fund such radical ideas. Nor has he endorsed the principle of income security embodied in the tax-benefits integration scheme recommended in the CSJ report of 2009 (or better still a basic income) that would allow the flexibility of labour markets to support the amount of part-time community work and volunteering needed to sustain such projects.

When questioned about precedents for the 'Big Society' approach during the election campaign, Michael Gove was one of the few Conservative spokesmen to try to give concrete examples. The one he quoted was the Charter Schools movement in the US, under which parents and teachers have taken over the running of educational establishments from school boards. In New Orleans after the devastation of Hurricane Katrina, these cooperatives rebuilt the whole system, achieving spectacular improvements in educational outcomes in pupils from notoriously deprived and underachieving districts.

Sceptics argue that these successes have relied on levels of enthusiasm and dedication among teachers and parents that are not sustainable over the long haul. The stress generated by the hours worked by all participants would lead to rapid burnout, and the lack of a structure to reproduce these early triumphs might result in equally spectacular failures over time. Although all this may be true, it would be important to try to find out whether these success stories could be replicated, and if a compromise between cooperative enthusiasm and structured organisation might emerge from some of these experiments.

Conclusions

In a typically provocative lecture to the RSA, Slavoj Žižek (2009b) argued that the post-crash economic landscape of affluent societies has revealed several paradoxical features. In this phase of capitalism, Žižek argues, large proportions of the population are dispensable for production, which now relies on the expertise and creativity of a very few talented and immensely wealthy people. Conversely, social democracy has become an inseparable part of this form of capitalism, but its institutions and the politics that informs them do not correspond to the economic realities of the new order. Žižek maintains that this explains the parallel emergence of the basic income proposal (granting the right *not* to make an economic contribution to the redundant workforce) and the idea of a new philanthropy, through which the super-wealthy donate part of their asset holdings to the disadvantaged, and receive special honour for doing so (Sloterdijk, 2009).

In this chapter I have argued that there are grounds for thinking that this situation can be remedied, if the basic income principle is combined with a radical devolution of the tasks performed by service workers (both public and commercial) to local communities and associations. Active participation and engagement in collective projects to improve the quality of life in such communities is not only feasible (because people are capable of cooperating for the common good by virtue of their endowments through evolutionary biology) but also desirable (because such involvement contributes far more to well-being than passive consumption of services). Proposals for redistributing wealth from mega-banks and business corporations to such local bodies might jeopardise the rate of economic growth (as might a basic income), but it could restore the index of well-being to an upward trajectory. It could also enable important aspects of the threat from climate change and resource depletion to be tackled in effective ways, through moral regulation and culture rather than solely by means of technical fixes.

All this has very important implications for the majority of the population who now work in services. It implies that neither employment in low-paid domestic, recreational, hospitality and tourism services in the private sector, nor in health, education and social care, should be seen as providing the basis for future policies for the labour market or for social provision. Instead, the principle determining patterns of work and organisation of these activities should be the self-organisation of citizens in communities and associations, with paid employees accountable to such bodies, and to local democratic authorities, and not simply to market forces on the one hand, or government targets and management systems on the other.

This obviously requires a long-term readjustment in the mindsets of both the public and those who work in services; but the economic crash, and the need to pay down the national debt in the UK and US, will demand a radical shift in this mindset in any case. Even before the crash there was a growing body of evidence for disillusion with the results of Third Way reforms of public services in the UK. A series of scandals concerning patient safety and well-being in NHS hospitals – often the ones most highly rated by official inspectors – had revealed that the priorities pursued by managers in search of the resources which flow from such ratings had led to neglect of basic care. In the case of Mid-Staffordshire NHS Hospital Trust, public concern and a high volume of complaints were simply overlooked (Healthcare Commission, 2009). Similarly, the scandal over the death of Baby Peter in Haringey showed that social workers and their supervisors were tied up in electronic systems for assessment and recording at the expense of direct contact with children at risk, and that complex arrangements for interagency collaboration could fail – yet none of this was picked up by inspectors at the time. The scandal triggered a crisis in the whole child protection system (Jordan, 2010, Chapters 1 and 2).

Furthermore, the attempt to make such services more accountable to local people, and to involve communities and associations in them, has already been recognised as a direction for policy to take. There are many examples of survivor groups, neighbourhood associations and community organisations which successfully mobilise people on local issues, despite a desperate lack of funds (Holman, 2000). It is easy to make the case for this approach to services in terms of improvements in well-being and quality of life, where Third Way approaches have failed (Jordan, 2007).

In the case of commercial services, in the UK the crash is already curbing expenditure on eating out, travel and some forms of entertainment, and redirecting attention towards neglected aspects of self-provisioning, such as cooking and growing vegetables. Allotments are seeing a renaissance, and a Landshare scheme is allowing people access to plots for growing food both in towns and in the countryside (BBC Radio 4, 'You and yours', 27 September 2009). The deeper question in the long term is whether new structures in the organisation of commercial services can emerge, in which voluntary action and community projects can mesh with business activity.

I have argued here that the examples of music and sport are instructive (see p 125); in both, a highly profitable superstructure of commercial performance is built on a dense network of unpaid activity, which extends through every community (Jordan, 2008, 2010). If cultures of group and communal collective action around recycling, conservation, activities for frail and disabled people, engagement of young people, exercise and fitness could develop, enabled by a basic income scheme, these might actually contribute to demand for paid services, but of a different kind from the ones produced under an individualistic regime.

All this depends on the crash being recognised as a symptom of underlying problems in social relations, and not simply as an economic phenomenon. In the UK, the scandal over MPs' expenses and the consequent loss of trust in politicians has led to soul-searching about issues of trust more generally, and how these relate to the type of society generated by three decades of individualism and pro-market policies (Seldon, 2009). The link between high levels of inequality, high rates of physical and mental illness, low trust and low rates of subjective well-being is now widely accepted (Wilkinson and Pickett, 2009). The implications of these findings for the professional services and for government policy are still being digested. Some commentators press for government to stop trying to micro-manage social relations, and to allow professionals more scope to rebuild their expertise.

> Government needs to start trusting institutions and individuals again. The all-pervasive "target" culture from government, with inspectors, micromanagement and surveillance, has failed to improve public services or corporate life. The quality of services provided by schools, the NHS and the police has declined because, for the last 20 years, the government has had a "presumption of mistrust". Professionals have been deskilled and institutions and services re-orientated around the achievement of targets, which are monitored on check-lists by Whitehall. This trend must be superseded by a "presumption of trust"; we need teachers, medics, police and social workers who are trustworthy, certainly, but also who feel trusted and have pride again in their profession. (Seldon, 2010, p 28)

This, I have argued, is part of the answer to how services can make a more positive contribution to quality of life. Seldon goes on to argue that schools should reflect 'communal rather than consumerist values', and that communities are necessary for happy and meaningful lives; he also suggests a greater role for moral regulation – 'morality and goodness are not dirty words, nor are they words we should be afraid to use' (Seldon, 2010, p 28).

Professional autonomy and greater accountability to communities are not necessarily easy to reconcile. Teachers, doctors and social workers tend to measure their value in terms of exclusive expertise and esoteric knowledge within their professional cultures; they resist the requirements of open communication with the public, and try to avoid roles in which they are answerable to non-professionals in their daily tasks. But both parts of this transformation will be necessary, if the future of work is to be a positive factor in the improvement of the quality of people's lives.

NINE

Conclusions

The Third Way can be represented as the latest in a long line of attempts to regulate capitalism in line with some version of morality. It came into being as a response to 15 years of neo-liberal dominance in the affluent Anglophone countries, and in the IMF and World Bank (the Washington Consensus). While European countries remained loyal to Social Democratic and Christian Democratic political traditions and institutional settlements in the 1990s, Third Way ideas have since gradually become more influential in Europe, and especially in the post-communist new accession countries of the European Union (EU), in the first decade of the new century. Meanwhile, other responses to globalisation under free markets emerged in Asia (Gough, 2004) and Latin America (Gott, 2005), in the first case as export-led industrial strategies to complement the finance-based economies of the US and UK, and in the second as reactions against the exploitative reliance of both these types of regime on raw materials from the developing world.

Capitalism needs to be regulated if human social units are to be able to flourish, and people allowed to improve their quality of life (Polanyi, 1944); it is now clear that the future of the planet depends on environmental regulation. But capitalism constantly adapts and changes in response to a new regulatory environment, and sets new challenges to regimes trying to implement their various ethical principles. It constantly takes new shapes and transforms itself, breaking out of institutional constraints and destroying systems of social conservation.

The Third Way was a response to the subversion of welfare states by globalisation in the 1980s. It argued that these economic forces could be turned to the advantage of populations, and channelled to ethically justifiable ends, through new types of contractual regulation which went with the flow of market dynamics, but allowed individuals the opportunities and choices to take control of their lives. It rejected an approach to public policy which gave priority to equality of outcomes and to security, in favour of one which increased options for people, conceived as self-responsible and self-developmental.

The extent to which this approach came to permeate the thinking of even the continent thought to be most resistant to it can be judged from the shift in discourses in EU policy documents in the first decade of the century. Although the European social model continued to be defended as the bastion of the mainstream, Third Way ideas on opportunity, activation and self-direction began to pervade these declarations, especially in relation to employment and training, and the future for the new generation.

> Europeans face unprecedented opportunities, more choice and improved living conditions. The European Union ... has been instrumental in creating those opportunities, by stimulating employment and mobility.... [T]he focus needs to be on empowering and enabling individuals to realise their potential while at the same time helping those who are unable to do so....The reality is that economic and social actions at the EU and national level are mutually reinforcing and complementary, which links together opportunity, access and solidarity. (EU, 2008, Section 1)

In this book I have argued that the economic crash has exposed the weaknesses in the Third Way approach to the regulation of capitalism. The phenomena it sought to address – the inability of welfare state systems to provide either adequate protection against poverty or the basis for economic dynamism – were already those associated with a previous stage of capitalist evolution. In allying itself with the growing dominance of financial intermediaries over all other economic agents in the affluent economies, and seeking to regulate them according to the principles derived from contract theory, the Third Way failed to recognise the set of new challenges emerging in the late 1990s.

Capitalism is good at hiding the harms it does to human well-being as well as good at convincing people that they have a stake in its order. In the affluent countries, 'cognitive capitalism' (Moulier Boutang, 2007) involved many more workers in activities which used their intellectual, creative or imaginative powers for commercial ends; it also allowed them to work in isolation or in small teams. The Third Way provided the framework in which this development could be matched by ideas and images of self-realisation. In defining the mainstream in terms of opportunity and choice, it disguised the authoritarian elements in its regulatory regime, and the impoverishments of social relationships these entailed.

But by the same token, resistance to the various forms taken by capitalism evolves along with each new manifestation of its power, and takes a shape which responds to its dominant legitimation. In the 1980s, the rise in crime, disorder, drug dealing and informal work for cash expressed the reactions of those working-class populations which had been marginalised from the economy, and the collective life of whom had been fragmented. The means of resistance they adopted were quasi-economic; for example, claimants of benefits in the UK justified cash work which was not declared to the authorities by reference to an ethic of enterprise and family responsibility (Jordan et al, 1992).

By contrast, by the new century the threat to the kind of order created by Third Way regimes took the form of Islamic fundamentalism and 'blood and soil' mobilisations, such as the BNP in the UK, or the violence against Indian students in Australian cities (BBC Radio 4, 'News', 7 January, 2010). In the former case the resistance was to individualism and materialism, as well as the perceived humiliation of the Muslim countries by the US and Israel; in the latter it was to globalisation and its consequences for social and political life in affluent countries. But both were collective and cultural, both in their means of mobilisation and in the intuitions and traditions to which they appealed. They expressed a revulsion against technocratic regimes which legitimated themselves in terms of individual self-development and personal realisation, at the expense of deep-rooted cultures of faith, solidarity and belonging.

Of course, Third Way protagonists perceive these manifestations of archaic tradition as bigoted and destructive forces of exactly the kinds that signal the dangers of moral and cultural mobilisation. In this view, individualism and reflexive self-responsibility are justified precisely because they supply the potential for a diverse yet inclusive order, which is protected from such violent and partisan movements. Indeed, in response to the rise of the BNP, the UK Minister for Communities, John Denham, went so far as to say that the success of policies to combat racism and discrimination, and to promote equality, had meant that poverty and class had again become the biggest factors in economic and social disadvantage – presumably a bid to justify New Labour's focus on measures to revive the economy and employment, and to discredit the appeal to white indigenous voters to define issues in racial terms (BBC Radio 4, 'Today', 14 January 2010).

Yet the argument of this book has been that moral issues and a collective conscience are unavoidable, and that the Third Way's version of a moral order has turned out to be flawed in crucial respects. In trying to develop the cult of self-improvement and personal realisation in the mainstream, with 'cognitive capitalism' and the financial sectors as its economic bulwarks, the Third Way approach lacked the means to give recognition to those large sections of the population which had neither the work roles nor the material assets through which that order was accessible. So the Third Way had to rely on its legal, regulatory and punitive paraphernalia to enforce its principles far more than its claims to legitimacy could justify.

The failure of New Labour's economic policies underlined the shortcomings of its social programmes. The sheer volume of UK citizens lacking the personal and material resources for the kinds of 'independence' prescribed by the Third Way demanded too much of its energy as a political project. The crash made obvious how far these sections of the population were falling short of the necessary conditions for joining the mainstream, particularly over home ownership. As each new cohort reached working age, more effort was required to push them into low-paid, part-time or short-term work. Since the moral order upheld by New Labour relied so heavily on self-responsibility in labour and property markets, this left the government without a credible strategy for social inclusion, citizenship and the common good.

Of course, this did not imply that the Conservatives' diagnosis of a 'Broken Britain' was an accurate one, or that the Big Society would fix the problems. But it did allow the coalition government to focus on reducing prison numbers, reforming the police and abolishing ABSOs as parts of its first responses to social issues after the election of May 2010. New Labour could be represented as having been authoritarian in expensive and ineffective ways by its successor regime.

It remains to be seen whether the coalition intends to continue to rely on programmes of conditionality, enforcement and stigmatisation in its benefits administration. I have argued that this would be inconsistent with the idea of encouraging participation in paid and unpaid work through a culture of involvement in local action to improve the quality of life in disadvantaged districts, which is implied by the Big Society approach. Unless policies seek to enable activities of these kinds, there is a risk that promising ideas about tax-benefit reform, which might point eventually towards basic incomes, will be discredited because of their associations with cuts in benefits rates and coercive measures.

Prospects for transformation

The real challenge of the post–crash situation is that attempts to shift the culture of individualism and narrow self-interest towards a politics of the common good run up against the insecurities and needs of an unstable economic situation. As Barack Obama discovered in his first year in office, the clamour for jobs and reliable incomes can drown out any efforts to address longer-term issues of ecology, climate change or health insurance. His reverse in the loss of the 'safe' senate seat in Massachusetts showed that the US electorate was impatient for economic recovery which would be reflected in employment and wages.

The creative destruction of global capitalism allows no breathing space for the long view. A year before his inauguration, Obama had spoken in Evansville, Indiana, about the need to defend US jobs from processes of industrial relocation to developing economies. A year after his inauguration, it was announced that production at the factory in Evansville making Whirlpool washing machines, on which the whole local economy was based, and where lifelong jobs at decent wages had been available, was to be transferred to Mexico (BBC Radio 4, 'Today', 19 January 2010).

Meanwhile in the UK, the long established firm of Cadbury's, with its Quaker tradition of concern for the welfare of its workers, had succumbed to a hostile takeover by the giant US foods company Kraft. Although New Labour ministers bemoaned this outcome, there was nothing consistent with their policies on embracing global market forces that they could do about it. But it made their aspirations for a revival of manufacturing and exporting in the UK look very shaky, especially when it was revealed that Kraft had financed their bid by borrowing from one of the banks, RBS, which was over 80 per cent owned by the UK taxpayers since its bail-out the previous year (BBC Radio 4, 'The world at one', 20 January 2010).

Even in China, where double-digit growth had been restored by the beginning of 2010, future patterns of development cannot simply be resumed on past lines. The massive stimulus package through which the government staved off recession focused on reconstructing the infrastructure, rather than on the exports which had fuelled 30 years of growth. It will be Chinese consumers whose demand will have to absorb a much higher proportion of its manufactures in future, as the US and UK try to rebalance their economies, and their consumers to pay off some of their debts (BBC Radio 4, 'Today', 21 January 2010).

The project of transformation advocated in this book is a very long-term one. It involves reversing many of the priorities of the last quarter of a century or more. But the first step in this process is recognising that economics cannot supply a substitute for moral forms of regulation, and that individuals cannot be induced to construct a good society by making them responsible for their own projects of self-fulfilment.

I have argued that the future of work and income will have to be renegotiated among citizens from a number of different ethical perspectives. Up to now, these have been seen as largely separate issues. In the affluent Anglophone countries, the economic growth perceived as necessary for full employment has been revealed as the product of the asset bubbles created by overblown and over-mighty financial intermediaries. As the moves to supply a new global regulatory architecture take shape, governments will be forced to think again about sources of employment, and how they are to be organised. The claims of the environment and of the quality of life of communities might then come together in some of the ways discussed in Chapter Eight.

At the same time, the costs and contradictions of the tax and benefits systems may begin to demand fresh attention, and governments may be led in the direction of a basic income approach, not out of any moral conviction, but for reasons of technical expediency. This in turn might accelerate some of the transformations of the world of work which are already starting to happen.

The post-crash environment has proved volatile. Political leaders have alternated between attempts to convey 'business as usual' messages to electorates, and efforts to harness the moral outrage and feelings of betrayal at large. Barack Obama's announcement of plans to severely restrict the capacities of retail (high street) banks to take part in merchant banking or hedge fund activities, or to use borrowed funds to trade in derivatives and the like, are an example of the latter which could have far-reaching consequences on the global economy (BBC Radio 4, 'Today', 22 January 2010).

The crash seems to have struck a deeper chord with others outside the mainstream of party politics, raising doubts about the supposed snug fit between democracy and capitalism on which the Third Way edifice had been constructed. The claim of symbiosis between the institutions fundamental to these political and economic systems rested mainly on the decentralised nature of power under capitalism – the notion that it facilitated the coordination of billions of decisions by morally sovereign individuals with different tastes and preferences, just as democracy did through the ballot box and representative government.

But in the aftermath of the crash the differential impacts on sections of populations, and the rapid recovery in the fortunes of those most responsible for it, led to fresh scepticism about the long-term viability of these arrangements, and the demand for new thinking about institutions and policies. Capitalism has an inbuilt logic which runs counter to the political equality which is embodied in democracy. Its tendency to inequality is intuitively recognisable as unjust and oppressive. It undermines democratic practices and cultures, and hence creates social contradictions. If the welfare state can no longer contain and steer it, then some other institutions must do so, in line with new moral and social forces, if democracy is to thrive.

Comments on these lines by the Cambridge political philosopher John Dunn evoked a thoughtful response from the former Conservative minister, Michael Portillo (whose father was a refugee from Franco's fascist Spain) in his radio programme 'Democracy on trial' (BBC Radio 4, 11 May 2010). Portillo acknowledged that the recent growth in inequality in the UK demanded remedies, since capitalism could command no love, loyalty or self-sacrifice of the kinds which had led people to lay down their lives for democracy in the period when it was most threatened worldwide, the mid-20th century. The triumph of US-sponsored democracy which had reached its zenith in the early 1990s was not the 'end of history', as Francis Fukuyama (1992) had trumpeted, because of the tendency of global capitalism to subvert its moral claims to liberation and empowerment.

Yet the measures taken to deal with the consequences of the crash in the two years after its impact were all reactive and ad hoc, rather than following coherent principles. Even Barack Obama's proposals for clipping the wings of Wall Street reflected opportunism on the back of popular sentiment rather than a thought-through plan for harnessing financial resources to socially desirable purposes. The vacuum left by the failure of the Third Way is still to be filled.

Balancing contractual and moral regulation

As we have seen throughout this book, both contractual and moral regulation are inescapable features of any complex society in which private resource holdings and corporate organisations supply the means for employment and income, but where people create a social order out of informal interactions. The role of government in such societies is to devise institutions which allow participation in a market economy on recognisably fair terms, and to enable citizens to act together and separately in pursuit of their well-being.

I have argued that the Third Way misled those who cared about equality and social justice into supposing that institutions enabling or derived from contractual relations could meet all these requirements, so long as specific arms of government exercised a watchful oversight, constantly providing themselves and the public with information, and tweaking the rewards and punishments for various kinds of actions. As the search for fuller data and better methods of surveillance intensified, and the regime of incentives and sanctions became more densely cross-hatched across the social landscape, it grew obvious that the economic model was neither free nor fair in its consequences – a revelation starkly highlighted by the crash and the financial bail-out.

[T]he very sector we bailed out with public money, run by incompetent people who are once again paying themselves bonuses, is now threatening to destabilise the next government unless it fires thousands of low-paid workers, cuts their wages and withdraws the services to millions of mostly poor people. It's as though you borrowed money against your home to save a wayward relative from penury only to have them roll up a week later in a brand new Porsche and tell you to cut your food bill or they'll repossess the property. (Younge, 2010, p 29)

But this book has been mostly about the less obvious side of the Third Way's failure – the establishment of a culture of individualism which makes people unable to recognise opportunities to act together to resist such affronts, either at the local, associative or community level, or as whole societies (or internationally). I have argued that the more subtly pernicious effects of the Third Way approach to government have been experienced as an inability to think beyond a narrow individual or familial self-interest, or at best in terms of collective action with others of similar incomes and tastes. Because people have been brainwashed or conditioned into thinking that the supreme virtue of citizenship is self-responsibility and material 'independence' (achieved by borrowing large sums of money from financial speculators), that their freedom is derived from their rights to switch and shift between membership organisations of all kinds (from service providers to churches and even political communities), and that the only source of value lies in market price, it is not surprising that they have not been able to play a full part in the construction of a post-crash moral transformation.

I have argued that this mindset evolved through the gradual expansion in the spheres of human interaction to which the assumptions of market economics were applied. In what was a ground-breaking text for this imperialistic venture, *The calculus of consent* (1962), Buchanan and Tullock argued that the institutions of constitutional democracy could be logically derived from the methodologically individualistic assumptions of micro-economics, and that they represented the best way to channel self-interested, utility-maximising behaviour to the benefit of all members of the community. They offered this rationale for political arrangements as an alternative to the collectivist justifications of participatory social movements and the solidarities of welfare states which were the dominant orthodoxies of the time, and which, they argued, relied on citizens' abilities to recognise and adopt the interests of society as a whole.

In their final chapter, entitled 'The politics of the good society', they dealt specifically with the question of how contractual and moral regulation might be balanced, and the trade-offs between them.

> It should be stressed that moral restraint is a substitute for institutional-constitutional restraint, and in a society with more of the former there will be less of the latter, and vice versa. Our quarrel with those who would rely primarily on the moral restraint of individuals to prevent undue exploitation of individuals and groups through the political process is, therefore, at base an empirical one. The assessment of man himself will, or should, determine the respective importance that is placed on institutional-constitutional and on moral limitations on the behaviour of individuals in political society. (Buchanan and Tullock, 1962, p 306)

But they went on to claim that behaviour in the moral and the political spheres was essentially governed by the same rationale (the search for consumer-style satisfaction and competitive advantage) as that in the market. This implied that any evidence on the relative effectiveness of moral and contractual regulation could be assumed to be valid under any set of arrangements, since individuals are essentially the same, irrespective of the regulatory environment in which they are living:

> If modern man is unduly interested in the emoluments of the affluent society (in creature comforts), he is unlikely to shed this cloak merely because he is placed in a slightly different institutional complex. A shift of activity from the market sector cannot in itself change the nature of man, the actor in both processes. The individual who seeks short-run pleasures through his consumption of "luxury" items sold in the market is precisely the same individual who will seek partisan advantage through political action. The man who spends his time at the television set or in his automobile in private life is not the man who is likely to vote for more taxes to finance libraries, concerts, and schools. (Buchanan and Tullock, 1962, p 306)

Here Buchanan and Tullock spelt out the precise assumptions behind the neo-liberal transformation of the 1980s, which in turn morphed into the Third Way. But they could not have guessed that this 30-year experiment would provide the test of their thesis – that people do not change, whether they live their lives under regimes of moral or contractual regulation.

I have argued that people were changed by the transformations launched in texts such as Buchanan and Tullock's. They came to be more narrowly self-interested, more zombie-like in their compliance with commercial expectations, less aware of the possibilities of collective resistance to exploitation and less conscious of the opportunities for inclusive, national or international solidarities. Because governments treated them as individuals who could at best act only to select the benefits of interdependence with others of similar incomes, tastes and needs as themselves, their capacities to participate in collective political and moral life were impoverished. I have argued that only a reversal of this orthodoxy, in the direction of a heightened awareness of broader common interests and a recognition of fellow citizens, can restore these stunted capacities.

Final reflections

The Third Way's dying fall was aptly symbolised by the New Labour leadership's election campaign of May 2010 – a limp performance with no vision for the future beyond 'protecting the recovery' through minimising public sector cuts. In the event, the outcome was less of a disaster than the government deserved, partly through the unmerited loyalty of the party's core support, and partly because the Conservatives were still mistrusted for their neo-liberal past – fears confirmed for many by the cuts in state benefits and public services announced in the emergency budget of 22 June, 2010. Especially in Scotland, Labour clung on to many seats where Third Way ideas had never really penetrated, while in Northern Ireland the Conservatives failed in their attempts to break the mould of tribal allegiances; the combined effects of these outcomes forced them into coalition with the less-than-resurgent Liberal Democrats.

The transformations advocated in this book will require both institutional innovations and culture shifts that appear to be well beyond the horizon of current political mobilisations, either in the affluent Anglophone countries or anywhere else. This is only partly because of the economic crash; it is mainly because the mindset encapsulated in the Third Way has gripped a large proportion of the mainstream populations of much of the world. In their current state of insecurity (adversity for many), people seek a mixture of partial protection through what remains of the state's powers, and the limited opportunities of collective action with others they recognise as being in situations like their own.

They do not look beyond their immediate situations to consider the origins of the crisis in fundamental imbalances in wealth, savings rates, sovereign funds and debts, nor consider the shortcomings of the collective institutions in which their daily decisions are formulated, nor take account of the long-term environmental consequences of their lifestyles. The purpose of any thinking behind any attempted transformation of the kind I have advocated would be to enable them to have such considerations in their minds in their deliberations (or snap judgements) about how to live, how to act with others and how to vote.

Social theorists have distinguished sharply between the formal, abstract 'systems' of government and corporate organisation, and the 'lifeworld' of everyday interactions, implying that moral regulation is confined to the latter (Habermas, 1987; Luhmann, 1977). But I have argued that even the largest-scale collective arrangements rely ultimately on some sense of loyalty and solidarity among members, moral sentiments the Third Way neglected to cultivate. If institutions lose their symbolic significance in binding people together, they quickly become no more than objects for instrumental advantage, as welfare state systems became under Third Way regimes. After all, democracy since ancient Athens has represented itself in terms of collectives which *embody* the people (juries and assemblies).

Even for the medium term, developments since the crash signal the need to take a longer view about how societies are regulated and social relations ordered. For example, the agreement by the Eurozone countries of the EU on a plan to make €750 billion in loans and guarantees available to support the debt-ridden governments of Southern Europe during the crisis in Greece's public finances was recognised as having long-term implications, but falling short of dealing with the full extent of the problems signalled by that threat. On the one hand, it indicated that the fiscal affairs of these countries required 'Germanisation' – accountability to the paymasters of the EU for their future prudence and transparency.

But on the other, the decision to allow the European Central Bank to start buying up Greek, Portuguese and Spanish government bonds previously held by mainly German banks indicated that the private savings of Northern European citizens could no longer be reliably loaned to Southern European governments through these commercial intermediaries, but required the guiding hand of an international organisation. This in turn pointed to troubling questions about how a country like Greece could ever regain its government solvency in the absence of any foreseeable prospect of economic growth, and about how others such as Ireland could expect to be viable over time without significant natural resources, or comparative advantage in any sector of production. And finally this suggested that the euro stood in need of a set of institutions for fiscal and political union at the EU level if it was to be viable in the face of the next crisis, perhaps not so far into the future.

In other words, innovations like this Greek rescue plan were pointing to underlying issues in the configuration of collective institutions required even to maintain the status quo, let alone allow the development of new directions beyond the Third Way.

At the national level, the cuts required by government deficits have tested the emerging alternatives to the Third Way. In the UK, the coalition government's initial measures during June and July 2010 led to the accusations of a return to a Thatcherite agenda of dismantling the welfare state. But they seemed in fact to reflect both the strengths and weaknesses of the Big Society analysis on which David Cameron claimed them to be based.

On the one hand, the 'bonfire of the quangos' – the closure of many of the boards, trusts and agencies through which New Labour had regulated and administered public services – indicated the coalition's rejection of the Third Way's theory and model criticised in this book. When Cameron repeatedly asserted that his policies sought a 'shift in the culture' of government, and a 'radical redistribution of power' to individuals and communities, he was appealing to an approach to regulation and citizenship based on associative bonds and mutual commitment, rather than mechanistic, abstract or formal systems, rules and incentives.

On the other hand, the specific innovations so swiftly adopted – the devolution of NHS funding to general practitioners (GPs) and the opportunity for schools to become independent 'academies' – were leaps in the dark, almost certain to produce very mixed outcomes. For every one GP practice that takes the chance to become a social enterprise, to create a range of activities and groups for its community and to develop new preventive approaches there will be several others that simply hand over financial management to commercial companies. For every new school started by parents or teachers, there will be others run by wealthy sponsors or specialised companies.

The two central weaknesses of the Big Society approach are therefore likely to loom large in the aftermath of these measures. First, it takes time for cultures of self-organisation in communities and groups to develop, and commercial interests will occupy the spaces left as Third

Way systems are closed down. Second, because wider solidarities are so weak, new organisations will be homogeneous and narrow in their membership, reflecting the fragmentation of society into neighbourhoods of similar incomes, age groups and lifestyles. The devolution of responsibility to this level will favour the better-off and more experienced; it will therefore contribute to greater inequalities of resources and power.

This book has tried to identify the collective institutions needed in order to avoid such negative outcomes, and to provide a basis for more equitable long-term policies.

References

6, P. (2000) *The politics of moral character: Cultural change and public policy*, London: Demos.

Abrams, F. (2002) *Below the breadline: Living on the Minimum Wage*, London: Profile Books.

Ackerman, B. and Alstott, A. (1999) *The stakeholder society*, New Haven, CT: Yale University Press.

Adler, M.D. and Posner, E.A. (2006) *New foundations of cost-benefit analysis*, Cambridge, MA: Harvard University Press.

Ahrne, G. (1990) *Agency and organisation: Towards an organisational theory of society*, London: Sage Publications.

Akerlof, G.A. and Shiller, R.J. (2009) *Animal spirits: How human psychology drives the economy, and why it matters for global capitalism*, Princeton, NJ: Princeton University Press.

Allen, K. (2010) 'The benefit buster helping the unemployed to help themselves', *The Guardian*, 30 April, p 33.

Ambady, N. and Rosenthal, R. (1993) 'Half a minute: predicting teacher evaluations from thin slices of non-verbal behavior and physical attractiveness', *Journal of Personality and Social Psychology*, vol 64, no 3, pp 431-41.

Angier, N. (2007) *The canon: A whirligig tour of the beautiful basics of science*, New York, NY: Houghton Mifflin.

Apel, K.-O. (1980) *Towards a transformation of philosophy*, London: Routledge.

Argyle, M. (1999) 'Causes and correlates of happiness', in D. Kahneman et al (eds) *Well-being: The foundations of hedonic psychology*, New York, NY: Russell Sage Foundation, pp 353-72.

Arthur, B. (1990) 'Positive feedbacks in the economy', *Scientific American*, February, pp 80-5.

Ashton-James, J. et al (2007) 'Mimicry and me: the impact of mimicry on self-construal', *Social Cognition*, vol 25, no 4.

Atkinson, A.B. (1995) *Public economics in action: The basic income/flat tax proposal*, Oxford: Clarendon Press.

Bacon, R. and Eltis, W. (1976) *Britain's economic problem: Too few producers*, London: Macmillan.

Barry, B. (1997) 'The attractions of basic income', in J. Franklin (ed.) *Equality*, London: Institute for Public Policy Research, pp 157-71.

Bass, B.M. (1990) 'From transactional to transformational leadership', *Organisational Dynamics*, vol 18, pp 15-31.

Bauman, Z. (2003) *Liquid love: On the frailty of human bonds*, Cambridge: Polity Press.

Beck, U. (1992) *Risk society: Towards a new modernity*, London: Sage Publications.

Beck, U. and Beck-Gernsheim, E. (1995) *The normal chaos of love*, Cambridge: Polity Press.

Beck, U. and Beck-Gernsheim, E. (2002) *Individualization*, London: Sage Publications.

Becker, G.S. (1996) *Accounting for tastes*, Cambridge, MA: Harvard University Press.

Bellah, R.N., Madsen, R., Sullivan, W.M., Swidler, A. and Tipton, S.M. (1985) *Habits of the heart: Individualism and commitment in American life*, Berkeley, CA: University of California Press.

Bentham, J. ([1776] 1832) 'A fragment on government', in J. Bowring (ed.) *The complete works of Jeremy Bentham*, vol 1, Edinburgh: Tait.

Bentham, J. ([1825] 1832) 'The rationale of reward', in J. Bowring (ed.) *The complete works of Jeremy Bentham*, vol 11, Edinburgh: Tait.

Beveridge, W. (1942) *Social insurance and allied services*, Cm 6404, London: HMSO.

Blair, T. (1996) Speech to Labour Party Conference, 1 October.

Blair, T. (1998a) *The Third Way: New politics for the new century*, Fabian Society Pamphlet 588, London: Fabian Society.

Blair, T. (1998b) 'Preface', in DSS, *New ambitions for our country: A new contract for welfare*, Cm 3805, London: The Stationery Office.

Bloch, E. (1961) *Naturrecht und menschliche Würde* [*Natural law and human dignity*], Frankfurt: Suhrkamp.

Blond, P. (2009a) 'The new conservatism can create a capitalism that works for the poor', *The Guardian*, 3 July, p 33.

Blond, P. (2009b) 'Without a concept of virtue our politics and our banks are doomed', *The Independent*, 1 June.

Blond, P. (2009c) 'Rise of the Red Tories', *Prospect*, 28 February, issue 155.

Blond, P. (2010), *Red Tory: How left and right have broken Britain, and how we can fix it*, London: Faber and Faber.

Blunkett, D. (2003) 'Active citizens, strong communities: progressing civil renewal', Scarman Lecture to the Citizens Convention, 11 December.

Blunkett, D. (2004) 'New challenges for race equality and community cohesion in the twenty-first century', Speech to the Institute for Public Policy Research, 20 June.

Bohman, J. (1996) *Public deliberation, pluralism, complexity and democracy*, London: MIT Press.

Bolton, P. and Dewatripont, M. (2005) *Contract theory*, Cambridge, MA: MIT Press.

Boseley, S. (2010) 'Mid Staffordshire NHS trust left patients humiliated and in pain', *The Guardian*, 24 February.

Bowles, S. and Gintis, H. (2002) 'Social capital and community governance', *Economic Journal*, vol 112, no 483, pp F419-36.

Bronk, R. (2009) *The romantic economist: Imagination in economics*, Cambridge: Cambridge University Press.

Buchanan, J.M. (1965) 'An economic theory of clubs', *Economica*, vol 32, pp 1-14.

Buchanan, J.M. (1967) *Public finance in a democratic process*, Chapel Hill, NC: University of North Carolina Press.

Buchanan, J.M. and Tullock, G. (1962) *The calculus of consent: Logical foundations of constitutional democracy*, Ann Arbor, MI: University of Michigan Press.

Buchanan, J.M. and Tullock, G. (1980) *Towards a theory of a rent-seeking society*, College Station, TX: Texas A&M University Press.

Buchanan, J.M. and Vanberg, V.J. (1991) 'The market as a creative process', *Economics and Philosophy*, vol 7, pp 321-49.

Bunting, M. (2008) 'From buses to blogs, a pathological individualism is poisoning public life', *The Guardian*, 28 January.

Bunting, M. (2009) 'In control? Think again. Our ideas of brain and human nature are myths', *The Guardian*, 24 August.

Burgess, M.J. (2000) *British fiction and the production of social order, 1740-1830*, Cambridge: Cambridge University Press.

Bynner, J. and Parsons, S. (2003), 'Social participation, values and crime', in E. Ferri, J. Bynner and M. Wadsworth (eds), *Changing Britain, changing lives: Three generations at the turn of the century*, London: Institute of Education, pp 261-94.

Cameron, D. (2009) 'The big society', Hugo Young Memorial Lecture, London, 10 November.

Cameron, D. (2010) 'Labour are now the reactionaries, we the radicals – as this promise shows', *The Guardian*, 9 April.

Carter, H. (2010) 'David Askew death: police say council was too slow to help', *The Guardian*, 12 March.

Cherlin, A. (2004) 'The de-institutionalization of American marriage', *Journal of Marriage and Family*, vol 66, no 4, pp 848-61.

Christakis, N.A. and Fowler, J.H. (2009) *Connected: The surprising power of social networks to shape our lives*, New York, NY: Little Brown.

Cialdini, R. (2001) *Influence: Science in practice*, New York, NY: Allyn and Bacon.

Cole, G.D.H. (1929) *The next ten years in British social and economic policy*, London: Macmillan.

Cole, G.D.H. (1935) *Principles of economic planning*, London: Macmillan.

Coleridge, S.T. ([1810] 1969) 'The friend', in S. Colson (ed.) *Collected works of S.T. Coleridge, vol IV*, Princeton, NJ: Princeton University Press.

Coleridge, S.T. ([1818] 1969) 'Lectures on European literature', in S. Colson (ed.) *Collected works of S.T. Coleridge, vol II*, Princeton, NJ: Princeton University Press.

Coleridge, S.T. (1825) 'Table talk', in S. Colson (ed.) *Collected works of S.T. Coleridge, vol XII*, Princeton, NJ: Princeton University Press.

Collier, P. (1998) *Social capital and poverty*, World Bank Social Capital Initiative, Working Paper No 4, Washington, DC: World Bank.

Collins, R. (2004) *Interaction ritual chains*, Princeton, NJ: Princeton University Press.

Conservative Party (2010) *An invitation to join the government of Britain (Election Manifesto)*, London: Conservative Party.

Coulson, S. (2001) *Semantic leaps: Frame-shifting and conceptual blending in meaning construction*, Cambridge: Cambridge University Press.

Cox, R. H. (1998) 'From safety nets to trampolines: labour–market activation in the Netherlands and Denmark', *Governance*, 18(1), pp 28–47.

Cranston, M. (1983) 'Are there any human rights?', *Daedalus*, vol 112, Fall.

Crocker, D. (2008) *Ethics of global development: Agency, capability, and deliberative democracy*, Cambridge: Cambridge University Press.

Cruddas, J. and Rutherford, J. (2010) 'The time has come for a new socialism: we can only thrive as individuals when we have a sense of belonging', *The Independent*, 1 April.

Cruddas, J. and Rutherford, J. (2009) *The crash: A view from the left*, London: Lawrence and Wishart.

CSJ (Centre for Social Justice, The) (2009) *Dynamic benefits: Towards welfare that works*, London: CSJ.

Curtis, Dame M. (1946) *Report of the Care of Children Committee*, Cmd 6922, London: HMSO.

Damasio, A. (1995) *Descartes' error: Emotion, reason and the human brain*, New York, NY: Harper Perennial.

Damasio, A. (2009) 'This time with feeling' (http//fora.tv/07/04/Antonio-Damasio).

Dasgupta, P. (2000) 'Social capital and economic performance', in P. Dasgupta and I. Serageldin (eds) *Social capital: A multifaceted perspective*, Washington, DC: World Bank.

Davy, H. (c.1799) *Collected works*, London: Royal Society.

Delanty, G. (2000) *Citizenship in the global age: Society, culture, politics*, Buckingham: Open University Press.

DH (Department of Health) (1998) *Modernising social services: Promoting independence, improving protection, raising standards*, Cm 4169, London: The Stationery Office.

DH (2005) *Independence, well-being and choice: Our vision of the future of social care for adults in England*, Cm 6499, London: The Stationery Office.

Dickerson, S.S. and Kemeny, M.E. (2004) 'Acute stressors and cortisol responses: a theoretical integration and synthesis of laboratory research', *Psychological Bulletin*, vol 130, no 3, pp 355-91.

Dobbie, W. and Fryer, R.G. Jr (2009) 'Are high-quality schools enough to close the achievement gap? Evidence from bold social experiment in Harlem', Harvard University (www.economics.harvard.edu/faculty/fryer/files/hcz%204.15.2009.pdf).

Dorling, D. (2009) Interview on 'Today', BBC Radio 4, 12 August.

Dorling, D. and Thomas, B. (2003) *People and places: A 2001 census atlas of the UK*, Bristol: The Policy Press.

Douglas, C. H. (1918) 'The delusion of super-production', *English Review*, December, pp 136-7

Douglas, C. H. (1919) 'The control of production', *The New Age*, 1 May, p.4.

Douglas, C.H. ([1920] 1974) *Economic democracy*, Sudbury: Bloomfield.

Douglas, C.H. ([1930] 1951) *The monopoly of credit*, Liverpool: KRP Publications.

Douglas, C.H. (1934) *Warning democracy*, London: Stanley Nott.

Douglas, M. (1970) *Natural symbols: Explorations in cosmology*, London: Barrie and Rockliff.

Douglas, M. ([1978] 1982) 'Cultural bias', in M. Douglas, *In the active voice*, London: Routledge and Kegan Paul, pp 183-254.

Douglas, M. (1982) 'Identity: personal and socio-cultural', *Uppsala Studies in Cultural Anthropology*, vol 5, pp 35-46.

Douglas, M. (1987) *How institutions think*, London: Routledge and Kegan Paul.

Douglas, M. (1996) *Thought styles*, London Sage Publications.

Driver, S. and Martell, L. (1997) 'New Labour's communitarianisms', *Critical Social Policy*, vol 17, no 52, pp 27-46.

Driver, S. and Martell, L. (2001) 'Left, right and the Third Way', in A. Giddens (ed.) *The global Third Way debate*, Cambridge: Polity Press, pp 37-49.

Dryzek, J. (1990) *Discursive democracy: Politics, policy and political science*, Cambridge: Cambridge University Press.

Dryzek, J. (1999) 'Transnational democracy', *Journal of Political Philosophy*, vol 7, no 1, pp 30-51.

DSS (Department of Social Security) (1998) *New ambitions for our country: A new contract for welfare*, Cm 3805, London: The Stationery Office.

Dunbar, R.I.M. (2008) 'The social brain hypothesis', (www.liv.ac.uk/evolpsyc/Evol_Anthrop_6.pdf).

Durkheim, E. ([1893] 1933) *The division of labour in society*, New York: Free Press.

Durkheim, E. (1898) 'Individualism and the intellectuals', *Revue Bleue*, vol 4, no 10, pp 7-11.

Durkheim, E. (1912) *Les formes élémentaires de la vie religieuse: Le systéme totemique in Australie*, Paris: Alcan.

Durlauf, S.N. and Fafchamps, M. (2004) *Social capital*, Working Paper 10485, Cambridge, MA: The National Bureau of Economic Research (www.nber.org/papers/W10485).

Ehrenreich, B. (2002) *Nickel and dimed: Undercover in low-wage USA*, London: Granta.

Elliott, A. and Lemert, C. (2005) *The new individualism: The emotional costs of globalization*, London: Routledge.

Elliott, L. (2010) 'Lighting a fire under the model economy', *The Guardian*, 5 April, p 24.

Esping-Andersen, G. (1990) *The three worlds of welfare capitalism*, Cambridge: Polity Press.

Esping-Andersen, G. (ed.) (1996) *Welfare states in transition: National adaptations in global economies*, London: Sage Publications.

Esping-Andersen, G. (1999) *Social foundations of post-industrial economies*, Oxford: Oxford University Press.

Etzioni, A. (1994) *The spirit of community: The reinvention of American society*, New York, NY: Touchstone.

EU (European Union) (2008) *European Union Renewed Social Agenda*, Brussels: European Commission.

Evason, E. and Woods, R. (1995) 'Poverty, deregulation of labour markets and benefit fraud', *Social Policy and Administration*, 29(1), pp 40-54.

Fehr, E. and Gächter, S. (2000) 'Co-operation and punishment in public goods experiments', *American Economic Review*, vol 90, no 4, pp 980-94.

Fehr, E. and Gächter, S. (2002) 'Altruistic punishment in humans', *Nature*, vol 415, pp 137-40.

Fehr, E. and Schmidt, K. (1999) 'A theory of fairness, competition and cooperation', *Quarterly Journal of Economics*, vol 114, pp 817–68.

Ferris, I. (2002) *The romantic national tale and the question of Ireland*, Cambridge: Cambridge University Press.

Fine, B. (2001) *Social capital versus social theory: Political economy and social science at the turn of the millennium*, London: Routledge.

Fitzpatrick, T. (1999) *Freedom and security: An introduction to the basic income debate*, London: Macmillan.

Fleckenstein, W.A. (2008) *Greenspan's bubbles: The age of ignorance at the Federal Reserve*, New York, NY: McGraw Hill.

Foldvary, F. (1994) *Public goods and private communities: The market provision of social services*, Aldershot: Edward Elgar.

Foley, M.W. and Edwards, B. (1999) 'Is it time to disinvest in social capital?', *Journal of Political Economy*, vol 19, no 2, pp 141–73.

Fourier, C. ([1836] 1967) *La fausse industrie, morceleé, répugnante, mensongére, et l'antidote, l'industrie naturelle, combinée, attrayante, véridique, donnant quadruple produit et perfection extrême en toute qualités*, Paris: Anthropos.

Frey, B. and Stutzer, A. (2002) *Happiness and economics: How the economy and institutions affect well-being*, Princeton, NJ: Princeton University Press.

Fukuyama, F. (1992) *The end of history and the last man standing*, New York: Free Press.

Fulford T., Lee, D. and Kitson, P.J. (2004) *Literature, science and exploration in the Romantic era: Bodies of knowledge*, Cambridge: Cambridge University Press.

Fullmer, J.Z. (2000) *Young Humphry Davy*, Washington, DC: American Philosophical Society.

Gershuny, J.I. (1983) *Social innovation and the division of labour*, Oxford: Oxford University Press.

Giddens, A. (1991) *Modernity and self-identity: Self and society in the late modern age*, Cambridge: Polity Press.

Giddens, A. (1992) *The transformation of intimacy: Sexuality, love and eroticism in modern societies*, Cambridge: Polity Press.

Giddens, A. (1994) *Beyond left and right: The future of radical politics*, Cambridge: Polity Press.

Giddens, A. (1998) *The Third Way: The renewal of social democracy*, Cambridge: Polity Press.

Giddens, A. (2000) *The Third Way and its critics*, Cambridge: Polity Press.

Giddens, A. (ed.) (2001) *The global Third Way debate*, Cambridge: Polity Press.

Gigerenza, G. and Todd, P.M. (1999) *Simple heuristics that make us smart*, New York, NY: Oxford University Press.

Gladwell, M. (2006) *Blink: The power of thinking without thinking*, Harmondsworth: Penguin.

Glendon, M.A. (2001) *A world made new: Eleanor Roosevelt and the Universal Declaration of Human Rights*, New York, NY: Random House.

Gneezy, U. and Rustichini, A. (2000) 'A fine is a price', *Journal of Legal Studies*, vol 29, pp 1-17.

Goffman, E. (1967a) 'On face work: an analysis of ritual elements in interaction', in *Interaction ritual: Essays in face-to-face behaviour*, New York, NY: Doubleday Anchor, pp 1-46.

Goffman, E. (1967b) 'The nature of deference and demeanor', in *Interaction ritual: Essays in face-to-face behaviour*, New York, NY: Doubleday Anchor, pp 47-96.

Gore, A. (1992) *Earth in the balance: Ecology and the human spirit*, Boston, MA: Houghton Mifflin.

Gott, R. (2005) *Hugo Chávez and the Bolivarian revolution*, London: Verso.

Gough, I. (2004) 'East Asia: the limits of productivist regimes', in I. Gough et al (eds) *Insecurity and welfare regimes in Asia, Africa and Latin America: Social policy in development contexts*, Oxford: Oxford University Press, pp 169-201.

Grist, M. (2009a) *Social Brain Project*, London: RSA Social Brain Project, December, Retweet 5.

Grist, M. (2009b) *Changing the subject: How new ways of thinking about human behaviour might change politics, policy and practice*, London: RSA Social Brain Project.

Guardian, The (2009) 'Peak oil: what does the data say?', 13 November.

Guardian, The (2010) 'Iain Duncan Smith vows to tackle "absurd" welfare dependency', 27 May.

Habermas, J. (1987) *The theory of communicative democracy, Vol 2: Lifeworld and system*, Cambridge: Polity Press.

Habermas, J. (1996) *Between facts and norms: Contributions to a discourse theory of law and democracy*, Cambridge: Polity Press.

Haidt, J. (2007) *The happiness hypothesis: Putting ancient wisdom to the test of modern science*, London: Arrow Books Ltd.

Halpern, D. (2010) *The hidden wealth of nations*, Cambridge: Polity Press.

Hart, O. (1995) *Firms, contracts and financial structure*, Oxford: Clarendon Press.

Hattersley, R. (2010) 'The price I wouldn't pay', *The Guardian*, 23 March.

Hayek, F.A. (1976) *The mirage of social justice*, London: Routledge and Kegan Paul.

Hazlitt, W. ([1825] 1932) 'The spirit of the age', in P.P. Howe (ed.) *The complete works of William Hazlitt, vol XIII*, London: Dent.

Healthcare Commission (2009) *Investigation into Mid-Staffordshire NHS Foundation Trust*, London: Commission for Healthcare Audit and Inspection.

Helliwell, J.F. (2003) 'How's life? Combining individual and national variables to explain subjective well-being', *Economic Modelling*, vol 20, pp 331-60.

Helliwell, J.F. and Putnam, R.D. (2005) 'The social context of well-being', in F.A. Huppert, N. Baylis and B. Keverne (eds) *The science of well-being*, Oxford: Oxford University Press.

Henley, J. (2009) 'Stoke-on-Trent: Britain's first green city', *The Guardian*, 19 November.

Herder, J.G. ([1772] 1969) 'An essay on the origins of language', in J.G. Herder, *Social and political culture*, Cambridge: Cambridge University Press.

Herschel, J. (1830) *A preliminary discourse on the study of natural philosophy*, London: Royal Society.

Herschel, W. (1786) 'On the construction of the heavens', *William Herschel Papers*, pp 241-8.

Herschel, W. (1811) 'Astronomical observations relating to the construction of the heavens', in J.L.E. Dreyer (ed.) *The collected scientific papers of Sir William Herschel*, London: Royal Society.

Hilbert, R.A. (1992) *The classical roots of ethnomethodology: Durkheim, Weber and Garfinkel*, Chapel Hill, NC: University of North Carolina Press.

Hirsch, F. (1977) *Social limits to growth*, London: Routledge and Kegan Paul.

Hirschman, A.O. (1977) *The passions and the interests: Political arguments for capitalism before its triumph*, Princeton, NJ: Princeton University Press.

Holman, B. (2000) *Kids at the door revisited*, Lyme Regis: Russell House.

Holmes, R. (2008) *The age of wonder: How the romantic generation discovered the beauty and terror of science*, London: Harper.

Honneth, A. (1995a) *The fragmented world of the social: Essays in social and political philosophy*, New York, NY: State University of New York Press.

Honneth, A. (1995b) *The struggle for recognition: The moral grammar of social conflict*, Cambridge: Polity Press.

Hoskin, M. (1963) *William Herschel on the construction of the heavens*, London: Osbourne.

Humboldt, A. von ([1847] 1849) *Cosmos: A sketch of a physical description of the universe*, London: Bohn.

Hume, D. ([1739] 1978) *A treatise of human nature* (ed L. Selby-Bigge), Oxford: Clarendon University Press.

Hurwicz, L. (1960) 'Optimality and information efficiency in resource allocation processes', in K. Arrow, S. Karlin and P. Suppes (eds) *Mathematical methods in the social sciences*, Stanford, CA: Stanford University Press.

Inman, P. (2010) 'Avarice: the true villain behind global slump', *The Guardian*, 12 April, p 30.

Iversen, F. and Wren, A. (1998) 'Equality, employment and budgetary restraint: the trilemma of the service economy', *World Politics*, vol 50, no 4, pp 507–46.

Jacobs, M. (2001) 'The environment, modernity and the Third Way', in A. Giddens (ed.) *The global Third Way debate*, Cambridge: Polity Press, pp 317–49.

Jamieson, L. (1998) *Intimacy: Personal relationships in modern societies*, Cambridge: Polity Press.

Jefferson, T. ([1784] 1903) *Notes on Virginia*, in *The writings of Thomas Jefferson, vol 2* (ed A. Lipscomb), Washington, DC: Jefferson Memorial Association.

Jenkins, S. (2008) 'Better to hand us all a grand than hurl billions at the banks', *The Guardian*, 10 December, p 33.

Jordan, B. (1973) *Paupers: The making of the new claiming class*, London: Routledge and Kegan Paul.

Jordan, B. (1985) *The state: Authority and autonomy*, Oxford: Blackwell.

Jordan, B. (1987) *Rethinking welfare*, Oxford: Blackwell.

Jordan, B. (1996) *A theory of poverty and social exclusion*, Cambridge: Polity Press.

Jordan, B. (1998) *The new politics of welfare: Social justice in a global context*, London: Sage Publications.

Jordan, B. (2004) *Sex, money and power: The transformation of collective life*, Cambridge: Polity Press.

Jordan, B. (2006a) *Social policy for the twenty-first century: New perspectives, big issues*, Cambridge: Polity Press.

Jordan, B. (2006b) *Rewarding company, enriching life: The economics of relationships and feelings* (www.billjordan.co.uk).

Jordan, B. (2007) *Social work and well-being*, Lyme Regis: Russell House.

Jordan, B. (2008) *Welfare and well-being: Social value in public policy*, Bristol: The Policy Press.

Jordan, B. (2010) *What's wrong with social policy and how to fix it*, Cambridge: Polity Press.

Jordan, B. with Jordan, C. (2000) *Social work and the Third Way: Tough love as social policy*, London: Sage Publications.

Jordan, B., Redley, M. and James, S. (1994) *Putting the family first: Identities, decisions, citizenship*, London: UCL Press.

Jordan, B., Agulnik, P., Burbidge, D. and Duffin, S. (2000), *Stumbling towards basic income: The prospect for tax-benefit integration*, London: Citizen's Income Trust.

Jordan, B., James, S., Kay, H. and Redley, M. (1992) *Trapped in poverty? Labour-market decisions in low-income households*, London: Routledge.

Judt, T. (2010a) 'What is to be done?', *The Guardian* ('Review'), 20 March, pp 2-3.

Judt, T. (2010b) *Ill fairs the land: A treatise on our present discontents*, London: Allen Lane.

Kahneman, D., Diener, E. and Schwartz, N. (eds) (1999) *Well-being: The foundations of hedonic psychology*, New York, NY: Russell Sage Foundation.

Kampfner, J. (2010) 'I want to vote for a progressive Labour platform. So I'm backing the Lib Dems', *The Guardian*, 9 March, p 28.

Keynes, J.M. (1936) *A general theory of employment, interest and money*, London: Macmillan.

Keynes, J.M. (1973) 'Essay on Alfred Marshall', in *The collected writings of John Maynard Keynes, vol VII*, London: Macmillan.

Kindleberger, C. (1967) *Europe's postwar growth: The role of labor supply*, Cambridge, MA: Harvard University Press.

Laffont, J.J. and Martimort, D. (2002) *The theory of incentives: The principal-agent model*, Princeton, NJ: Princeton University Press.

Latham, M. (2001) 'The Third Way: an outline', in A. Giddens (ed.) *The global Third Way debate*, Cambridge: Polity Press, pp 25-35.

Layard, R. (2005) *Happiness: Lessons from a new science*, London: Allen Lane.

Layard, R. (2006) 'Happiness and public policy: a challenge to the profession', *Economic Journal*, vol 116, no 510, pp C24-33.

Layard, R. and Dunn, J. (2009) *A good childhood: Searching for values in a competitive age*, London: Good Childhood Enquiry/Penguin.

Leadbeater, C. (2008) *We-think*, London: Profile.

Levitt, S.D. and Dubner, S.J. (2006) *Freakonomics*, London: Penguin.

Lewis, W.A. (1954) 'Development with unlimited supplies of labour', *Manchester School*, vol XXII, May, pp 139-91.

Locke, J. ([1698] 1976) *Two treatises of government* (ed P. Laslett), Cambridge: Cambridge University Press.

Lonergan, E. (2009) *Money*, Art of Living Series, London: Acumen Publishing.

Lonergan, E. (2010) 'Reflections on life, the universe and the meaning of money', *The Guardian* ('Friday interview'), 8 January.

Luhmann, N. (1977) 'Differentiation of society', *Canadian Journal of Sociology*, 2, pp 29-53.

McGilchrist, I. (2009) *The master and his emissary: The divided brain and the making of the western world*, New Haven, CT: Yale University Press.

MacIntyre, A. (1981) *After virtue: A study in moral theory*, London: Duckworth.

Macho-Stadler, I. and Pérez-Castrillo, J.D. (2001) *An introduction to the economics of information, incentives and contracts* (2nd edn), Oxford: Oxford University Press.

Marschak, J. (1955) 'Elements in the theory of teams', *Management Science*, vol 1, pp 127-37.

Marshall, A. ([1890] 1927) *Principles of economics*, London: Macmillan.

Marske, C.E. (1987) 'Durkheim's "cult of the individual" and the moral reconstitution of society', *Sociological Theory*, vol 5 (Spring), pp 1-14.

Maurin, E. (2004) *Le ghetto francais*, Paris: Editions du Seuil.

Meade, J.E. (1938) *Consumers' credits and unemployment*, Oxford: Oxford University Press.

Mill, J.S. ([1848] 1994) *Principles of political economy*, Oxford: Oxford University Press.

Mill, J.S. ([1859] 1912) 'On liberty', in *Utilitarianism, liberty and representative government*, London: Dent.

Mill, J.S. ([1864] 1965) 'Bentham', in his *Dissertations and discussions*, London: Penguin.

Milner, D. (1919) 'The state bonus scheme: arguments for a simple step forward' *The Ploughshare*, July, pp 155-7.

Milner, D. (1920) *Higher productivity by a bonus on national output: A proposal for a minimum income for all varying with national productivity*, London: Allen & Unwin.

Monbiot, G. (2009) 'If the state won't save us, we need a licence to print our own money', *The Guardian*, 20 January, p 25.

Moulier Boutang, Y. (2007) *Le capitalisme cognitif: La nouvelle grande transformation*, Paris: Editions Amsterdam.

Mueller, D.C. (1979) *Public choice*, Cambridge: Cambridge University Press.

Newman, A. L. (2002) 'When opportunity knocks: economic liberalisation and stealth welfare in the United States' *Journal of Social Policy*, 32 (2), 179-98.

Nissan, D. and Le Grand, J. (2000) *A capital idea*, London: Fabian Society.

Nordhaus, W. and Tobin, J. (1972) *Is growth obsolete?*, New York, NY: National Bureau of Economic Research (NBER)/Columbus University Press.

Nozick, R. (1974) *Anarchy, state and utopia*, Oxford: Blackwell.

Offer, A. (2006) *The challenge of affluence: Self-control and well-being in the United States and Britain since 1950*, Oxford: Oxford University Press.

O'Neill, O. (1996) *Towards justice and virtue*, Cambridge: Cambridge University Press.

Paine, T. ([1791] 1906) *The rights of man: Being an answer to Mr Burke's attack on the French Revolution*, London: Dent.

Pareto, V. ([1896] 1966) 'Cours d'économie politique', in S.E. Finer (ed.) *Vilfredo Pareto: Sociological writings*, London: Pall Mall Press, pp 97-122.

Pareto, V. (1909) *Manuel d'économie politique*, Paris: Alcan.

Pareto, V. ([1916] 1966) 'Treatise on general sociology', in S.E. Finer (ed.) *Vilfredo Pareto: Sociological writings*, London: Pall Mall Press, pp 167-331.

Pateman, C. (1988) *The sexual contract*, Cambridge: Polity Press.

Pateman, C. (2004) 'Democratizing citizenship: some advantages of a basic income', *Politics and Society*, vol 32, no 1, pp 89-106.

Pigou, A.C. (1920) *The economics of welfare*, London: Macmillan.

Pogge, T. (2002) *World poverty and human rights*, Cambridge: Polity Press.

Polanyi, K. (1944) *The great transformation: The political and economic origins of our time*, Boston, MA: Beacon Press.

Purnell, J. (2010) 'Where is the vitality and vision to win?', *The Guardian*, 11 January, p 30.

Raban, J. (2010) 'Parson Blond's foggy sermon', *The Guardian* ('Review'), 24 April, pp 18-19.

Rawls, J. (1971) *A theory of justice*, Oxford: Blackwell.

Rawls, J. (1985) 'Justice as fairness: political not metaphysical', *Philosophy and Public Affairs*, vol 14, pp 223-51.

Rose, N. (1996) *Inventing ourselves: Psychology, power and personhood*, Cambridge: Cambridge University Press.

Rowlingson, K., Wiley, C. and Newburn, T. (1997) *Social security fraud*, London: Policy Studies Institute.

Rumford, Count ([1795] 1970) 'Of food, and particularly of feeding the poor', in S.C. Brown (ed.) *Collected works of Count Rumford*, vol III, Cambridge, MA: Harvard University Press.

Sandel, M. (1982) *Liberalism and the limits of justice*, Cambridge: Cambridge University Press.

Sandel, M. (2009a) 'The prospects for a politics of the common good', BBC Reith Lectures, BBC Radio 4, June.

Sandel, M. (2009b) *Justice: What's the right thing to do?*, London: Allen Lane.

Sandel, M. (2010) 'Introduction: as frustration with politics builds, it is time to define what we mean by a good life', *The Guardian* (supplement on 'Citizen ethics'), 20 April, p 1.

Sanfrey, A.G. et al (2003) 'The neural basis of economic decision-making in the ultimatum game', *Science*, 300, June.

Santore, D. (2008) 'Romantic relationships, individualism and the possibility of togetherness: seeing Durkheimian solidarity in theories of contemporary intimacy', *Sociology*, vol 42, no 16, pp 1200-17.

Schumpeter, J. ([1943] 1994) *Capitalism, socialism and democracy*, London: Routledge.

Scruton, R. (2009) 'Why beauty matters', BBC 2 television, 28 November.

Seager, A. (2009) 'Solar power from Sahara a step closer', *The Guardian*, 1 November.

Seeleib-Kaiser, M., Van Dyk, S. and Roggenkamp, M. (2005) *What do parties want? An analysis of programmatic social policy aims in Austria, Germany and the Netherlands*, Working Paper 01/2005, Bremen: Centre for Social Policy Research.

Seldon, A. (2009) *Trust: How we lost it and how to get it back*, London: Biteback Publishing.

Seldon, A. (2010) 'This year, Britain must finally grasp the nettle of our chronic loss of trust', *The Guardian*, 1 January.

Sen, A. (1999) *Development as freedom*, Oxford: Oxford University Press.

Sen, A. (2009) *The idea of justice*, London: Allen Lane.

Sennett, R. (2008) *The craftsman*, London: Allen Lane.

Sennett, R. and Cobb, J. (1973) *The hidden injuries of class*, New York, NY: Vintage Books.

Shackle, G.L.S. (1992) *Epistemics and economics – a critique of economic doctrines*, London: Transaction Books.

Shepherd, J. (2009) 'Poorest miss a day of school each week, Tory study claims', *The Guardian*, 28 December.

Shepherd, J. (2010) 'Rich students widen the "gulf" in access to top universities', *The Guardian*, 19 May, p 5.

Sloterdijk, D. (2009) 'Die Revolution der gebender Hand', *Frankfurter Allgemeine*, 13 June.

Smith, A. ([1759] 1948) 'The theory of moral sentiments' in H.W. Schneider (ed.) *Adam Smith's moral and political philosophy*, New York, NY: Harper and Row, pp 7-280.

Smith, A. ([1776] 1976) *An inquiry concerning the nature and causes of the wealth of nations* (eds R.H. Campbell and A.S. Skinner), Oxford: Clarendon Press.

Spragens, T. (1981) *The irony of liberal reason*, Chicago: Chicago University Press.

Stiglitz, J.E. (2001) 'An agenda for development for the twenty-first century', in A. Giddens (ed.) *The global Third Way debate*, Cambridge: Polity Press, pp 340-57.

Stiglitz, J.E. (2002) *Globalization and its discontents*, London: Allen Lane.

Stiglitz, J.E. and Greenwald, B. (2003) *Towards a new paradigm in monetary economics*, Cambridge: Cambridge University Press.

Stiglitz, J.E., Ocampo, J.A., Spiegel, S., Ffrench-Davis, R. and Nayyar, D. (2006) *Stability with growth: Macroeconomics, liberalisation and development*, Oxford: Oxford University Press.

Taylor, C. (1989) *Sources of self: The making of modern identity*, Cambridge: Cambridge University Press.

Taylor, M. (2009) 'Reflections on social evils and human nature', in D. Utting (ed.) *Contemporary social evils*, Bristol: The Policy Press, pp 215-24.

Tett, G. (2009) *Fool's gold: How unrestrained greed corrupted a dream, shattered global markets and unleashed a catastrophe*, London: Little, Brown.

Thaler, R.H. and Sunstein, C.R. (2008) *Nudge: Improving decisions about health, wealth and happiness*, London: Penguin.

Thompson, M., Ellis, R.J. and Wildavsky, A. (1990) *Cultural theory*, Boulder, CO: Westview Press.

Tiebout, C. (1956) 'A pure theory of local expenditures', *Journal of Political Economy*, vol 42, pp 416-24.

Tocqueville, A. de ([1836] 1968) *Democracy in America* (eds J.P. Meyer and M. Lerner), London: Collins.

Treanor, J. and Elliott, L. (2010) 'IMF proposes two taxes for world's banks', *The Guardian*, 21 April.

Tullock, G. (1967) *Towards a mathematics of politics*, Ann Arbor, MI: University of Michigan Press.

Twenge, J.M. (2006) *Generation me*, New York, NY: Simon and Schuster.

Van Parijs, P. (1992) 'The second marriage of justice and efficiency', in P. Van Parijs (ed.), *Arguing for basic income; Ethical foundations for a radical reform*, London: Verso, pp 215-40.

Van Parijs, P. (1995) *Real freedom for all: What (if anything) can justify capitalism?*, Oxford: Clarendon Press.

Van Praag, B. and Ferrer-i-Carbonell, A. (2004) *Happiness quantified: A satisfaction calculus approach*, Oxford: Oxford University Press.

Van Trier, W. (1995) *Everyone a king: An investigation into the meaning and significance of the debate on basic incomes with special reference to three episodes from British inter-war experience*, Leuven: Department of Sociology, Catholic University of Leuven.

Vickrey, W. (1945) 'Measuring marginal utility by reactions to risk', *Econometrica*, vol 13, pp 319-33.

Waddan , A. (1997) *The politics of social welfare: The collapse of the centre and the rise of the right*, Cheltenham: Edward Elgar.

Wainwright, M. (2009) 'Newcastle-upon-Tyne takes top spot as Britain's greenest city', *The Guardian*, 19 November.

Waldrop, M.M. (1994) *Complexity: The emerging science at the edge of order and chaos*, Harmondsworth: Penguin.

Walmsley, C. and de Sousa, R. (2010) 'Philosophies of science', Paper given at an International Summer School on 'Theory and Philosophy', Blackwater Castle, Cork, Ireland, 3 May.

Walras, L. (1877/1954) *Elements of Pure Economics, or The Theory of Social Wealth*, London: Allen and Unwin..

Walzer, M. (1983) *Spheres of justice*, Oxford: Blackwell.

Warfield Rawls, A. (1989) 'An ethnomethodological perspective on social theory', in D.T. Helm (ed.) *The interaction order*, New York, NY: Irvington, pp 7-20.

Weber, M. (1905) *The Protestant ethic and the spirit of capitalism*, London and Boston, MA: Unwin Hyman.

Whale, J. (2000) *Imagination under pressure, 1789-1832: Aesthetics, politics and utility*, Cambridge: Cambridge University Press.

White, S. (1998) 'Interpreting the Third Way: not one road, but many', *Renewal*, vol 6, no 2, Spring.

Wicksell, K. ([1896] 1958) 'A new principle of just taxation', in R.A. Musgrave and A.T. Peacock (eds) *Classics in the theory of public finance*, London: Macmillan, pp 72-116.

Wilkinson, R. and Pickett, K. (2009) *The spirit level: Why more equal societies almost always do better*, London: Allen Lane.

Williamson, O.E. (1975) *Markets and hierarchies: Analysis and anti-trust implications – A study in the economics of internal organisation*, New York, NY: Free Press.

Wilson, D.S., O'Brien, D.T. and Sesma, A. (2009) 'Human prosociality from an evolutionary perspective: variation and correlations at a city-wide scale', *Evolution and Human Behavior*, vol 30.

Wilson, T. (2002) *Strangers to ourselves: Discovering the adaptive unconscious*, Cambridge, MA: Harvard University Press.

Wolin, S. (1960) *Politics and vision: Continuity and innovation in Western political thought*, New York: Little Brown.

Wollstonecraft, M. ([1796] 1995) *A vindication of the rights of woman* (ed S. Tomaselli), Cambridge: Cambridge University Press.

Woolcloth, M. (1998) 'Social capital and economic development: towards a synthesis and policy framework', *Theory of Society*, vol 27, no 2, pp 151-208.

World Bank (2001) *World Development Report 2000/2001: Attacking poverty*, Washington, DC: World Bank.

Wright, E.O. (2004) 'Basic income, stakeholder grants and class analysis', *Politics and Society*, vol 32, no 1, pp 79-88.

Younge, G. (2010) 'The people have spoken. Don't let the markets shout them down', *The Guardian*, 10 May, p 29.

Zhang, J. (2007) 'Rural labour transfer and construction of new countryside in China', *China Economist*, vol 6.

Žižek, S. (2009a) Interview, *New Statesman*, October.

Žižek, S. (2009b) Lecture to the Royal Society of the Arts, London, 22 November.

Index